IMAGES
of America

A JOURNEY THROUGH

ARKANSAS

HISTORIC U.S. HIGHWAY 67

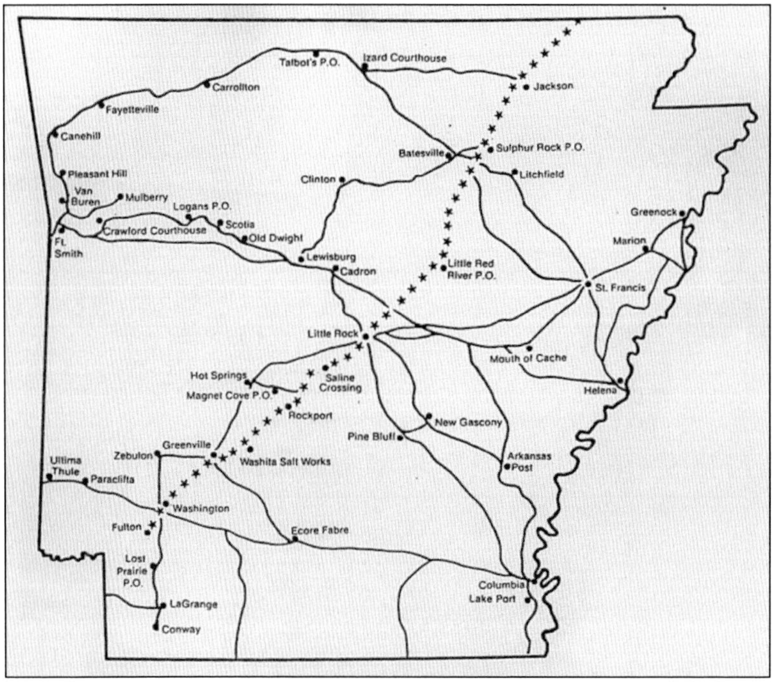

Long before the designation of this route as U.S. Highway 67, the general path of the road bisected the state as the most important land route in Arkansas. Originally the route began as a military road called the Southwest Trail around 1803; it is shown on the above map in 1830, when it still served as the primary link between St. Louis and Texas. At its beginning, the road was hacked out of the wilderness, for Arkansas was still a wild, unexplored territory that had been obtained from France as a part of the Louisiana Purchase. At the time of the 1830 map above, the road stopped at Fulton in southwest Arkansas; travelers often caught a Red River steamboat there, bound for Texas. At the time of this map, Texarkana, Malvern, Hope, and other towns on today's Highway 67 route had not yet been formed. On the lower map from 1880, the paths of the state's then booming railroads are shown. Once again the main route was laid out from northeast to southwest, bisecting the state along the lines of the Southwest Trail and the future path of U.S. Highway 67. By this time the town of Newport had been incorporated, as well as Texarkana.

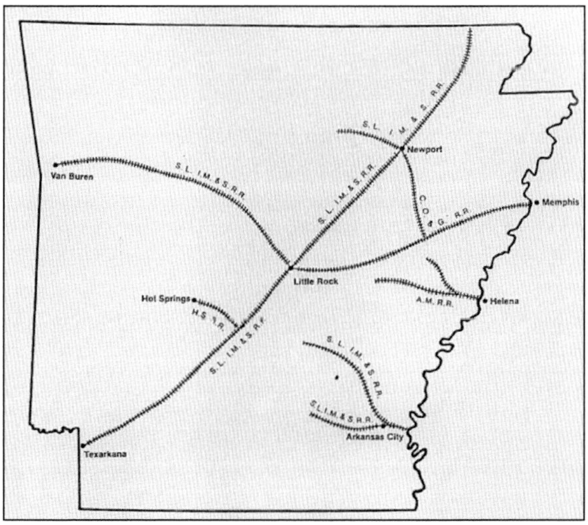

IMAGES
of America

A JOURNEY THROUGH ARKANSAS HISTORIC U.S. HIGHWAY 67

Ray Hanley

ARCADIA
PUBLISHING

ISBN 978-0-7385-0052-2

Published by Arcadia Publishing
Charleston, South Carolina

Printed in the United States of America

Library of Congress Catalog Card Number: 99-65712

For all general information contact Arcadia Publishing at:
Telephone 843-853-2070
Fax 843-853-0044
E-mail sales@arcadiapublishing.com

Visit us on the Internet at www.arcadiapublishing.com

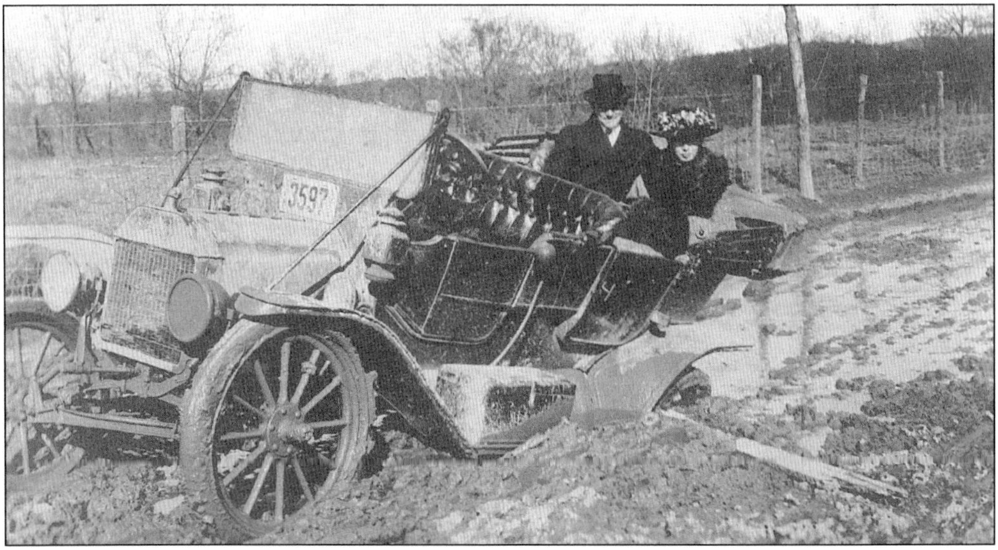

The automobile age reached much of Arkansas before its roads were ready, as evidenced by the plight of this couple somewhere in southwest Arkansas around 1915. It very likely took a farmer with a team of mules or oxen to extract this horseless carriage from the mire of the road. The first roads through the state followed the paths of least resistance, such as the old Native American trails and wagon paths. These did not always adapt well to narrow-tired automobiles.

Dedication

To my son Joseph who came into our family this year on one of those unexpected turns of life. May all the highways of his life lead to good places, and may he find faith and wisdom to handle the bumps, turns, and detours along the road he will travel.

Contents

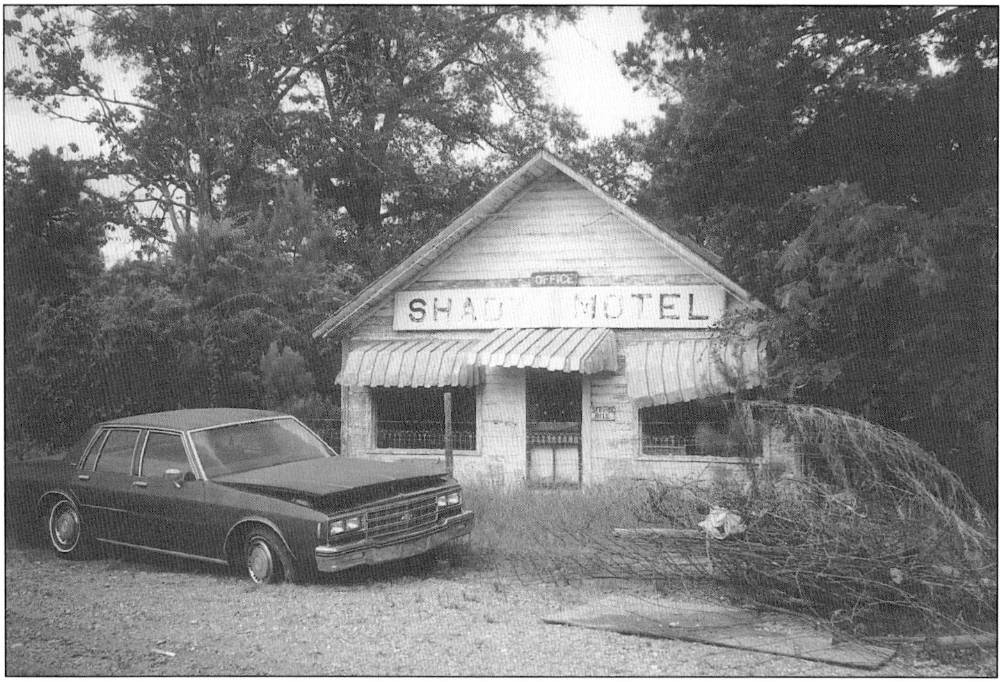

"Service Bell" reads the sign next to the screen door on the office of the Shady Motel, located on Highway 67 between Arkadelphia and Gurdon. However, for many long years it would have only been the ghosts of travelers past who rang the bell in search of a room. The decaying relic, with its fading sign and overgrown yard, is representative of the passage into history of the once-thriving family-owned enterprises that slipped away with the coming of Interstate 30 a few short miles away, which took away the traffic and the guests. (1999 photo by Ray Hanley.)

ACKNOWLEDGMENTS

This book is possible because of the input of dozens of people, many of whom still live along the route of the historic road and who share a pride in its history. Special thanks go to Mary Nell Turner of Hope; Tom Moore at Arkansas State University; Jimmy Bryant at the University of Central Arkansas; Wendy Richter with the Clark County Historical Association; Jamie Simmons with the Texarkana Museums; John Teeter at the Depot Museum in Prescott; Steve Heye with the Arkansas Highway Department; Mary Lea Vines of Corning; David Fray of the Benton Services Center; Adam Harris of the Pocahontas Chamber of Commerce; Vernon King, Ray Bowlin, and Mr. and Mrs. Wade James of Pocahontas; Jon LeMay of LeMay Photography of Little Rock; Phyllis Holmes of Newport; Eddie Best of the White County Historical Society; Mary Cheatham with the Hot Spring County Library; Mr. and Mrs. Charles Butler of Malvern; Lynn Ewbank of the Arkansas History Commission; and last, but far from least, my wife, Diane, for her usual invaluable editing job.

INTRODUCTION

In the history of American highways, the fabled old Route 66 is often called the "Mother Road of America." U.S. Highway 67 might as easily be called the "Mother Road" of Arkansas.

Roads and highways have been defining marks of civilization since at least the time of the Roman Empire. When the first settlers arrived on the eastern coast of the United States, it took little time before they began to carve out rough roads, often following game and Native American trails. Frequently, the roads were built first for military purposes, to move troops and supplies from post to post, making it possible to offer some degree of defense to outlying settlements. Such is the case with the beginnings of the Arkansas section of U.S. Highway 67, which is very likely the most historic route in the state.

The Southwest Trail was first a Native American path bisecting, from the northeast to the southwest, the area that would someday become the state of Arkansas. Spanish explorers, the U.S. Army, and early settlers used the trail. The military and commercial uses of the route become apparent in looking at maps from the early 1800s, when the trail connected St. Louis and Texas, then a part of Mexico.

The Southwest Trail entered Arkansas at the northeast in what would become Clay County, north of Corning, at Hix's Ferry on the Current River. Said to be the first river ferry in the state, Hix's Ferry was crucial to opening the trail into Arkansas. The ferry was operated by William Hix, who sold it to Payton Pitman in 1806. Some historical accounts say as many as 2,500 Cherokee wagons passed over the ferry in the 1830s during the forced relocation of the peaceful tribe from Georgia to the Indian Territory of Oklahoma via the "Trail of Tears."

The Southwest Trail continued through the center of the state, following the natural boundaries between the foothills of the Ozark and Ouachita Mountains, detouring around swamps and other obstacles. At Fulton in southwest Arkansas, the trail ended; hardy souls bound for Texas crossed the Red River into the wilderness or boarded a southbound steamboat. In 1831, Pres. Andrew Jackson signed an appropriations bill in the amount of $15,000 for the improvement of the Southwest Trail, an action that designated the route as a "National Road," the era's closest equivalent to today's Interstate Highway designation.

With its 1831 designation as a "National Road," the history of the route began to be recorded, as more travelers were drawn to explore its winding path through the Arkansas wilderness. In 1834, the noted British traveler and geologist George Featherstonhaugh traveled the new federal road and recorded some of his observations:

We are happy to learn that a road has been cut out through the Arkansas Territory, (by the) authority of the United States, called the Military Road. Entering upon the road from Batesville to Little Rock, we found the trees had been razed close to the ground and the road was distinguished by blazes cut into some of the trees standing on the roadside so it could not be mistaken–a great comfort to travelers in such a wilderness. One or more settlers here, having quarreled about the direction of the military road, have taken the liberty to cut roads resembling it and blazed trees to their own cabins–in consequence we go out of our way.

As the 19th century advanced, the road continued to be improved, and its route was continually shifted to avoid mountains, streams, and swamps, causing a situation that perpetually confused travelers. Yet shift as it might, the route seemingly never varied more than 20 miles or so either north or south of what later became United States Highway 67, so designated in the late 1920s.

The financing of Arkansas' highways was crippled for years by provisions in the 1874 state constitution that gave almost all power over roads, ferries, and bridges to the 75 counties. Efforts beginning in 1907 to establish local road improvement districts represented the state's initial attempt to improve the situation. In 1911, the state assigned an engineer to each county and levied a $5 tax upon each motor vehicle in order to raise funds. Local feuding and a lack of coordinated state leadership were persistent problems into the 1920s.

The requirement for counties to pay for their roads was a problem from the beginning, as evidenced by one law that reportedly stayed on the books of some counties until the 1920s. Records from Walnut Ridge, among other towns, show that every male citizen was required to donate six days of labor per year on the roads in his area or pay a fine of $1 per day, a sum that might easily have equaled a day's wage. When the conscript law was repealed in the 1920s, new government money was becoming available, along with local levies that made possible tractors, culverts, iron bridges, and even convict labor. The improvements on Highway 67 and various feeder roads along its route came rapidly after that time.

By the 1920s, the route that would soon receive the Highway 67 designation was a rough connection of two federally denoted National Trails. The Lakes to the Gulf Highway ran from northeast Arkansas in Clay County, slanting southwest toward Little Rock. It was graded but largely unpaved. It connected in Little Rock with the Bankhead Highway (named for Senator Bankhead, the father of actress Tallulah Bankhead), which came in from Memphis and then bisected southwest Arkansas and exited the state at Texarkana. The Bankhead, which ran from Washington, D.C., to San Diego, California, was unpaved in Arkansas, except for a section between Little Rock and Benton. The Bankhead Highway had veered off the path that Highway 67 would later follow, most markedly by veering from Benton to Hot Springs. Highway 67 would in places follow it exactly, in other places veering off by a few blocks to a few miles. Yet, as maps found later in this book will show, it is roughly along these two roads that towns soon to be humming with activity grew. With the Highway 67 designation came paving and, with that, bustling commerce to serve the ever-expanding number of automobiles. In 1930, the *Clay County Courier* told of the significance of the incremental paving of the highway with the following headline: "Road Which Bisects Arkansas Is One of Main Routes of the Nation." The story declared that "National Highway 67 between St. Louis and Texarkana, traffic observers believe, is destined to be a link in the most important northeast-southwest highway in this country." The section of that route leading into Corning was gravel at the time of the article but would be paved with a concrete slab later in that year.

Evidence of the road's impact on Arkansas life can be found in 1932, when Arkadelphia sought to promote itself nationwide as an "overnight stop for tourists" on the newly designated U.S. Highway 67. It was said on *Ripley's Believe It or Not* that, at that time, the southwest Arkansas town had more service stations than churches.

The picture postcard era began in Arkansas just after 1900, before the first mile of the old Southwest Trail was paved. Postcards can provide a valuable historical legacy, recording the changes in towns that at first were often just a few business blocks divided by a muddy dirt street, more dependent on rail travel than upon the wagons that had to traverse the rough road. The sampling of cards and photos used for this work show how the dirt streets came to be paved and how Highway 67 passed through the heart of Main Street U.S.A. It was by this road that much of the nation came to know Arkansas first hand, as travelers came from St. Louis to Texas or from the east through Memphis to strike Highway 67 at Little Rock for the trip into the southwest.

Hundreds of thousands of Americans who would have never seen Arkansas otherwise, would travel the state over the years thanks to U.S. 67. Many would pass through downtown Walnut Ridge, visit the town square at Pocahontas, view Little Rock from the Broadway bridge over the Arkansas River, or eat at the Checker Cafe in downtown Hope, little realizing the small town would one day produce a U.S. President. The businesses that lined the road provided a living for thousands of Arkansans and brought them into daily contact with visitors from across the nation in an era before interstates and franchised sameness forever changed the character of automobile travel. Many of these motorists who stayed in the quaint, one-of-a-kind tourist courts and ate in the locally owned cafes often mailed home a postcard and wrote notes about their impressions of Arkansas.

As near as can be determined, there has never been an effort to compile a book on the historic Arkansas Highway 67. Readers will note that the book begins in the northeastern part of the state, where US 67 enters above Corning, and progresses along the route through Little Rock and other towns to a conclusion at Texarkana, where the road leaves the state for Texas and eventually the Mexican border.

The route that began as a wilderness trail for Native Americans and pioneers has changed markedly in the past hundred years. In places today, the simple road has been covered over by interstate highway, with exit ramps marking the few points where a motorist can pause on his journey. In other sections, a four-lane freeway has bypassed the historic route, though never more than a few miles from the original trail. The last stretch of Highway 67 still in use as a primary route in Arkansas, a section between Newport and the Missouri line, will be bypassed by a four-lane freeway within the next few years. In this site again, history will be repeated as locally owned businesses that grew up to serve the motoring public will find themselves passed by and struggling to survive. Before the spreading interstate further drains the commercial life from the route, it is hoped that this book will inspire readers to remember and perhaps seek out what remains of the once-bustling artery, for it is a part of the heritage of our state.

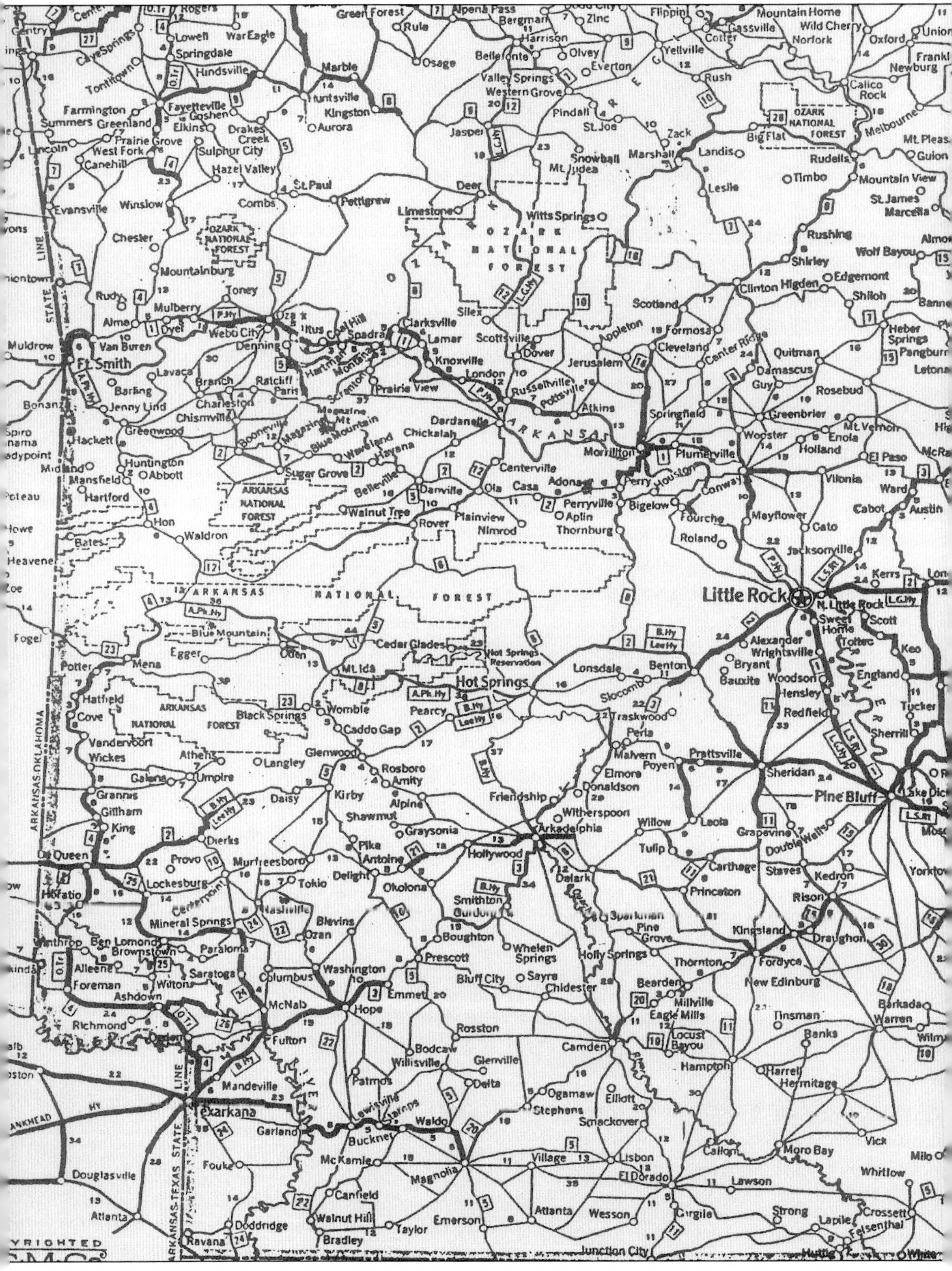
Rogers
Lowell
War Eagle
Springdale
Cave Springs
Tontitown
Hindsville
Fayetteville
Goshen
Elkins
Farmington
Greenland
Summers
Prairie Grove
Lincoln
West Fork
Canehill
Drakes Creek
Sulphur City
Hazel Valley
Evansville
Winslow
Chester
Mountainburg
Rudy
Alma
Mulberry
Dyer
Webb City
Ozark
Van Buren
Ft. Smith
Muldrow
Lavaca
Barling
Jenny Lind
Greenwood
Hackett
Huntington
Abbott
Mansfield
Hartford
Hon
Waldron
Bates
Branch
Ratcliff
Paris
Charleston
Chismville
Booneville
Magazine
Blue Mountain
Sugar Grove
Denning
Altus
Coal Hill
Hartman
Spadra
Clarksville
Lamar
Knoxville
London
Prairie View
Scranton
Dardanelle
Chickalah
Havana
Waveland
Belleville
Danville
Ola
Casa
Centerville
Adona
Perryville
Aplin
Thornburg
Plainview
Nimrod
Rover
Walnut Tree
Russellville
Pottsville
Atkins
Dover
Scottsville
Silex
Jerusalem
Appleton
Morrilton
Plumerville
Perry
Houston
Bigelow
Conway
Fourche
Roland
Mayflower
Cato
Jacksonville
Little Rock
N. Little Rock
Sweet Home
Scott
Keo
England
Tucker
Sherrill
Alexander
Wrightsville
Bryant
Bauxite
Woodson
Hensley
Redfield
Benton
Lonsdale
Slocomb
Traskwood
Hot Springs
Hot Springs Reservation
Cedar Glades
Mt. Ida
Womble
Black Springs
Pearcy
Caddo Gap
Glenwood
Rosboro
Amity
Langley
Athens
Umpire
Galena
Daisy
Kirby
Alpine
Shawmut
Graysonia
Pike
Antoine
Delight
Okolona
Murfreesboro
Provo
Dierks
Lockesburg
Tokio
Nashville
Mineral Springs
Ben Lomond
Brownstown
Paraloma
Saratoga
Wilton
Ashdown
Foreman
Alleene
Winthrop
Richmond
Ogden
Fulton
McNab
Columbus
Washington
Hope
Emmet
Prescott
Boughton
Blevins
Ozan
Gurdon
Smithton
Whelen Springs
Bluff City
Sayre
Chidester
Rosston
Bodcaw
Willisville
Patmos
Glenville
Delta
Lewisville
Stamps
Buckner
Waldo
McKamie
Magnolia
Canfield
Walnut Hill
Taylor
Bradley
Emerson
Atlanta
Wesson
Village
Lisbon
El Dorado
Junction City
Camden
Ogamaw
Stephens
Elliott
Smackover
Calion
Texarkana
Mandeville
Garland
Fouke
Doddridge
Ravana
Douglasville
Queen
Gillham
King
Grannis
Wickes
Vandervoort
Cove
Hatfield
Mena
Potter
Egger
Oden
Arkadelphia
Hollywood
Friendship
Witherspoon
Donaldson
Malvern
Elmore
Perla
Poyen
Prattsville
Sheridan
Leola
Willow
Tulip
Carthage
Princeton
Dalark
Sparkman
Pine Grove
Holly Springs
Thornton
Bearden
Millville
Eagle Mills
Locust Bayou
Hampton
Harrell
Hermitage
Moro Bay
Vick
Fordyce
Kingsland
New Edinburg
Tinsman
Banks
Warren
Barkada
Rison
Kedron
Staves
Draughon
Grapevine
Double Wells
Pine Bluff
Lake Dick
Lawson
Strong
Lapile
Crossett
Felsenthal
Huttig
Whitlow
Milo
Cargile
Harrison
Bergman
Zinc
Olvey
Everton
Bellefonte
Valley Springs
Western Grove
Green Forest
Rule
Osage
Alpena Pass
Marble
Huntsville
Kingston
Aurora
Jasper
Pindall
St. Joe
Flippin
Yellville
Cotter
Gassville
Mountain Home
Wild Cherry
Norfork
Oxford
Union
Newburg
Calico Rock
Melbourne
Rush
Zack
Marshall
Landis
Leslie
Big Flat
Timbo
Rudells
Mountain View
St. James
Marcella
Guion
Snowball
Mt. Judea
Deer
Limestone
Witts Springs
St. Paul
Pettigrew
Combs
Toney
Rushing
Shirley
Clinton
Higden
Edgemont
Shiloh
Wolf Bayou
Scotland
Formosa
Cleveland
Center Ridge
Damascus
Guy
Quitman
Heber Springs
Pangburn
Rosebud
Springfield
Greenbrier
Wooster
Holland
Enola
Mt. Vernon
Vilonia
El Paso
Ward
Cabot
Austin
Kerrs
Horatio
OZARK NATIONAL FOREST
ARKANSAS NATIONAL FOREST
ARKANSAS
STATE LINE
ARKANSAS-OKLAHOMA
ARKANSAS-TEXAS STATE LINE
BANKHEAD HY

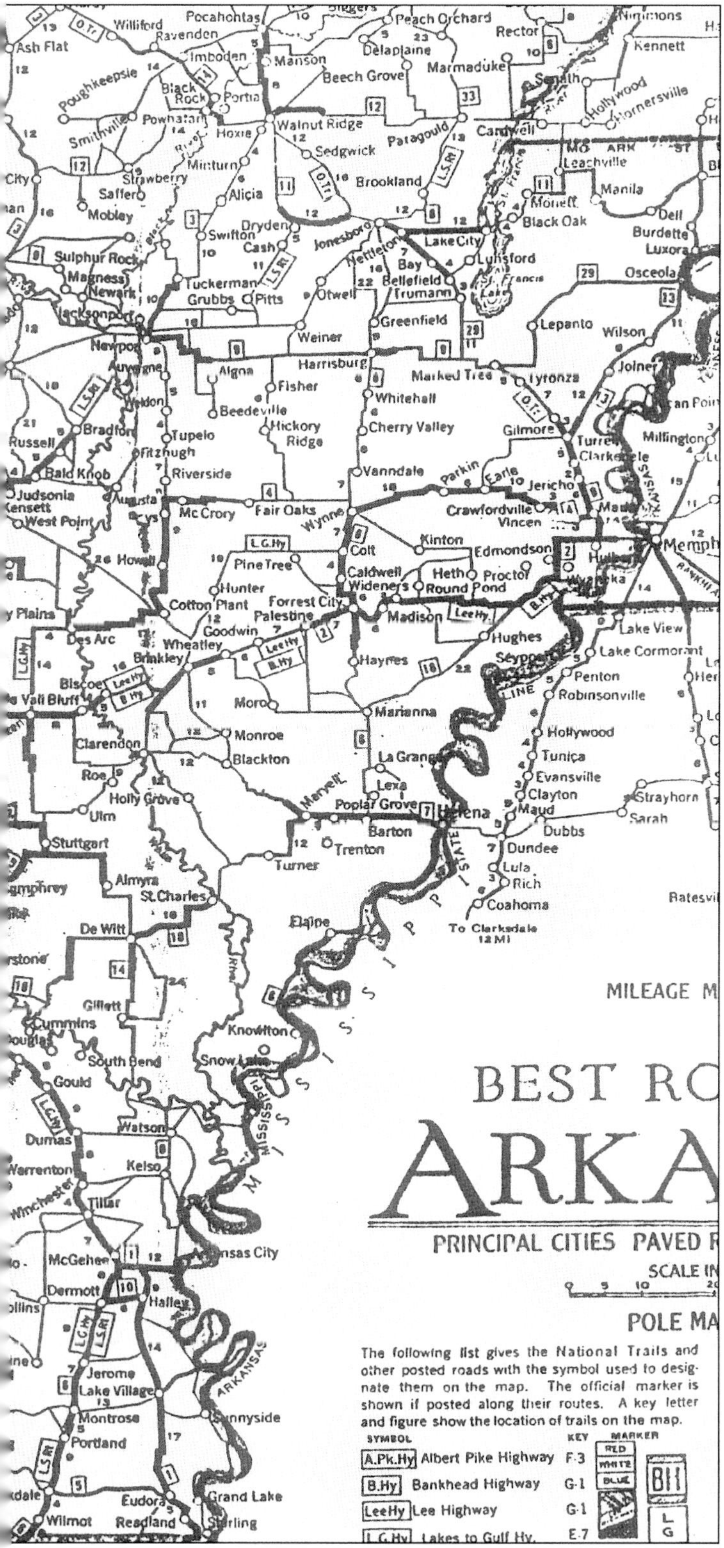

This 1920 map details the jumbled path of the route that would become Highway 67 within a decade. Fragmented local road districts, a lack of coordinated state leadership, and inadequate funding had left much of the route unpaved and in poor condition. Limited federal funding had come with the designation of the route from the Missouri line north of Corning to Little Rock as part of the "Lone Star Route." Heavy rains often left this section of highway impassable for days, stranding travelers in hotels in places like Corning and Pocahontas. In Little Rock, the route was picked up by the Bankhead Highway, which ran from Washington, D.C., to San Diego, California, and followed the winding, mostly unpaved road into Texas as it passed through southwestern Arkansas.

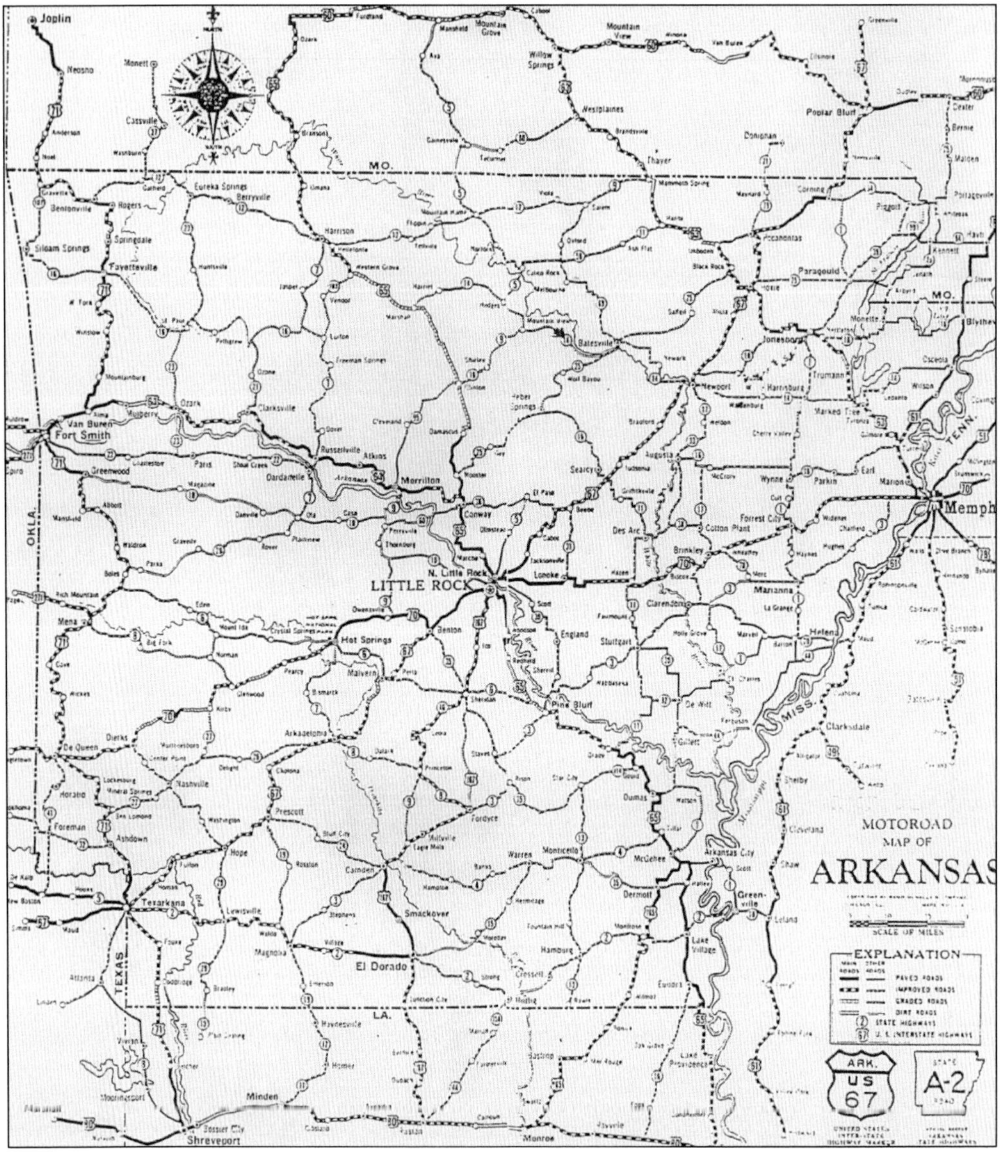

By the time of this 1930 map, the federal government had finished Highway 67, but not the paving. Sometimes following exactly, other times shifting a few blocks or few miles, Highway 67 replaced the Lakes to the Gulf and Bankhead Highways. Funding from the federal government and the slow emergence of coordinated state leadership in highway development was helping the route to improve. Much of the road had been straightened and concrete bridges were being constructed. However, with the exception of a short stretch on either side of Little Rock and a few miles below Corning, the entire highway was still unpaved.

One

Clay County to White County

Corning to Beebe

Highway 67 had its beginning as the Southwest Trail, crossing into Arkansas north of Corning at Hix's Ferry on the Current River. Over most of this century, countless travelers got their first glimpse of Arkansas leaving the flat farmland of southwestern Missouri to enter Clay County en route to the county seat of Corning.

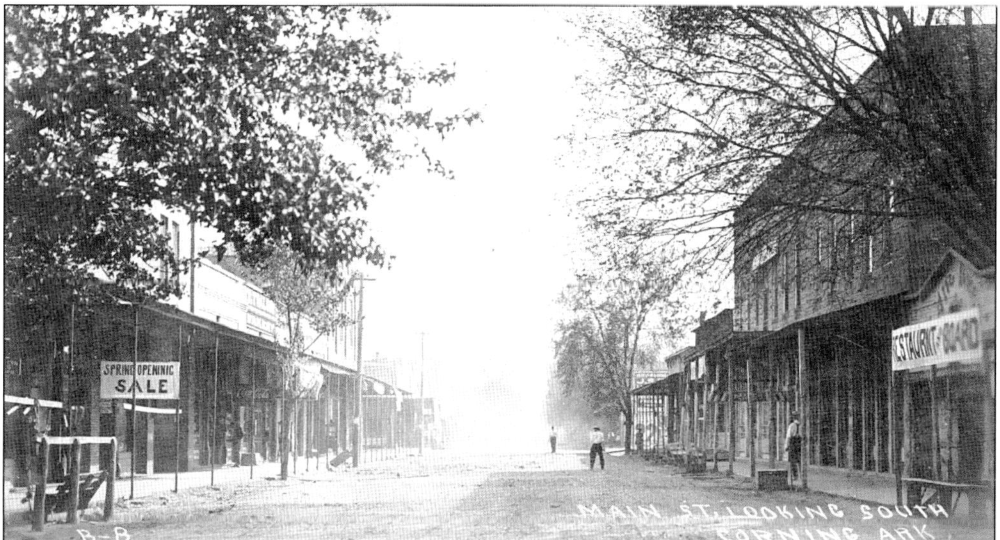

Highway 67 enters Arkansas about 15 miles north of Corning in Clay County, passing through flat farm fields en route to the small town that shares dual Clay County seat honors with the city of Piggott. Corning was founded in 1872 on the grade of the Cairo & Fulton Railroad and was originally called Hecth City, the name of the brothers who founded the town. People came to prefer the name Carpenter's Station, which came from the name of the depot agent. After a community split, the name became Corning in 1873, honoring the civil engineer who built the rail line. Before the coming of the highway, the town was served by dusty farm roads that brought horse and wagon traffic, as in this view where farmers have come to shop the spring sale (at left) and to eat at the restaurant seen to the right. The writer of the 1910 card complained of "skeeters."

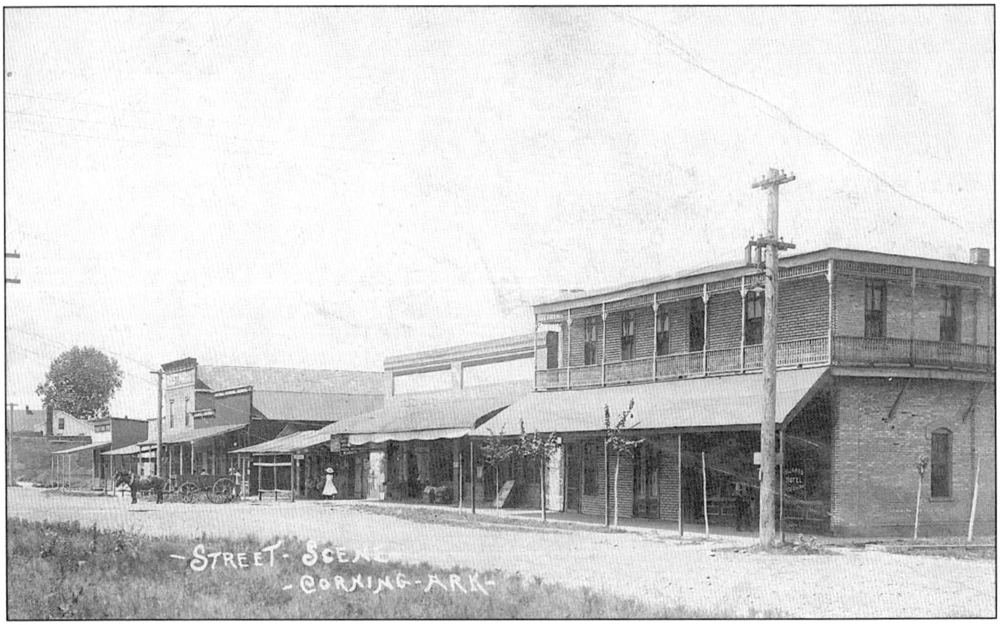

The St. James Hotel, seen on the corner in this 1912 view, was the largest in Corning and was built around the turn of the century. The hotel was across from the depot, and for the first few years, it housed many rail passengers who had reason to stop over in Corning. By the 1920s, when automobile traffic began to come through Corning on the rough dirt and gravel highway, the St. James often put up these travelers as well, sometimes when they were stranded in town because the highway was washed out or flood waters had stopped the ferry service. The hotel burned in 1926, and one man died in the blaze.

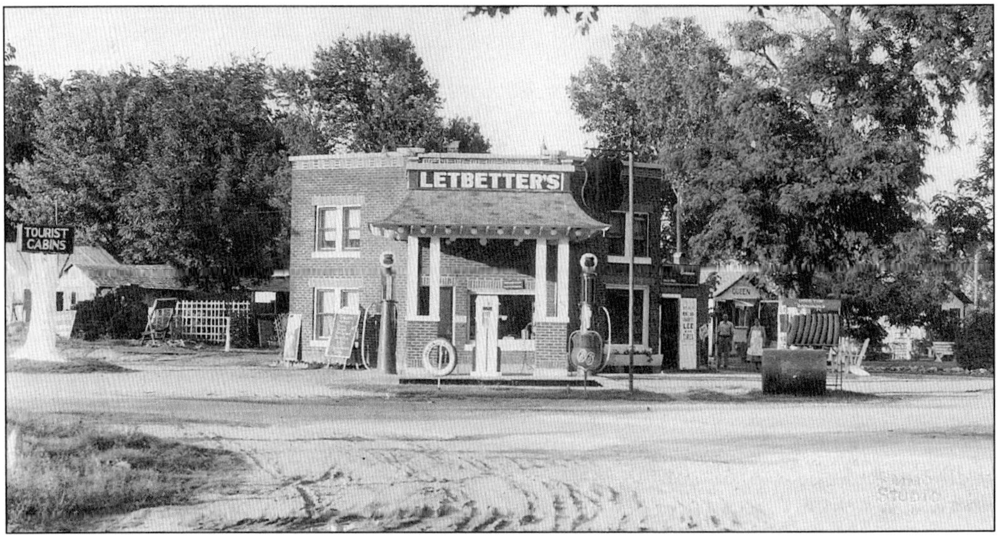

First graveled and then paved in the mid-1930s, Highway 67 began to sprout tourist courts, and among the most unique was Letbetter's Tourist Camp. The business, which began in the 1930s, was centered behind and to either side of the gas station and restaurant shown above, before the road was paved. The large building was among the busiest in Corning for years because it also housed the bus station. By the 1940s, buses ran day and night through Corning because of its location along the important highway connecting St. Louis and Texas.

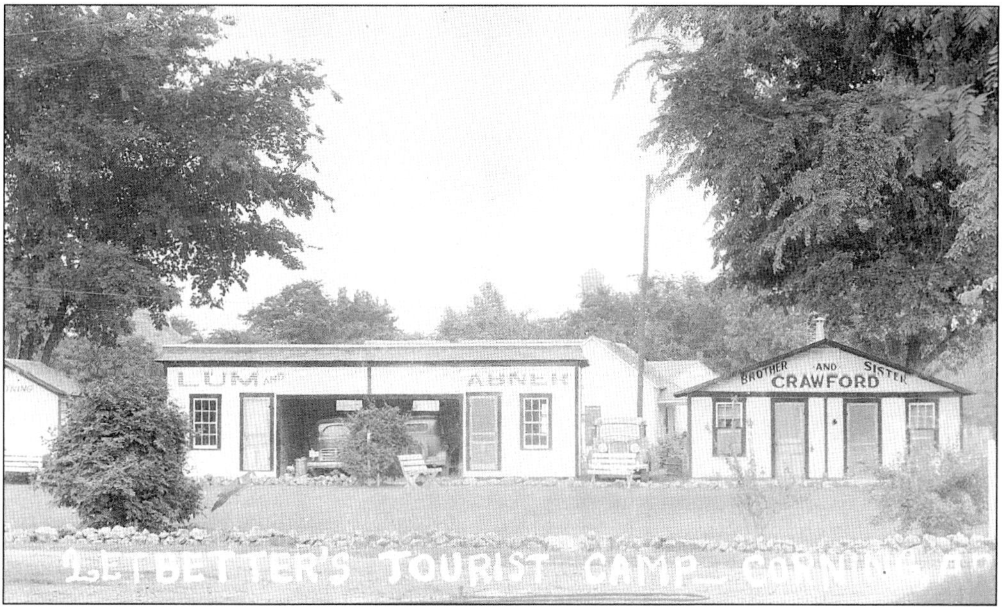

Above are some of the c. 1940 Letbetter's tourist cabins, which bore the names of characters from popular radio programs. The "Lum and Abner" cabins, to the left in this view, each had a garage for the guest's car. To the right are cabins named for "Brother and Sister Crawford" from the *Amos 'n Andy* program. Letbetter's Tourist Cabins were spread around a large lawn of shade trees and benches for the guests, a welcome respite from the hot Arkansas summer in an era before air conditioning. The cabins below are named "Amos" and "Queen," also for characters in the *Amos 'n Andy* radio program. The tourist court was torn down years ago; today, a fast food restaurant and gas station occupy the site.

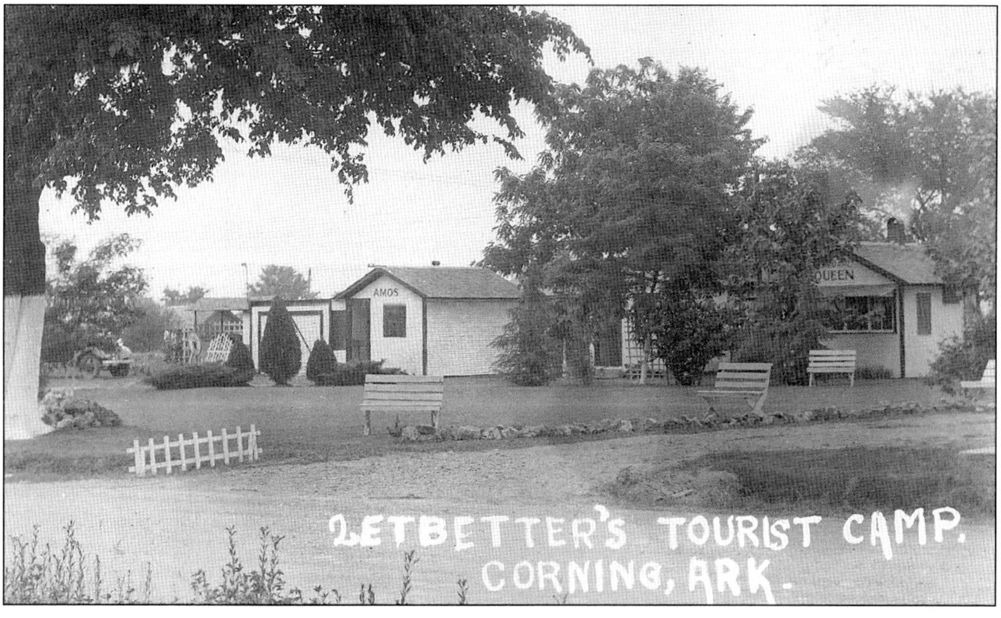

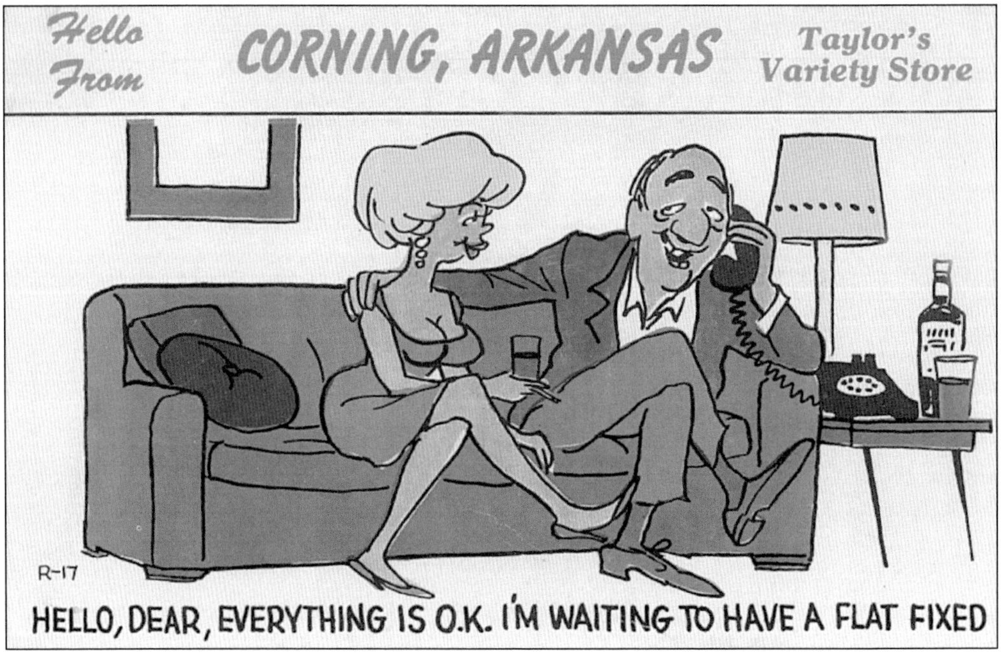

In the 1950s, some of the local Highway 67 businesses, such as Taylor's Variety Store, sold a series of postcards designed to catch the eye of travelers who sent home a note with Corning, Arkansas, imprinted on the cartoons.

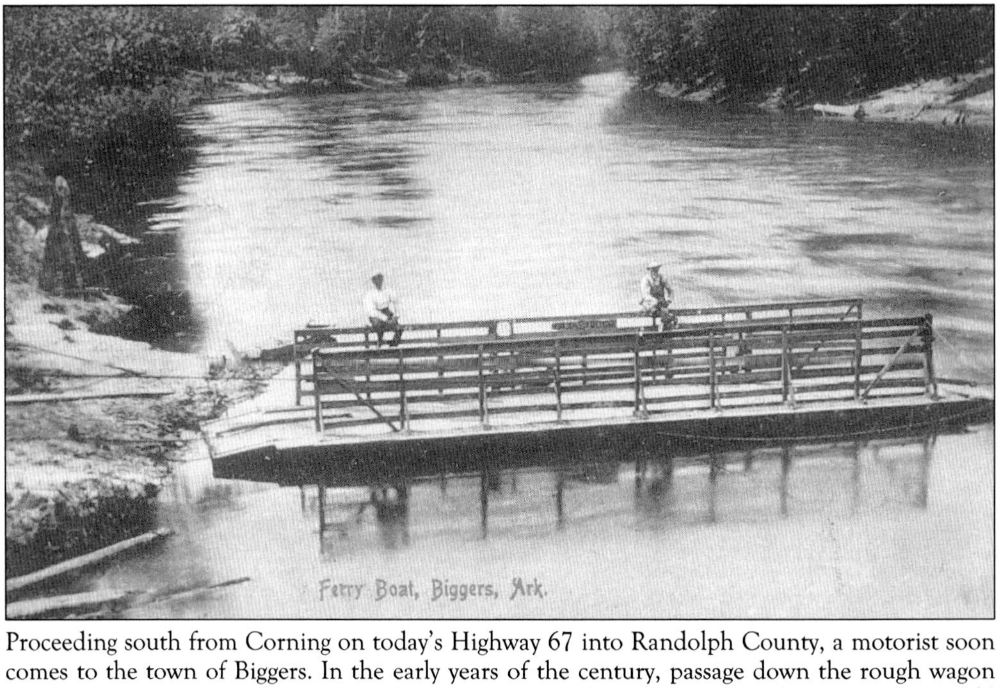

Proceeding south from Corning on today's Highway 67 into Randolph County, a motorist soon comes to the town of Biggers. In the early years of the century, passage down the rough wagon road required a ferry crossing at the Current River outside of Biggers. The ferry operators would pull the boat across the river by hand using a cable; this, for many years, was the only way to get wagons, horses, and pedestrians across. Floods often shut down the ferry and stranded travelers, sometimes for days. This picture was taken *c.* 1910.

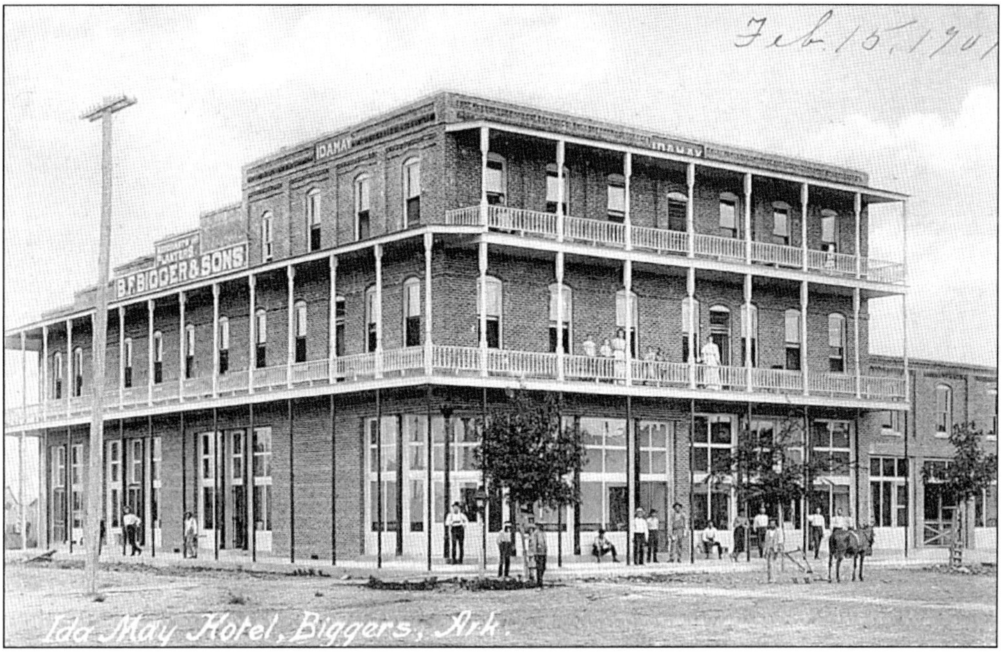

B.F. Biggers founded the Randolph County town that bore his name in 1889, setting up a distillery and a ferry service over the Current River. In 1900, Biggers erected the Ida Mae Hotel (misspelled as "May" on the card), naming the 24-room establishment after his wife, Ida, and his daughter Mae. In this 1910 view, a mule and plow are seen in the street, while a number of men pose on the sidewalk and women and children pose on the balcony. As the nearby rough road improved over the years, the hotel offered the only lodging in the small town. The hotel survived until 1962, when it was destroyed by fire. The card's message wished D.R. Davis "all possible success at West Point."

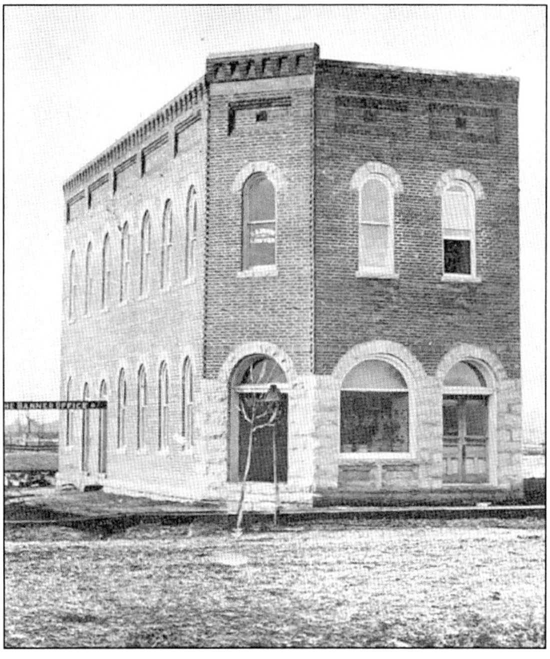

The Bank of Biggers was established in 1903 with capital assets in the sum of $20,000 and was a part of a "fine business block," as described by local town boosters. The community was supported primarily by stave mills and local farmers. The card's 1910 message read, "Hopeful this will find you the same rite & tell me what I asked you to tell me all the news." Today, Biggers is still marked by a city limits sign on Highway 67 some 12 miles north of Pocahontas, but all traces of the business district, including the bank, are now gone.

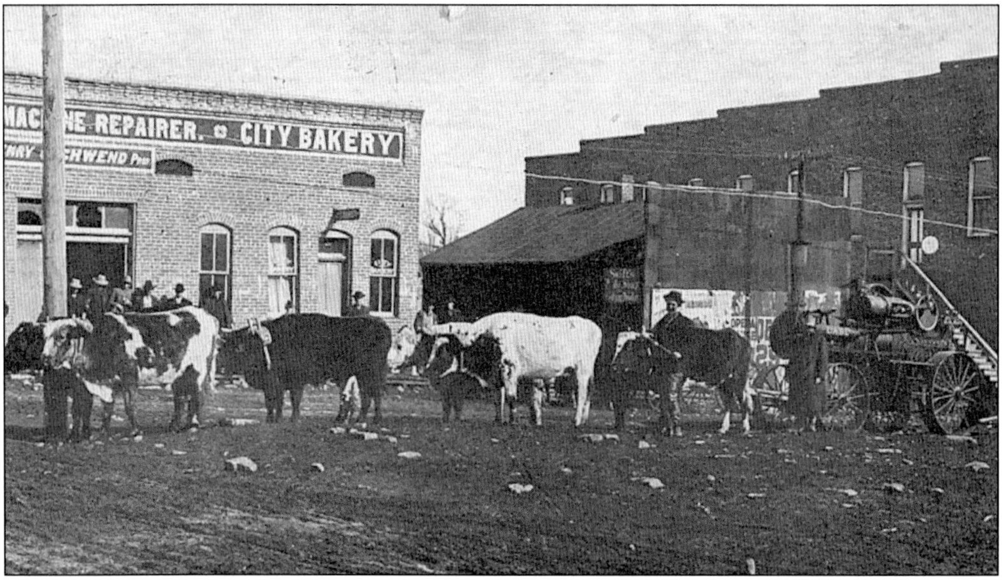

A dozen miles down Highway 67 from Corning today brings travelers to Pocahontas, a town that got its start when Dr. Ranson Bettis built a house around 1815 at what is today the corner of Bettis Street and Highway 67. First known as Bettis Bluff, the town became Pocahontas in 1835. During the first two decades of the 20th century, much of the commerce of the community moved by river or, later, by rail, as the road through town remained unreliable, especially after heavy rains. Often it took oxen to move wagons and freight, as in this case on the Pocahontas square, c. 1905. The beasts are apparently pulling a Case steam tractor to the machinery repair shop to the left, next the City Bakery.

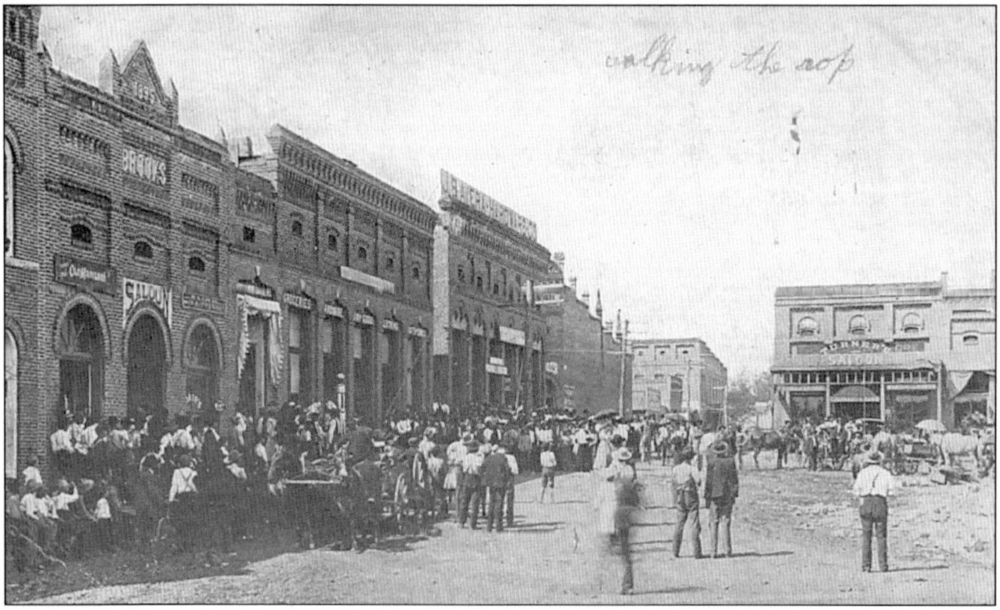

The classical town square of Pocahontas was often crowded with commerce and people, perhaps drawn by at least two saloons visible in the 1914 view above. J.B. Avera's Hardware can be seen in the distance on the left, and Turner's Saloon is at the far right on what was likely a busy Saturday, when the area's farmers came to town with their wagons and buggies for supplies.

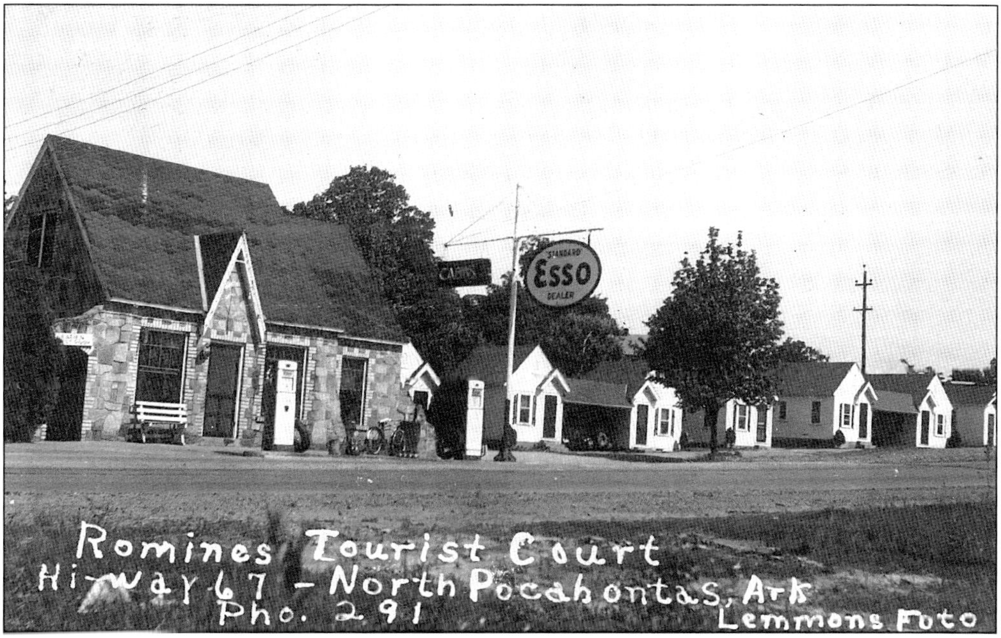

In 1936, the promise of a paved Highway 67 led a man named Romine to develop a tourist court around an Esso station on the north side of Pocahontas. The business's phone number was 291, and a night in one of the cabins most likely cost between $2 and $3 when this card was made around 1940. In the 1940s, Romine's lost much of its business when Highway 67 was rerouted four blocks to the south. Remarkably, as seen in the photo below, the court still survives on what is now N. Marr Street, where it has been converted to apartments. The office building is to the left; the area is now a quiet residential street totally bypassed by the highway traffic a few blocks south. (1999 photo by Wade James of Pocahontas, who spent his honeymoon at the Romine Court in 1940.)

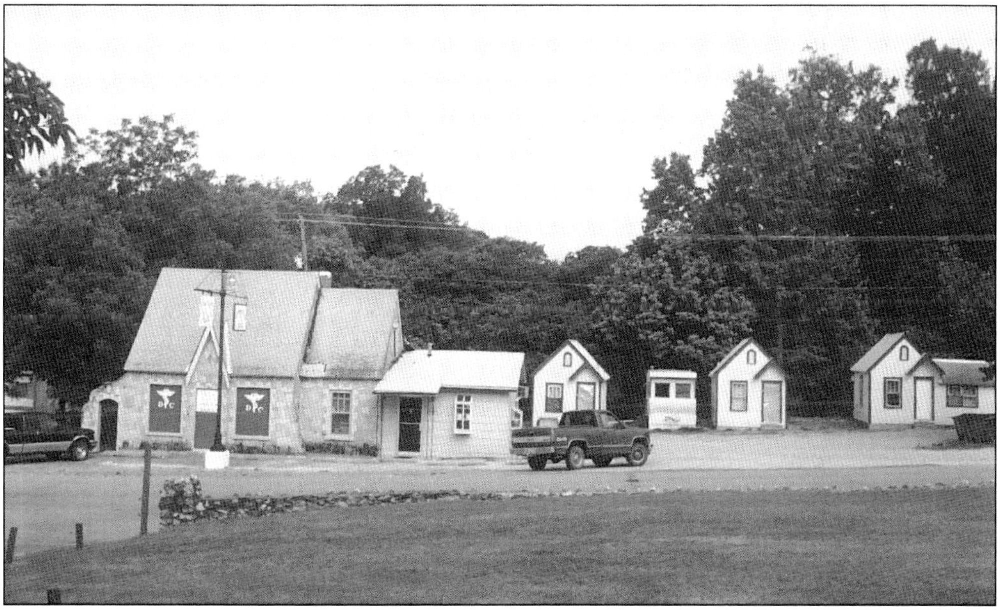

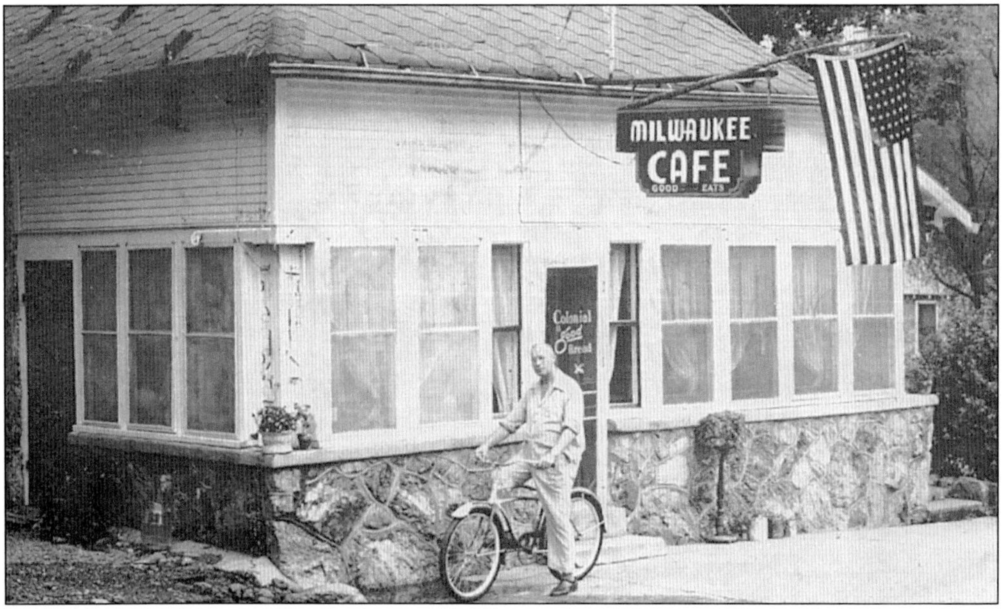

The Milwaukee Cafe was located near the Romine Court and was operated by Louis Froelich. Presumably, he is the gentleman seated on a bike in front of the door that has "Colonial is Good Bread" painted on the wire screen. The best theory on how a cafe in Pocahontas, Arkansas, came to have the Milwaukee name is that Froelich was a Wisconsin native. The cafe closed years ago, and the building reportedly later served as a grocery store. Today, as indicated by the photo below, the one-time cafe survives as a private residence on a long bypassed section of highway, now N. Marr Street. Without this postcard there would be no clue that the building once housed a cafe located on the edge of the busiest highway in Arkansas. (1999 photo by Wade James of Pocahontas.)

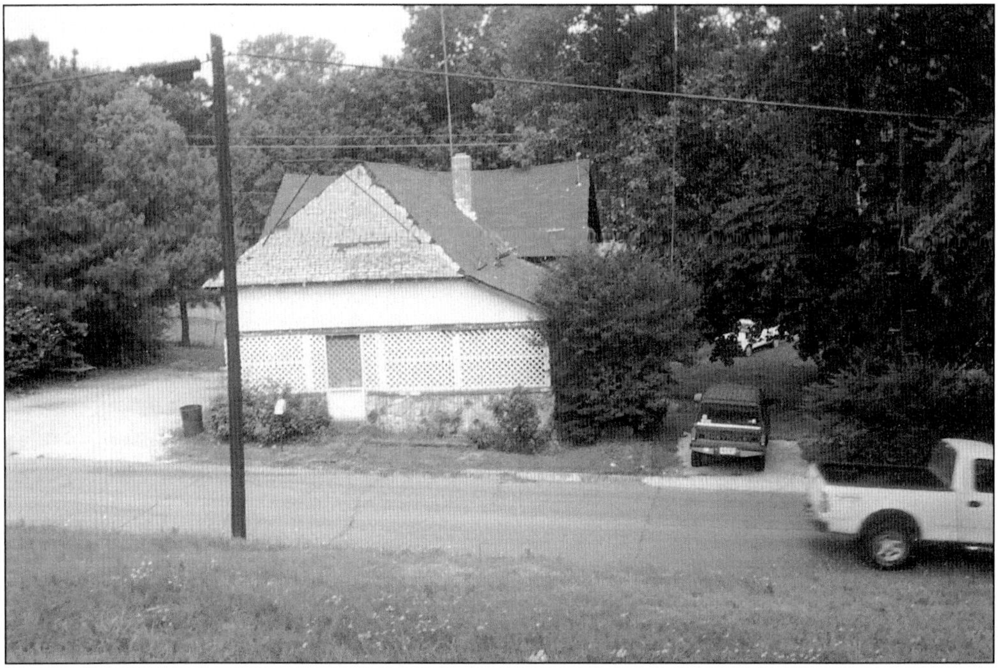

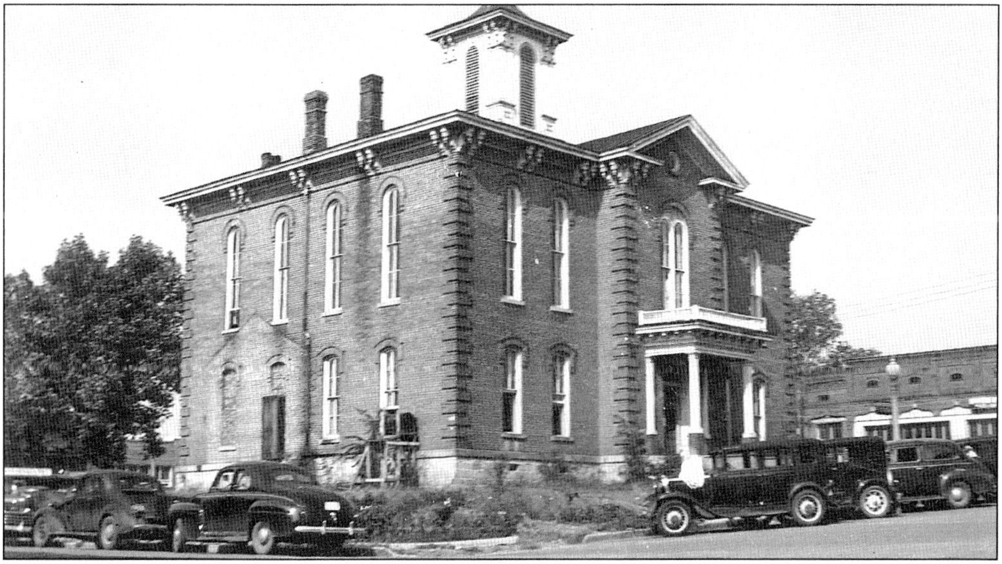

Today, Highway 67 passes three blocks south of the Pocahontas Courthouse square, but for many years, the highway circled the courthouse, which was built in 1872 and is seen here around 1940. A local story tells of a one-legged man who was able to drive his car on straight roads, overcoming, somehow, the obvious problem of its clutch. He is said to have remarked that if not for all the shifting required to circle the town square, he could drive all the way to St. Louis. Today, a new courthouse is in service just off the square; the old one is restored and houses the area chamber of commerce.

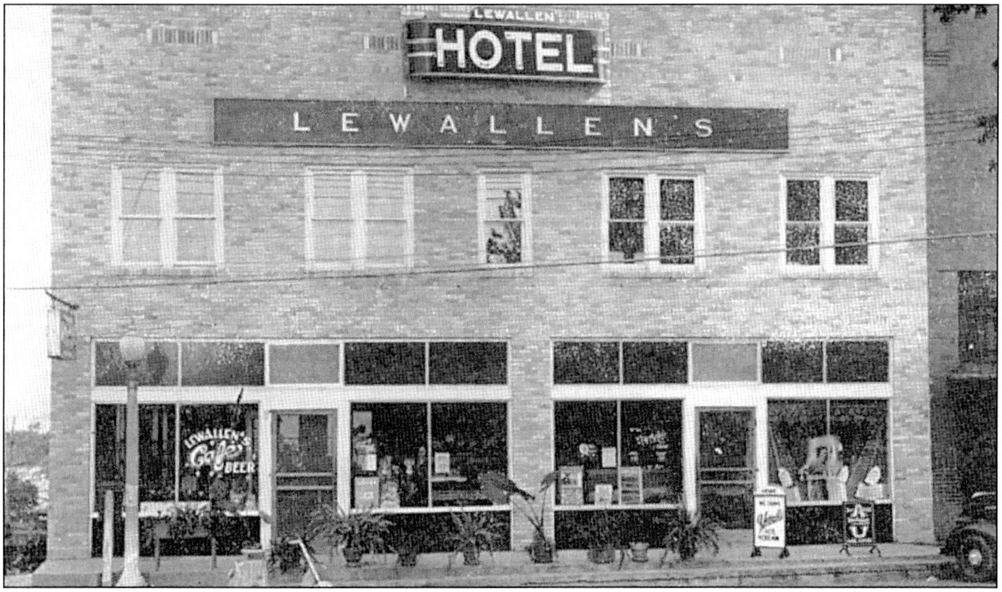

In 1937, when Highway 67 circled the courthouse, Mr. and Mrs. James Lewallen built a hotel on the south side of the courthouse square. A few years later, Ray Bowlin and his son Paul leased out the bottom of the hotel and opened the first in what became a small chain of furniture stores. The building has been used in many diverse ways over the years, including not only as a hotel and furniture store, but also as a cafe under various names and a bowling alley in the full basement. The building still stands today, but serves other commercial purposes; the hotel closed years ago.

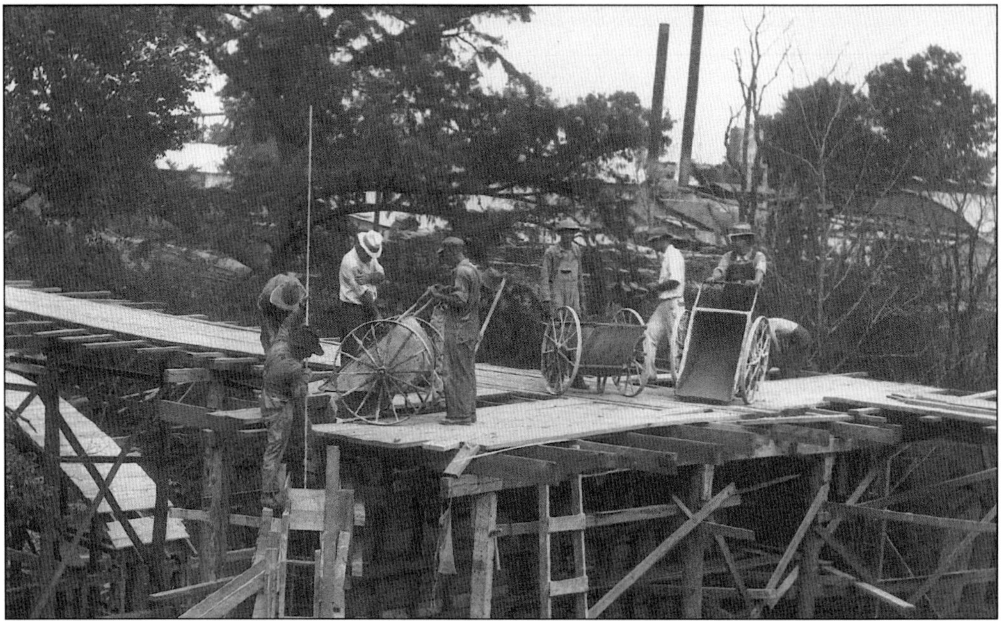

In 1934, Highway 67 was being paved with concrete slab, and to accompany the improved road, a new automobile bridge was under construction across the Black River, south of downtown Pocahontas. The job appears to have involved work done among the tops of the huge trees that lined the banks of the river. The men are pushing cement-laden wheelbarrows to fill the complex wooden forms for the concrete bridge supports. They likely felt fortunate to have such arduous employment during the Depression years. The bridge was replaced in recent years with a wide, modern span. (Photos courtesy of University of Central Arkansas Archives.)

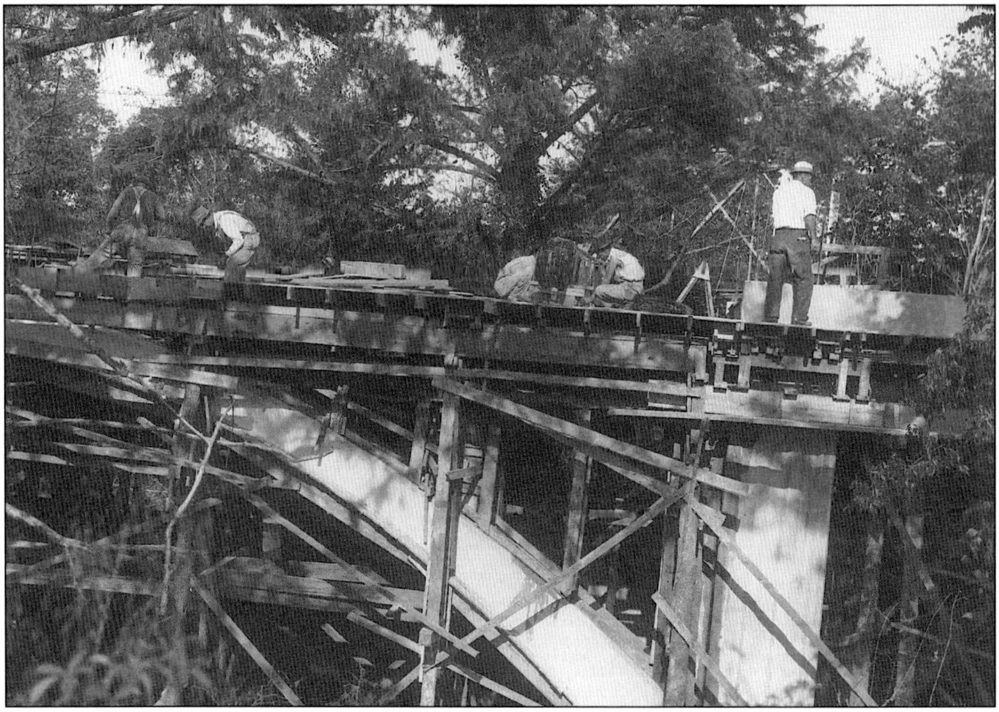

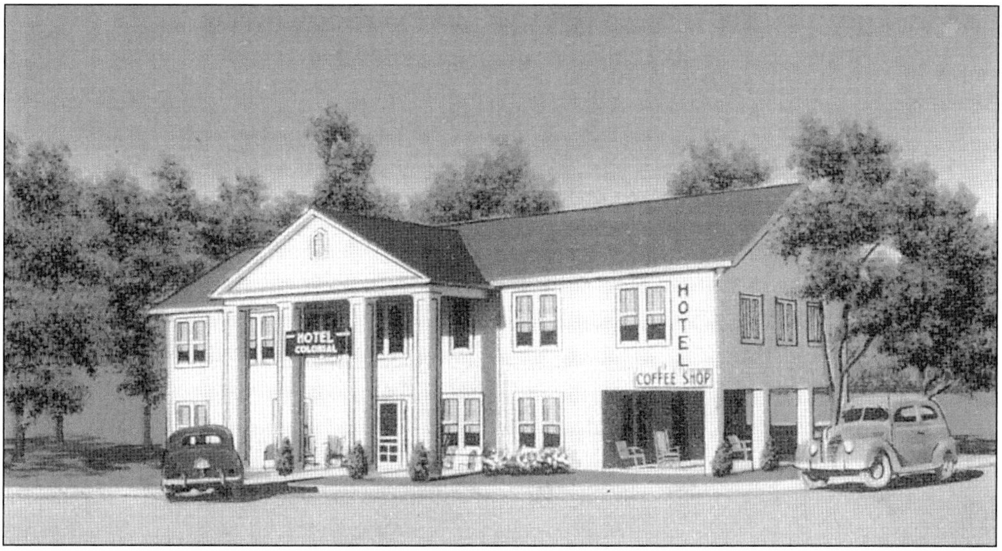

A few blocks from downtown, at the junction of Highways 67 and 62, the Hotel Colonial displayed its stately columns to attract motorists passing through Pocahontas, c. 1940. The proprietor, Mrs. R.K. Baker, also advertised the coffee shop in the right end of the hotel. A few years later, the Hotel Colonial was remodeled, and Jerry's Steak House and Cafe opened at the end of the building. The hotel was torn down years ago, and its site is now home to Pocahontas Savings & Loan.

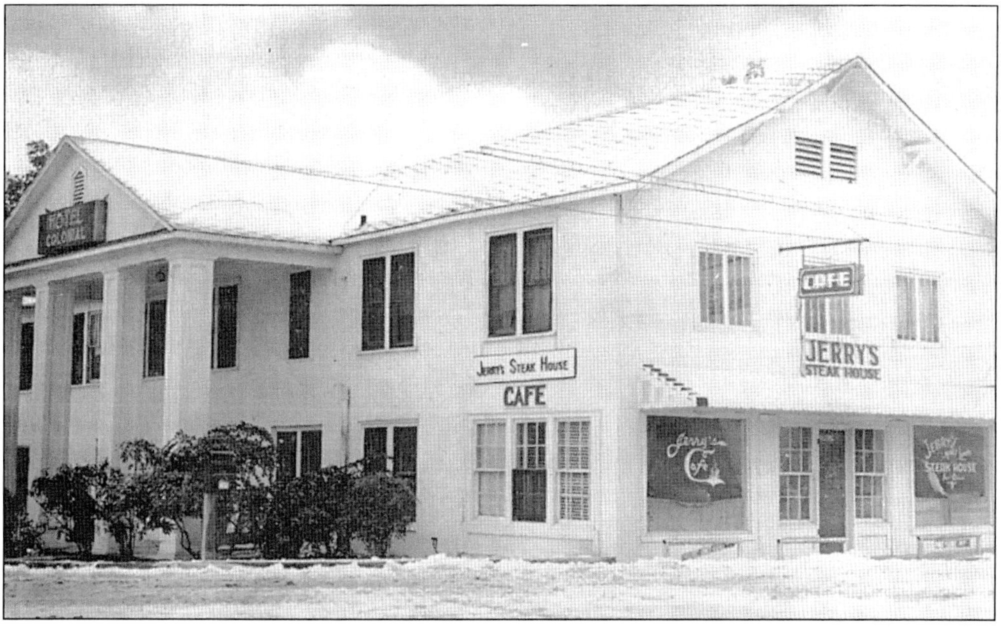

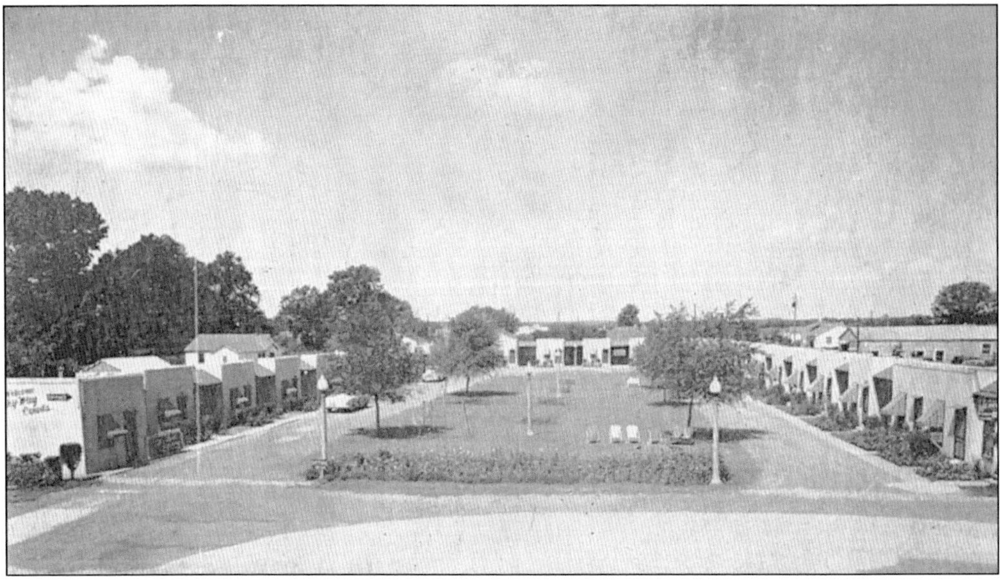

The paved road and new bridge erected over the Black River in 1934 helped give rise to tourist-related businesses along Highway 67 on the south side of Pocahontas. The Sky-Way Courts wrapped around a large grassy lawn and advertised many amenities, including 30 units with carports, air conditioning, innerspring mattresses, free ice, daily newspapers, and a television in the lobby. The name of the court came from the fact that there was an Army training landing strip across the road. Today, some of the buildings still stand, though the court went out of business years ago. The above image was taken *c.* 1940. Mrs. Stella James ran the Silver Grill and Restaurant on the highway, luring motorists with its advertised steaks, chops, Southern fried chicken, and seafood. The grill was built in 1937 and purchased by Mrs. James in the 1940s; she is seen in the lower right panel of this *c.* 1945 postcard. The grill closed in the 1980s and was torn down around 1995.

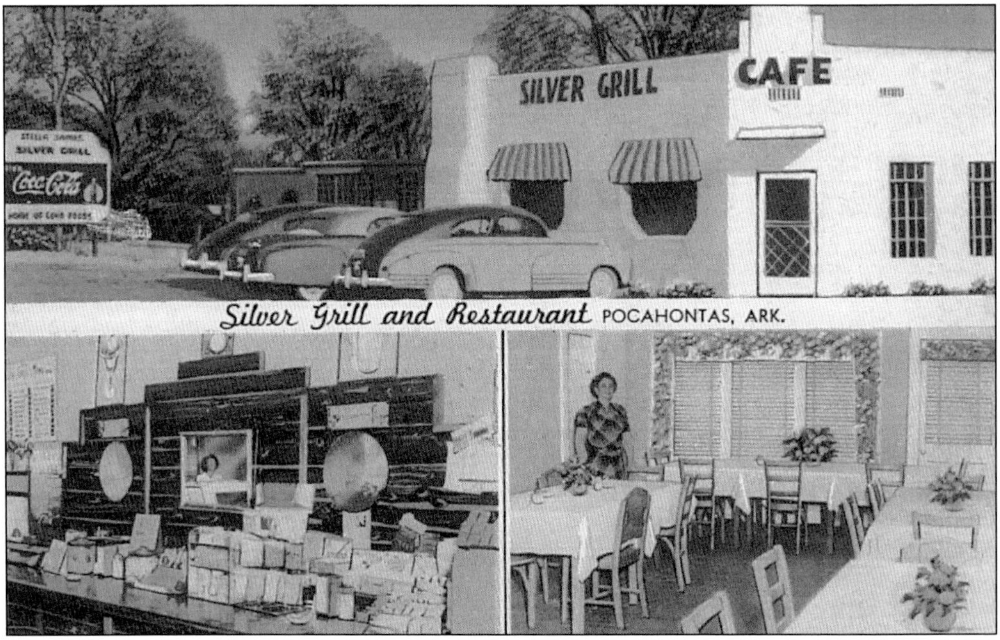

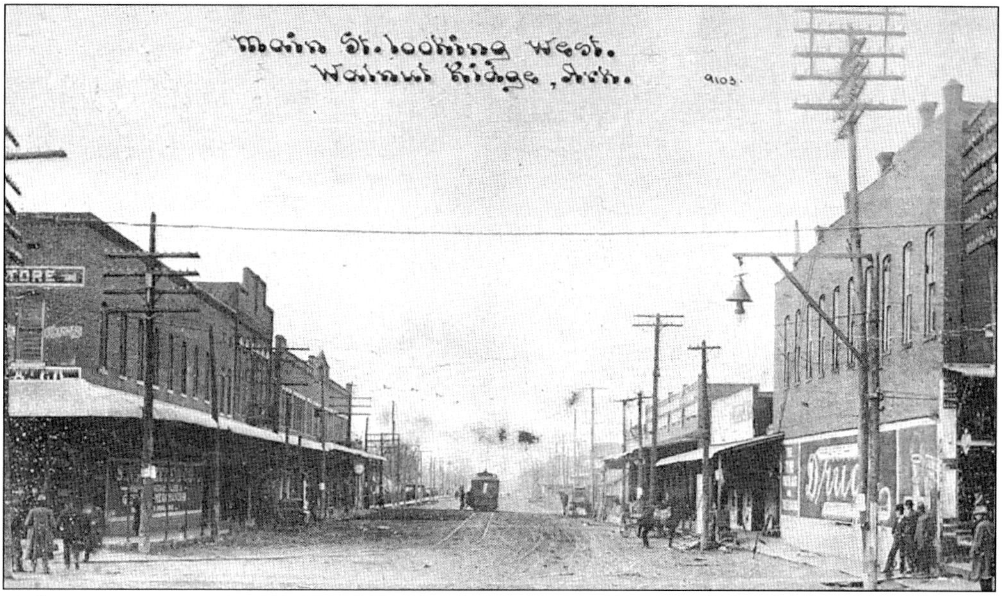

Today, an easy, quick ride between farm fields brings travelers down Highway 67 into the Lawrence County seat of Walnut Ridge. The relative isolation provided by early-20th-century modes of transportation allowed the town and its close neighbor, Hoxie, to develop into thriving communities. Founded in 1883 after the coming of the railroad, Walnut Ridge presumably was named for the walnut trees in the area. In the 1912 view above, the future path of Highway 67 down Main Street was still dirt but boasted a streetcar in the distance.

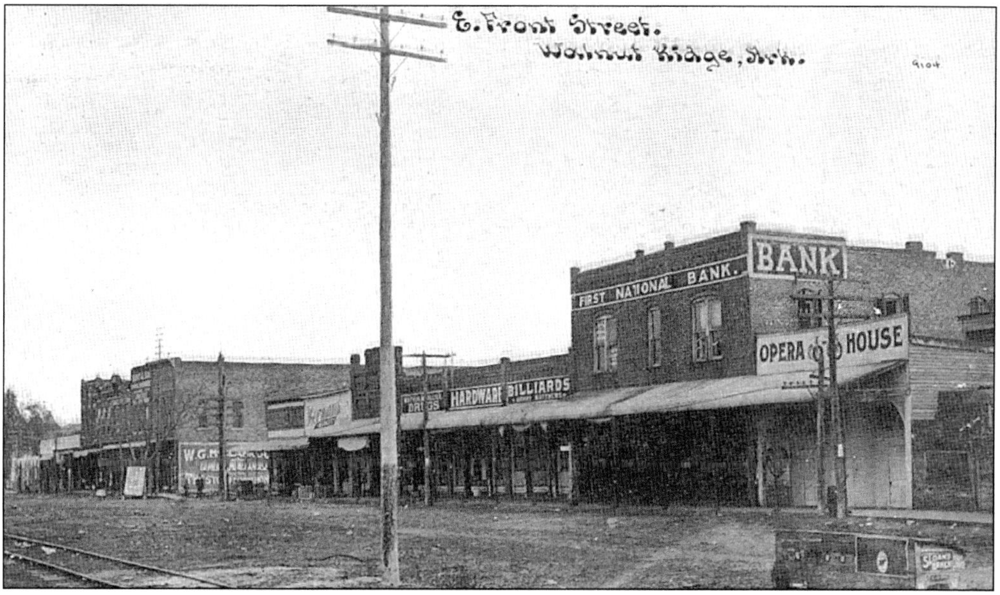

Today, Highway 67, as it has since at least the 1920s, comes down Main Street in Walnut Ridge and turns right in front of the rail track bed seen in the foreground in this view from around 1910. A motorist stopped at the traffic light looking across the tracks would today see most of the same buildings, although all now serve markedly different uses. Gone is the wooden opera house, but other businesses still operate in the former First National Bank, the billiard hall, and the pharmacy that operated adjacent to the Opera House.

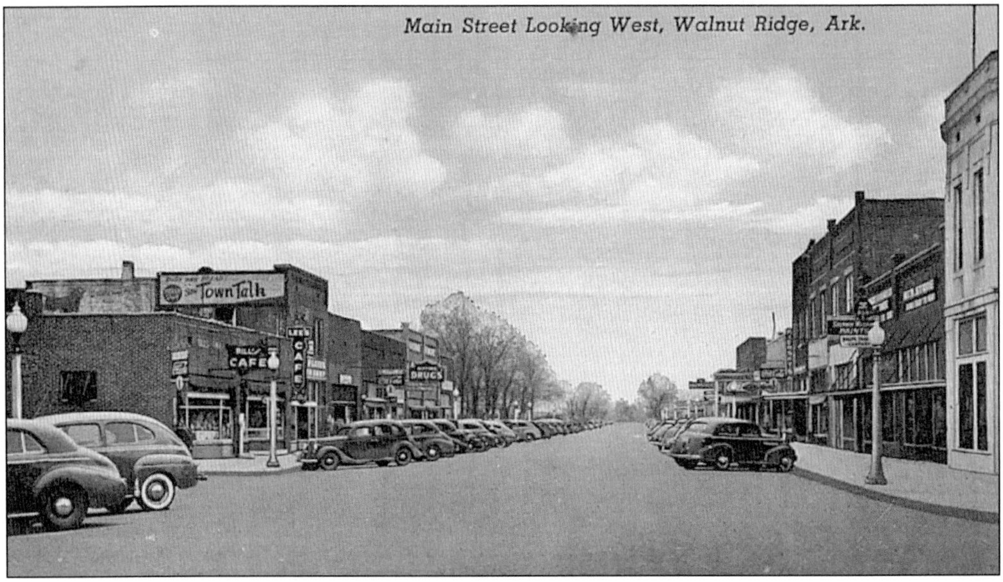

From the 1920s to the present time, Highway 67 has passed down Walnut Ridge's Main Street, bringing commerce to the merchants lining the street. Seen here around 1940 in a view looking west are competing eateries on the left side of the street; Bill's Cafe and Lee's Cafe are apparently next-door neighbors. A sign painted on one building advertises Town Talk bread.

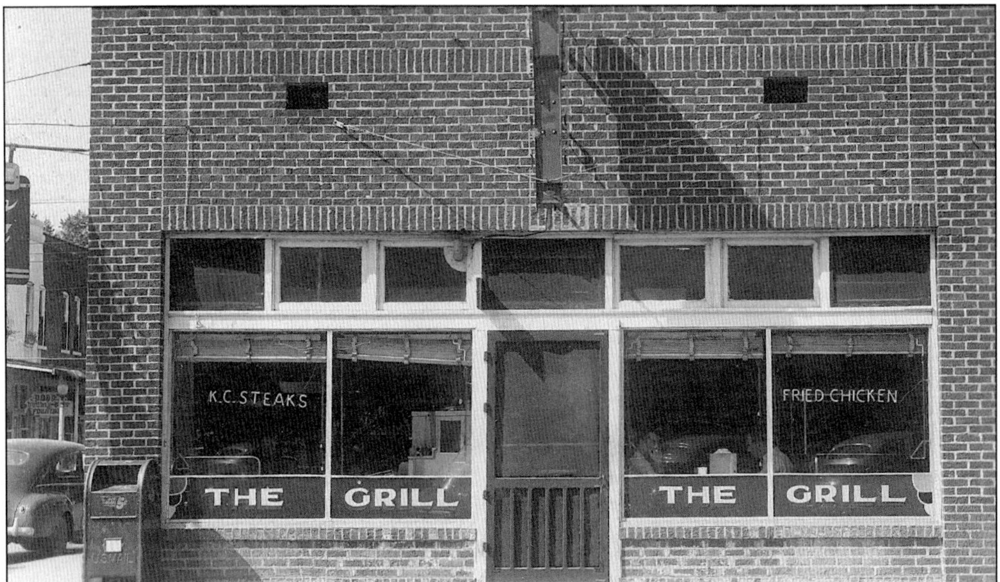

In the card above, mailed in 1948, Bill's Cafe on the corner had become The Grill, specializing in Kansas City steaks and fried chicken. Many hungry travelers over the years have parked at the curb on Main Street in order to dine here. That includes the men visible through the window to the right of the screen door, gazing out onto the passing traffic as they enjoyed a meal a few feet from the busiest highway in Arkansas. A postcard such as this could have been mailed at the mailbox on the sidewalk that has a sign reading, "Air Mail 5 cents." In recent years, the building no longer houses a restaurant but has served as a shoe store, among other things.

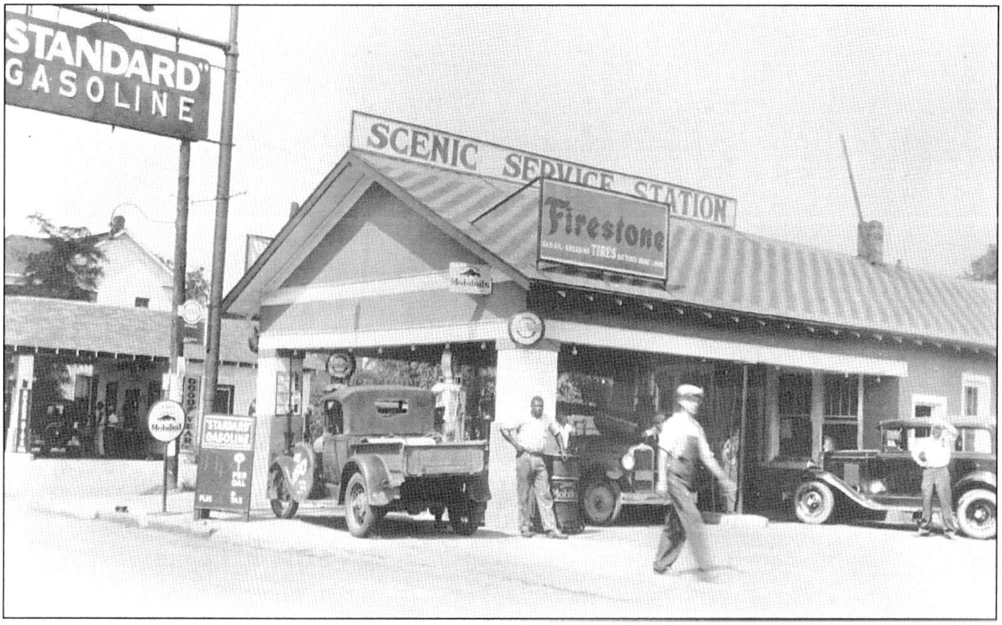

As the first automobiles began rolling through Walnut Ridge, the gas stations were not far behind. Mr. Bunk Spikes opened the Scenic Service Station on the unpaved highway on the south side of the town in the 1920s. In this photo from 1930, Spikes offered Standard Gasoline, Firestone tires, and Mobil oil. The chalkboard at the corner of the left pump shows the price of gas was only 11¢ per gallon. (Courtesy of Tom Moore of Jonesboro.)

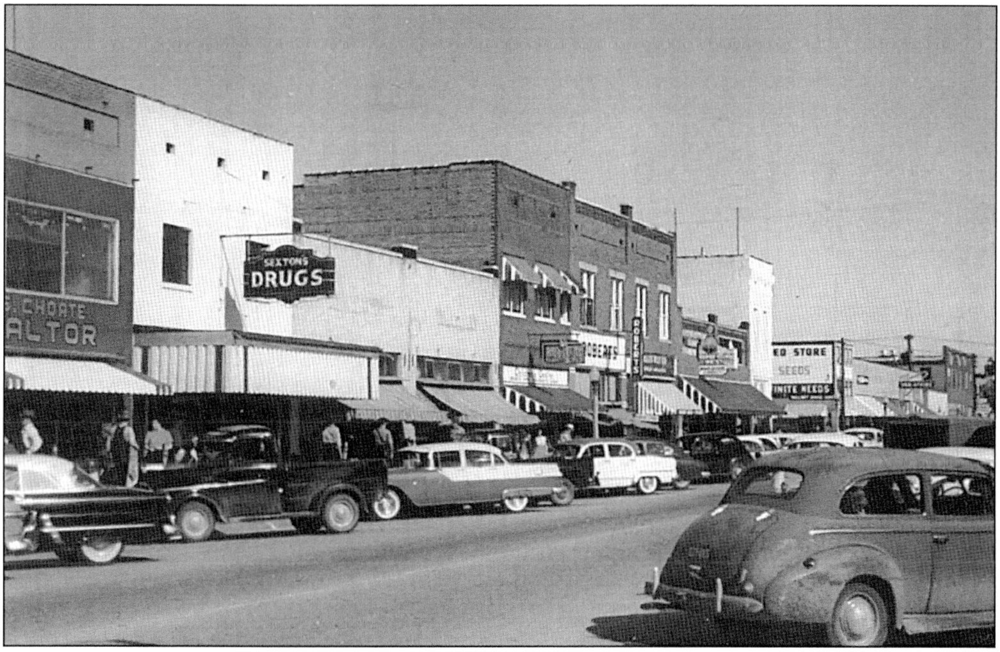

During the 1950s, before any shopping centers had been erected at the outer edges of town, a parking place on Walnut Ridge's Main Street section of Highway 67 was often at a premium. In the above card, every parking place was taken as shoppers patronized such places as Sexton's Drugs, which is still in business today at the same location.

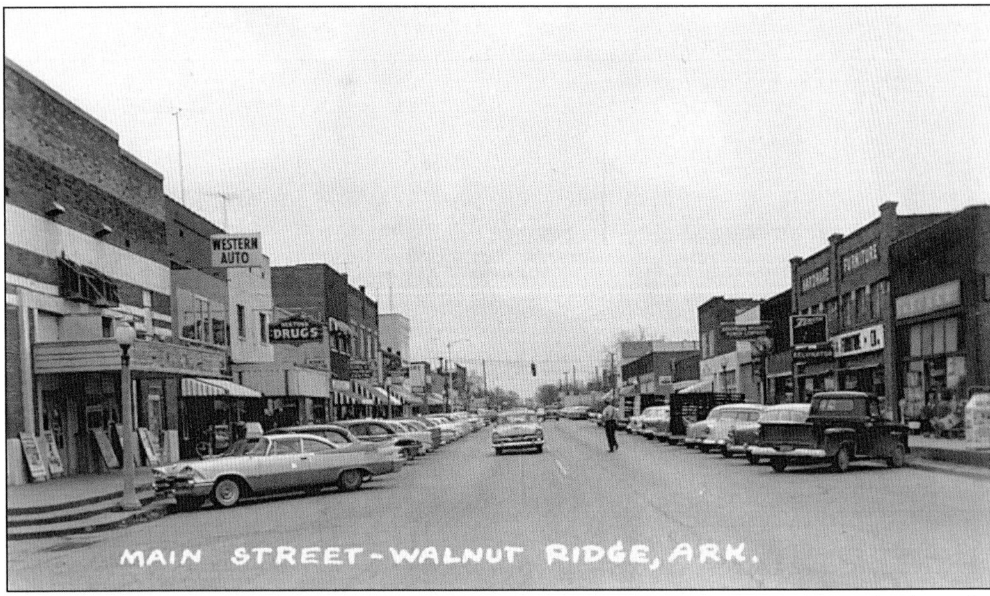

In the photo above, taken farther down the street, a Kroger grocery store is on the far right, looking quite different from its modern suburban descendants. The local movie theater can be seen on the left, perhaps an attraction for people passing through town and needing a break. Posters of coming attractions stand on the sidewalk. Today, the movie theater no longer shows films but is under restoration for other entertainment plans.

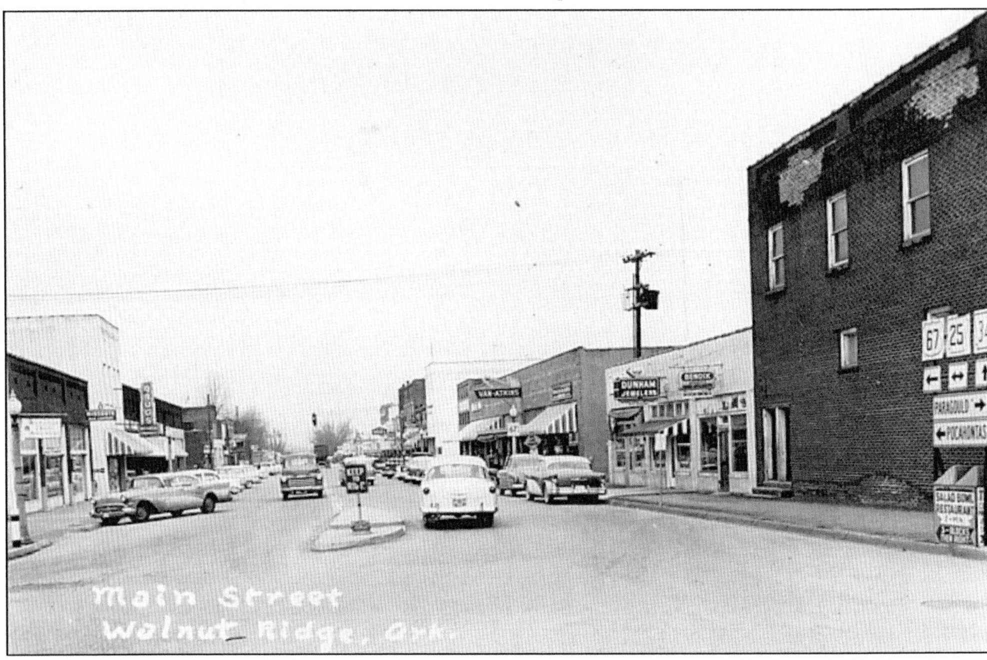

In the c. 1957 card from Walnut Ridge, above, Highway 67 has just turned the corner coming north from Hoxie, as the sign to the right points. The car is heading toward Pocahontas down Walnut Ridge's Main Street. Beneath the Highway 67 marker is a sign reading "Salad Bowl Restaurant, 2 minutes, three blocks then right." The Salad Bowl was a fixture on the northern edge of Walnut Ridge for decades.

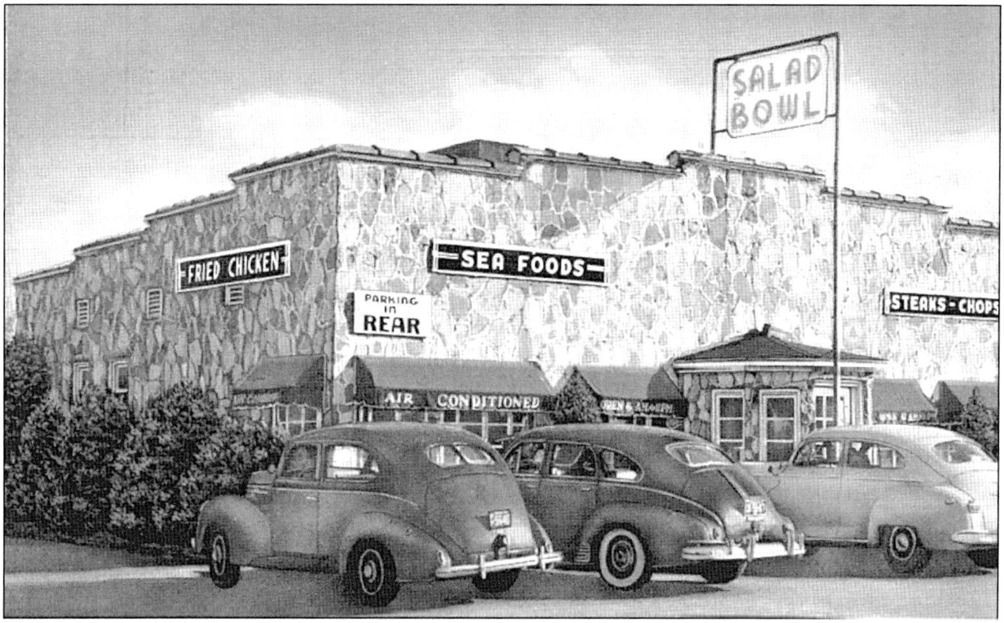

The *c.* 1950 card above proclaims that the eatery was "Recommended by American Automobile Association and Duncan Hines." The card's message reads, "This picture on this card is where we have just finished eating our breakfast, having a nice trip, just traveling and eating & sleeping."

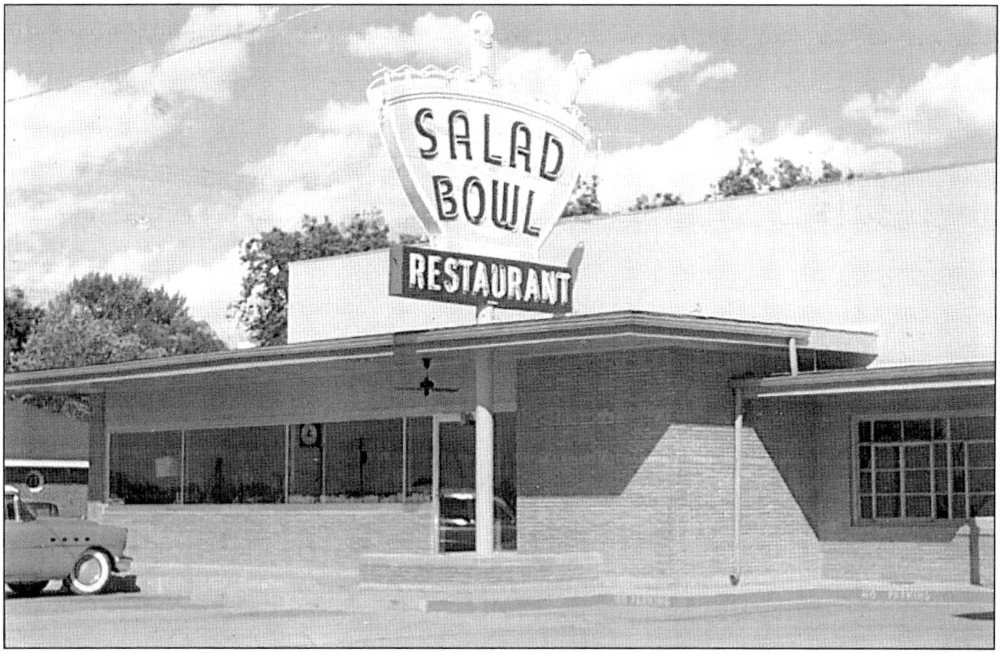

The popularity of the Salad Bowl was augmented by billboards that dotted Highway 67 as far north as the Missouri line and urged travelers to hold off their appetites until they reached Walnut Ridge and the Salad Bowl. By the late 1950s, the Salad Bowl had moved to a newer building right on Highway 67, where it operated well into the 1970s; the establishment is gone today.

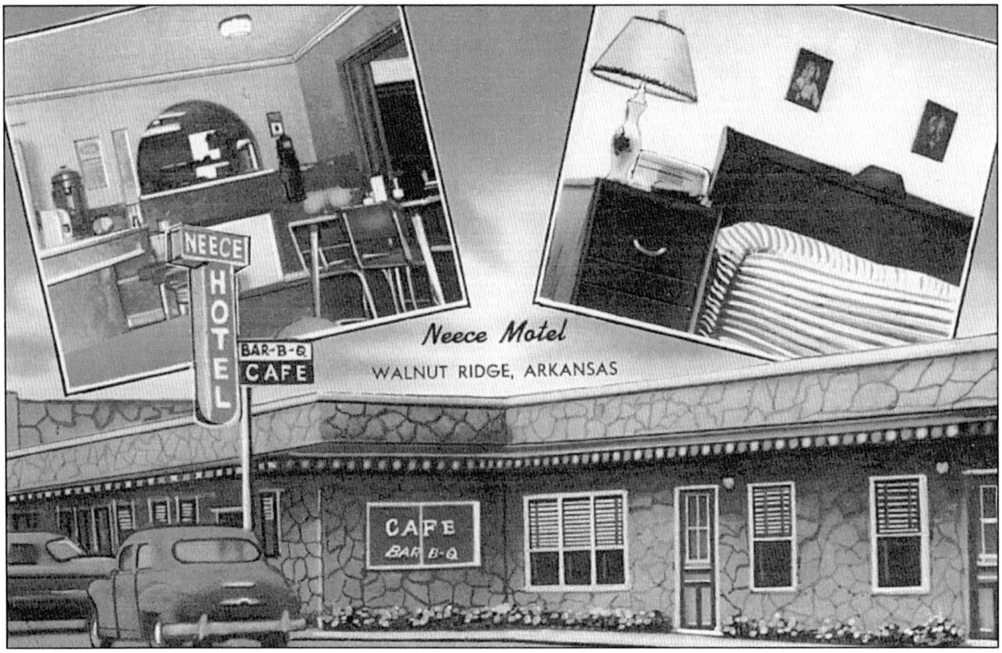

"When you motor in or near Walnut Ridge, may we have the pleasure of serving you?" was the message imprinted on the back of this *c.* 1945 view of the Neece Motel, located on Highway 67 on the north side of town. Mr. and Mrs. Melville Neece, the proprietors, also advertised free radio in each room and an adjoining cafe and service station.

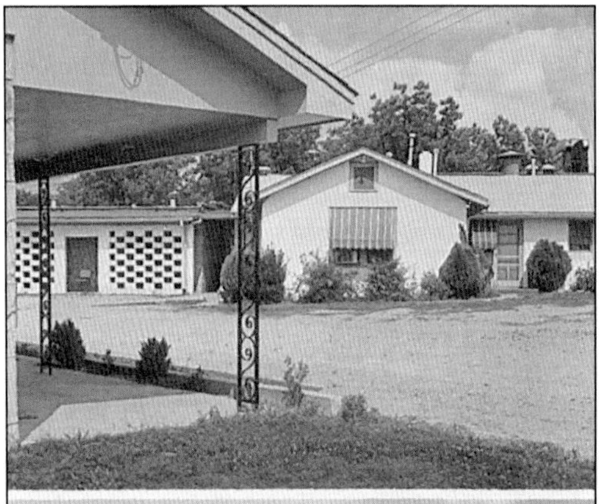

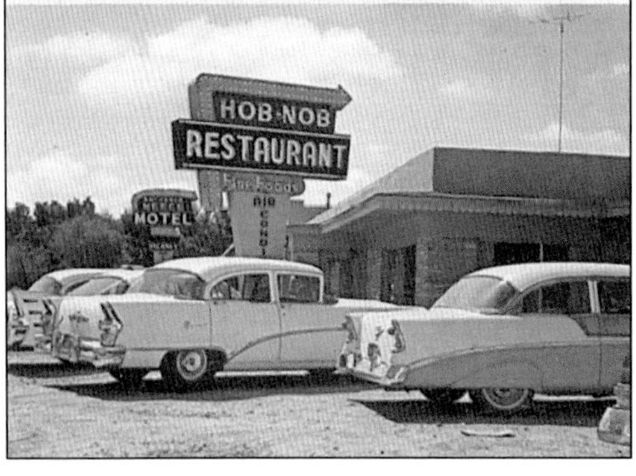

By the mid-1950s, the Neece Motel had modernized its 17 rooms, added televisions in each, and opened the 24-hour Hob-Nob Restaurant next door. The message on the card read, "Albert put Myrna in hospital here today, don't know yet if they can keep her from losing the baby." The motel no longer operates today, but the Hob-Nob still serves hungry travelers.

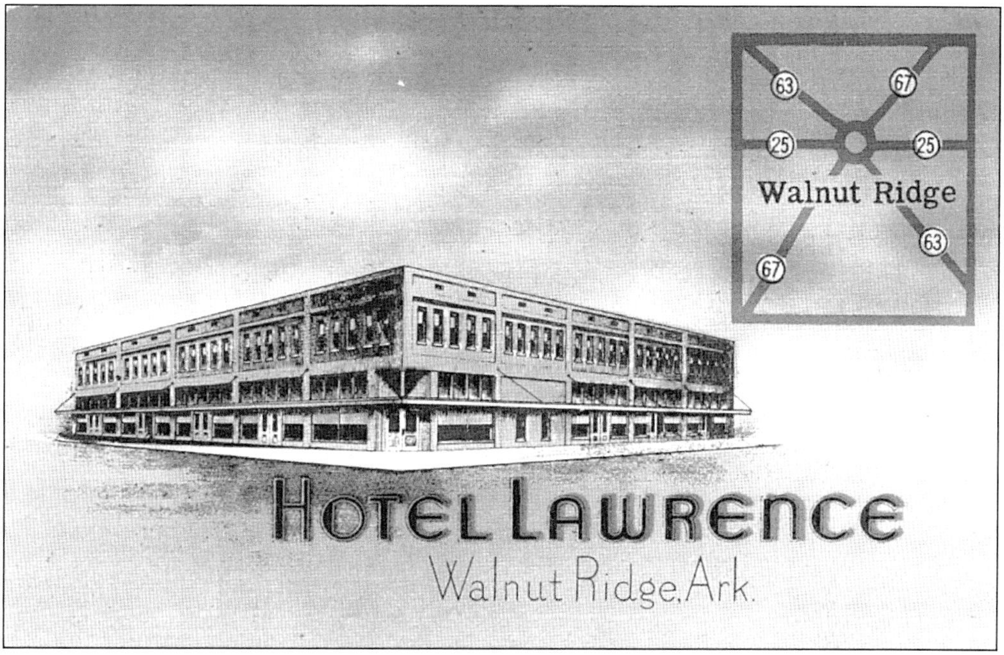

Located a block off Main Street/Highway 67 in Walnut Ridge, Hotel Lawrence was the premier lodging in the city from the 1920s into the 1940s. Later boarded up and neglected, as motorists were drawn to newer motels on the edge of town, the proud old hotel fell to the wrecker's ball many years ago.

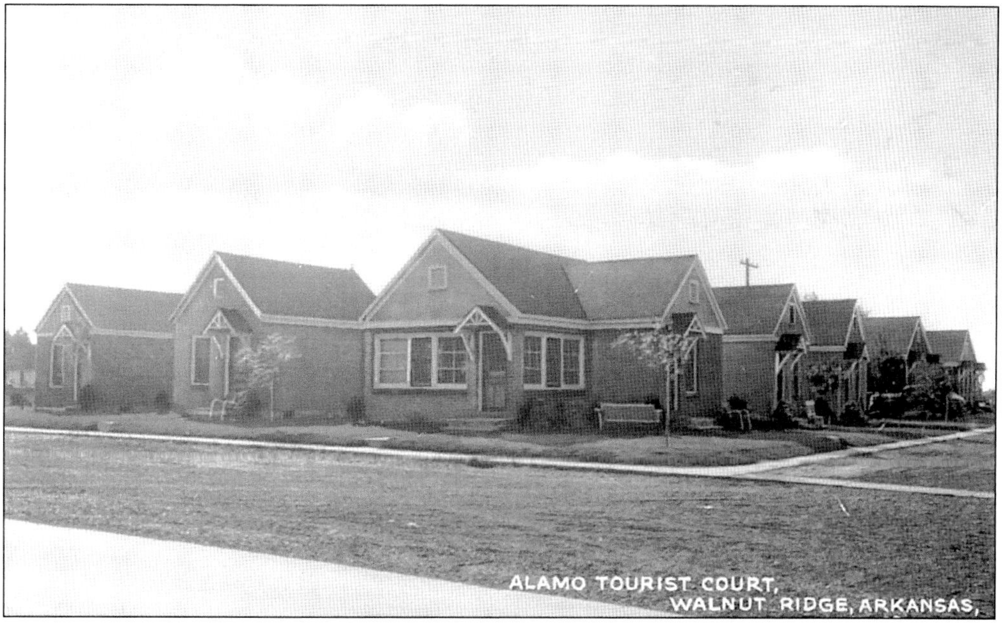

On the south side of Walnut Ridge the choice of lodging for Highway 67 motorists was the Alamo Court, an affiliated group of tourist courts that developed across the south and southwest in the 1940s. The individual cabins surrounding a lawn were in marked contrast to compact downtown hotels. The tourist court phenomenon spread across the nation as the ranks of the motoring public continued to expand. This picture was taken in 1941.

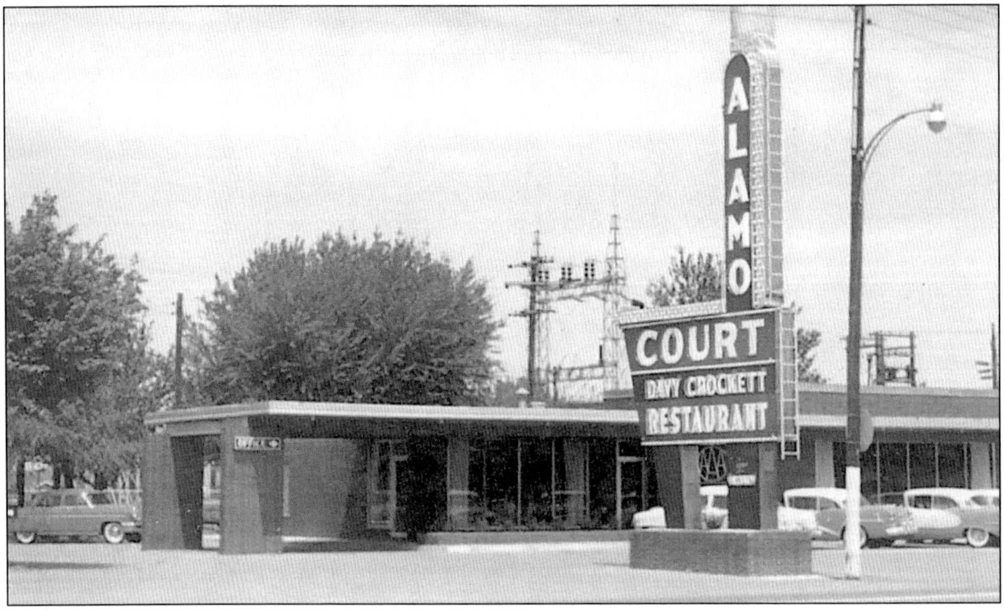

In the 1950s, the business was remodeled into the conventional motel layout of the era, and the Davy Crockett Restaurant was added. The business wanted to get the maximum mileage out of the "Alamo" label at a time when Walt Disney and Fess Parker were making a household word of the frontier legend who died at the famous battle. The Alamo Court, with more modern buildings, still provides lodging for travelers today.

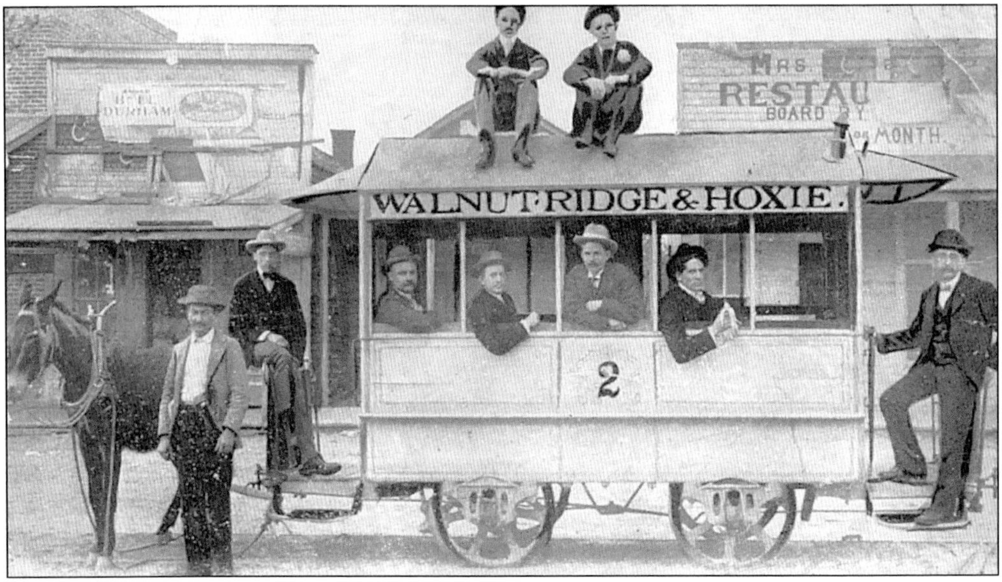

The small town of Walnut Ridge, with some 5,000 citizens, is joined at its southern limits by the slightly smaller town of Hoxie. Today, both towns are bisected by Highway 67, which passes the back-to-back city limit signs. The towns share more than a century of history, not the least of which involves the transit that has moved people from one town to the other along the path of today's Highway 67. During the 1890s and into the new century, a mule-drawn car line served as public transit, operating as a less-expensive alternative to the electric car that ran on the opposite side of the tracks. This is a c. 1900 image.

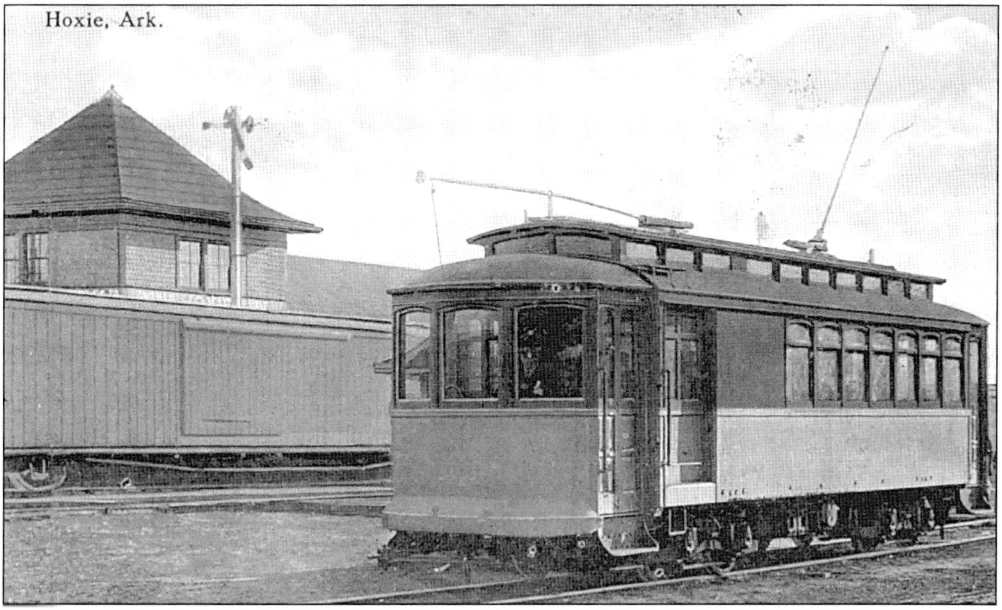

Above can be seen the electric trolley across the tracks, parked in front of the Hoxie Depot around 1910. The card's message reads, "Only car in Hoxie. One man is conductor & motorman." Today the trolley is long gone, but Highway 67 still joins the towns.

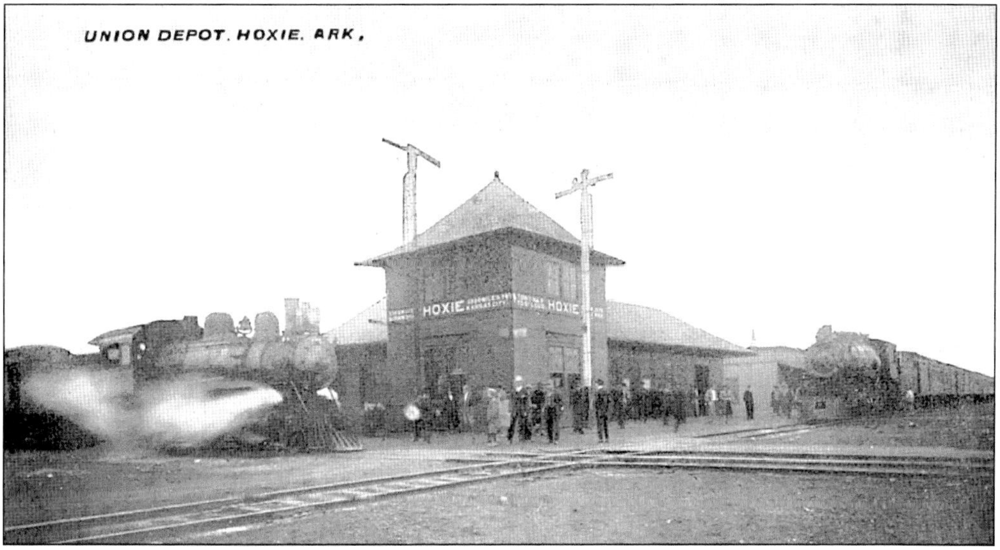

Motorists driving along Highway 67 through Hoxie today note the train tracks still in use a few yards to the east of the road. Hoxie was laid out in 1883 on the Kansas City, Ft. Scott & Gulf Railroad, where the tracks crossed just southeast of Walnut Ridge. The railroad has been a part of the town's heritage and the subject of postcards over the years. The town was born when Mrs. Mary Boas sold railroad officials on the route of a new line through her 450-acre farm south of Walnut Ridge by offering a free right-of-way. The town grew up around the tracks and was greatly enhanced when the Missouri Pacific Railroad opened a roundhouse and repair shop there in 1902. In this c. 1910 view, two trains are converging at the Hoxie station, and steam billows from the train on the left. The depot is gone today, but freight trains still rumble through town.

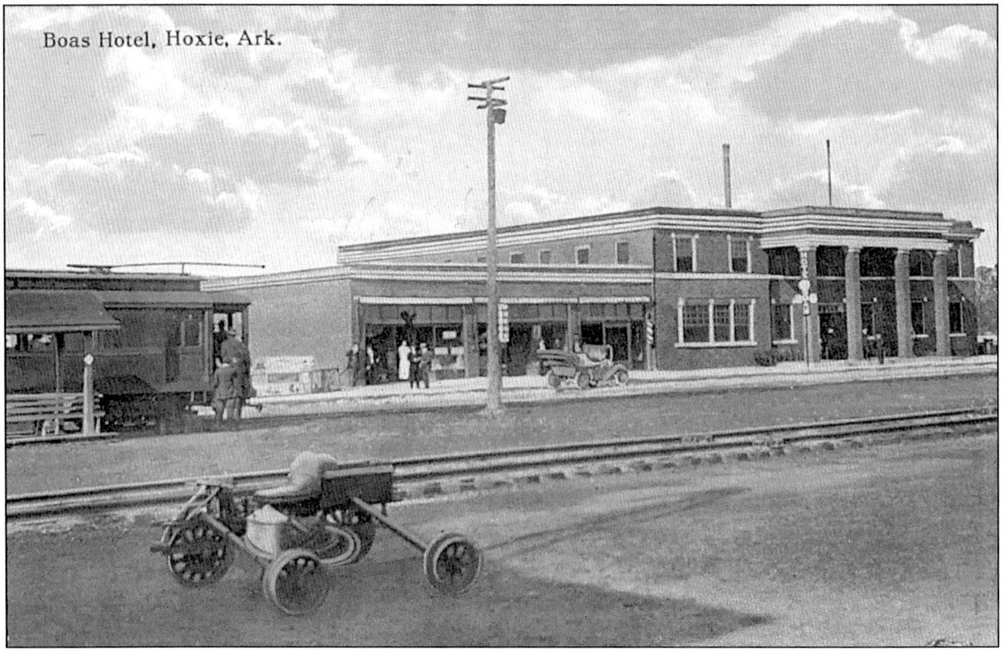

The Boas Hotel was first erected as a wooden-frame building to house railroad workers and passengers. Early in the century, the Boas family built this more substantial brick hotel across from the tracks and depot. It later served Highway 67 passengers until being demolished in the 1940s.

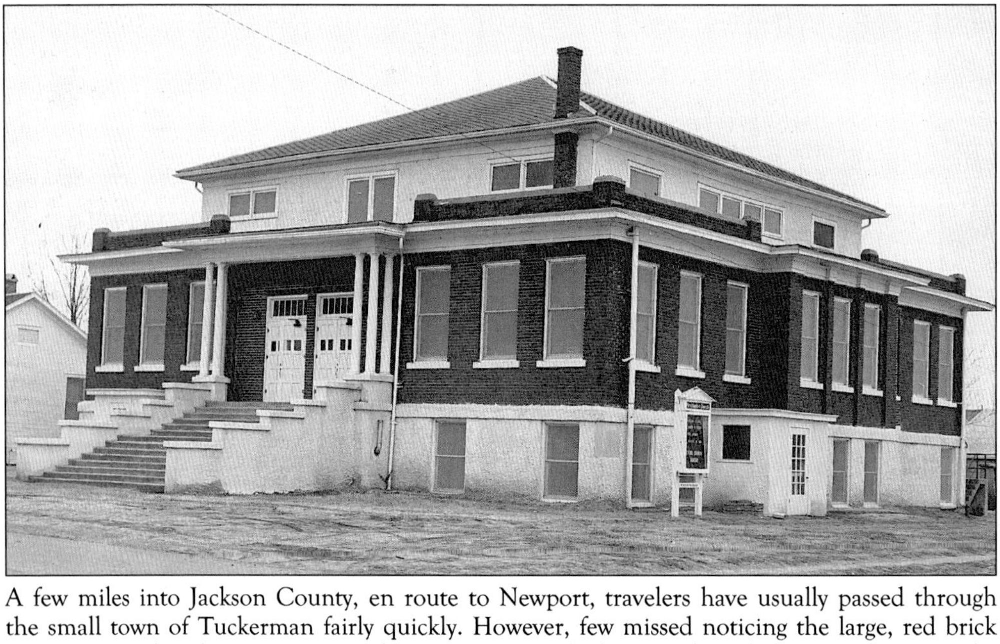

A few miles into Jackson County, en route to Newport, travelers have usually passed through the small town of Tuckerman fairly quickly. However, few missed noticing the large, red brick First Baptist Church on a corner in close proximity to the busy road. Built in the early 1920s, the landmark church's history says it once oversaw the baptizing of 121 people on a single Sunday, accomplished by three preachers working in shifts. The church still meets today in the same building. (Courtesy of Phyllis Holmes of Newport.)

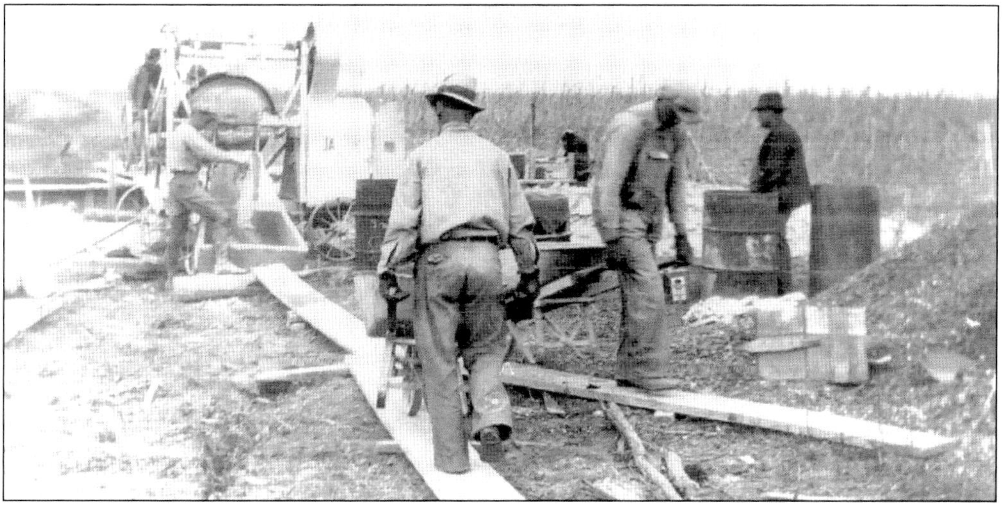

In 1934, when the photo above was made, near the point where Lawrence and Jackson Counties meet, men were hard at work laying the slabs of concrete that would eventually complete the paving of Highway 67 through the state. Seen here working beside a harvested farm field, laborers toil to push wheelbarrows of concrete across the planks that prevented them from getting bogged down in the mud. The construction crews of the era lacked the massive equipment used today, and much of the labor was manual, a factor that caused the paving to take years. As seen from the newspaper headlines, there were doubts to be overcome as to whether or not the road would even be finished. The towns along the highway formed an association to successfully lobby Congress for the funding that finally paid for the completion of the paving project. By the late 1930s, this motorist was enjoying the fruits of the hard work of the men who had spread tons of concrete onto the previously dirt track of Highway 67. The car in this view is in northern Jackson County, en route to Newport. (Courtesy of UCA Archives.)

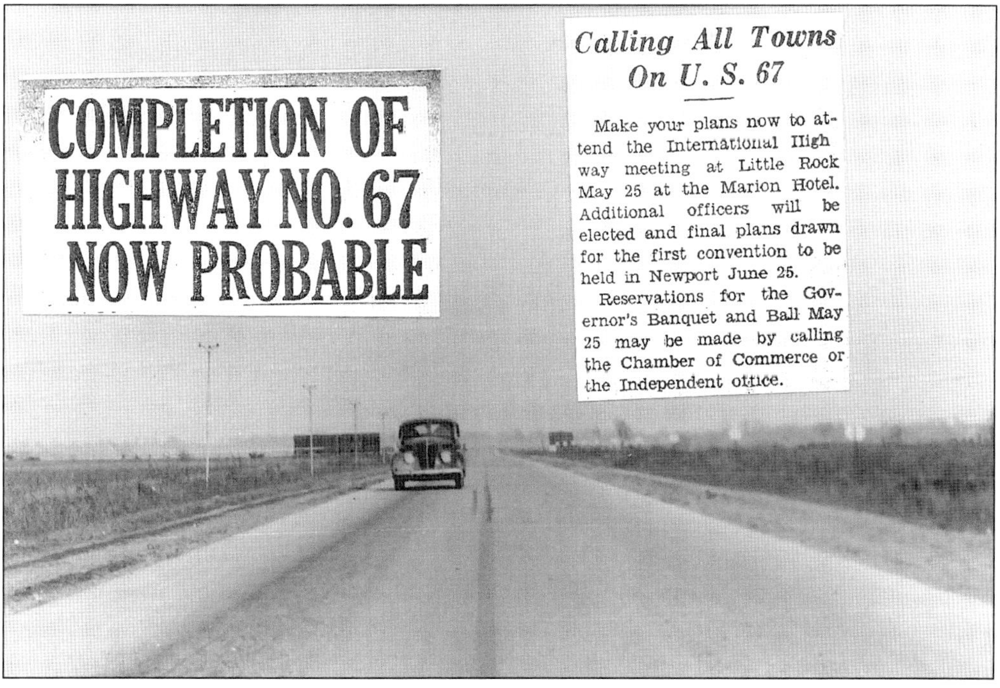

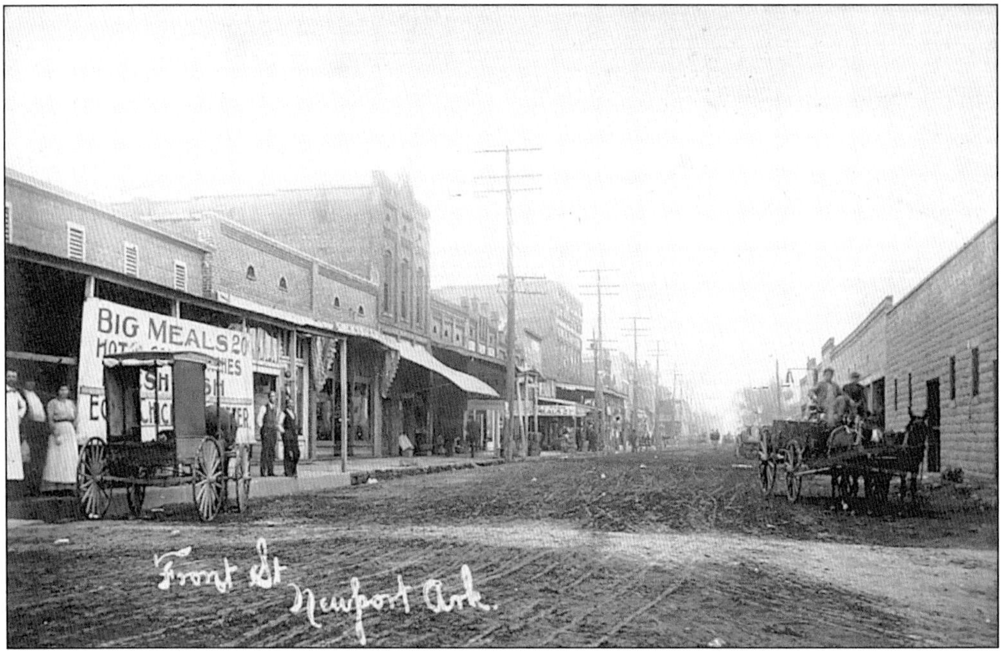

As the 20th century draws to a close, a new four-lane interstate Highway 67 is replacing the old highway and has bypassed the Jackson County seat of Newport. The town had its start in 1827 when David Litchfield began a ferry service on the White River, an element of town life that would persist into the 20th century. Over the better part of two centuries, the town's fortunes have been determined by the commerce of the river, changing only with the coming of the modern highway system. Newport's main thoroughfare was Front Street, seen above around 1905, when two competing businesses each advertised "Big Meals" for 20¢. As seen in the c. 1900 image below, with the area roads still rough and primitive, travelers depended on a ferry to cross the sometimes-wide White River in a manner little changed from the birth of the town seven decades before.

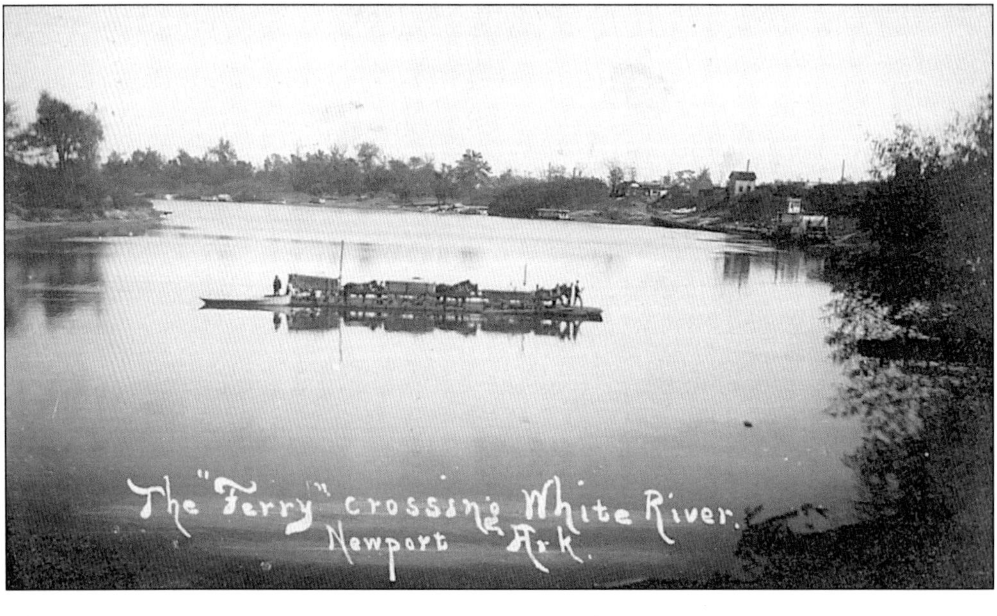

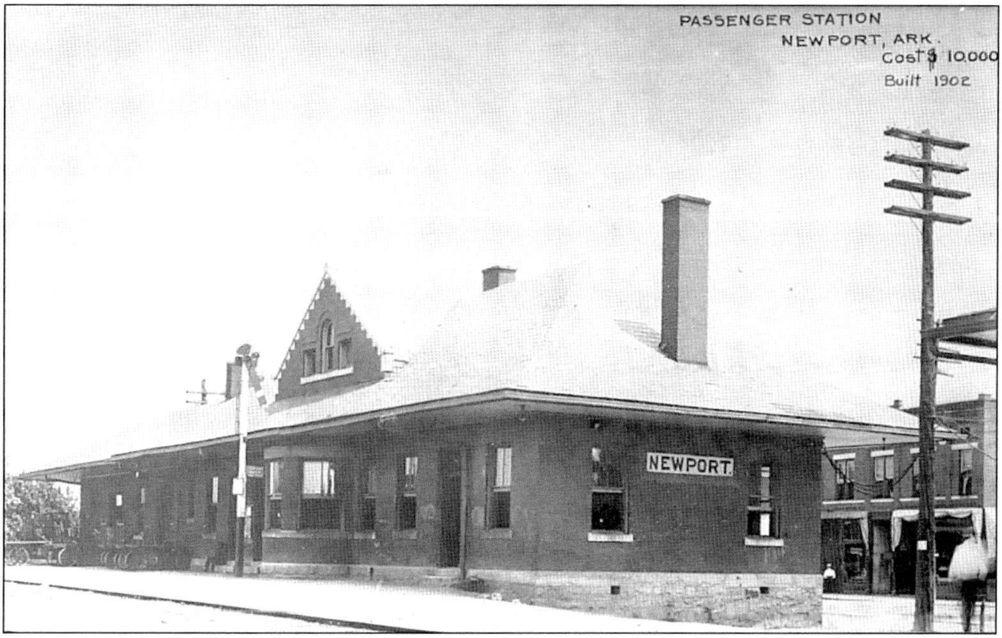

Transportation made a major advance through Newport in 1902 with the construction of a $10,000 depot for the Iron Mountain Railroad across Front Street from the main business district. Though improved rail service lessened the dependence on river commerce in an era when roads were still poor, the White River still made its presence known. On a cold winter night in February 1916, days of rain caused a split in the levee and Front Street was flooded, including the area around the depot. The depot is seen to the left of the men standing in the cold water. Note the stranded peanut wagon against the pole to the right. The depot survived floods and the eventual demise of rail travel and stands today proudly restored. It is one of only about 20 of the state's original train depots that have survived intact, an accomplishment of which Newport is rightfully proud.

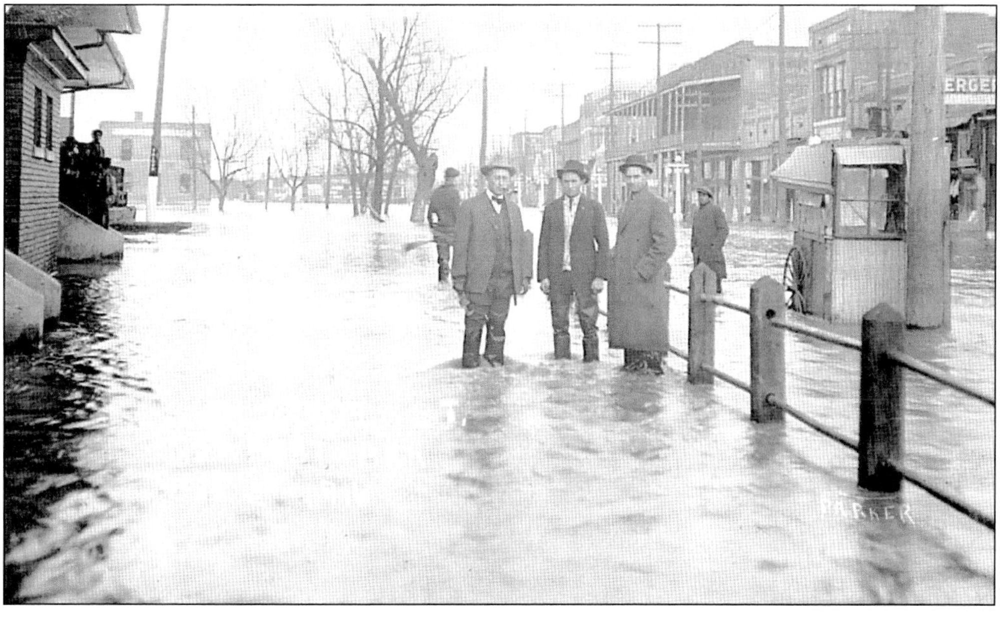

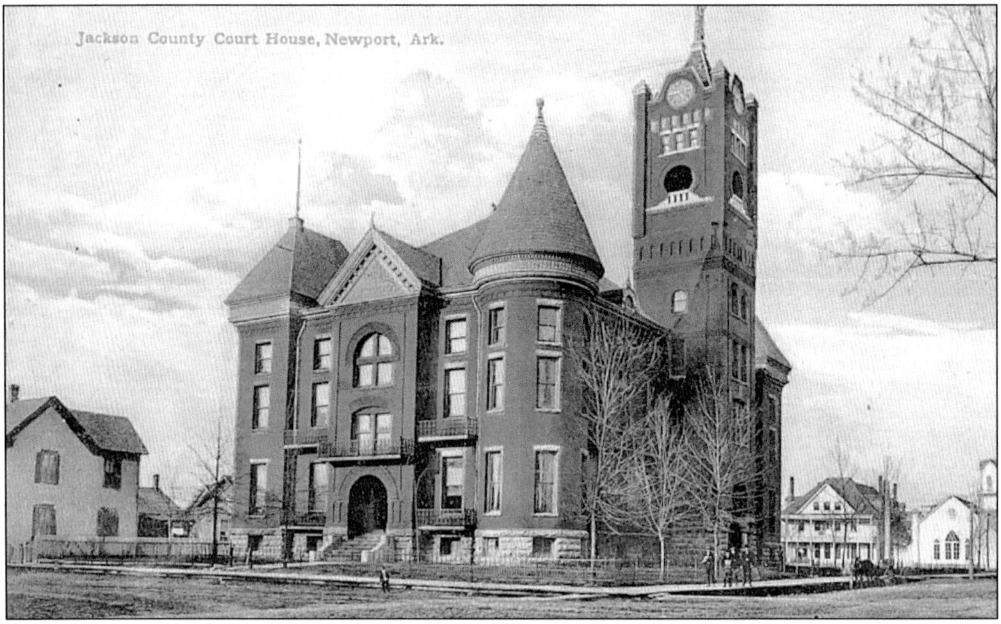

From the time of its construction in 1892, the Jackson County Courthouse has been the dominant feature of the Newport skyline, a landmark that often drew motorists off Highway 67 a block away for a closer look. Having survived floods that filled the basement and more than a century of history, the wonderful building still stands and makes a drive into downtown Newport a worthwhile detour off the now somewhat distant four-lane highway.

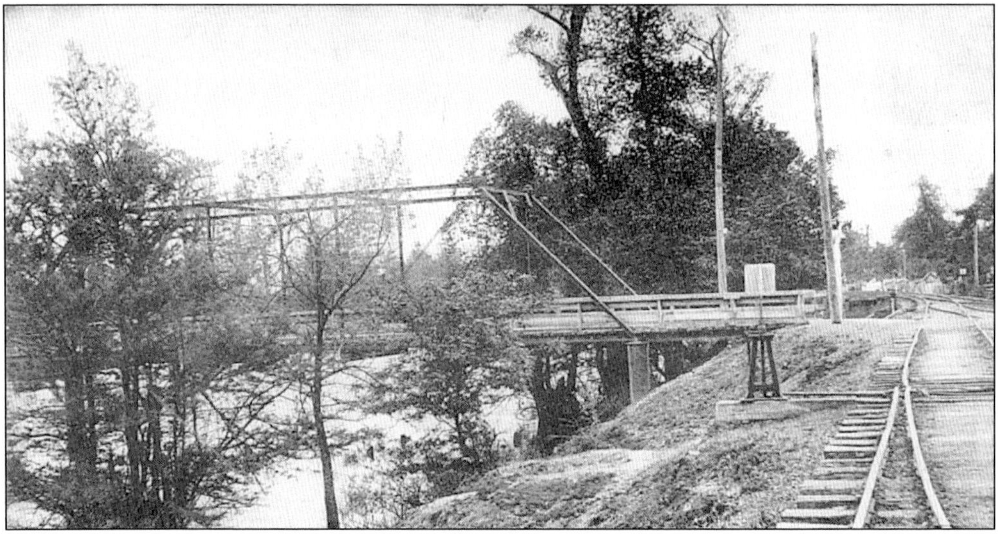

In the 1950s, a roadside park was established along Highway 67 in Newport on the edge of Newport Lake, an old White River slough that was home to ducks and other wildlife and fauna. The lake is seen here around 1905, edged by train tracks and crossed by an iron wagon bridge, where one day Highway 67 would cross the lake on a man-made causeway. In 1958, visitors from 47 states and 9 foreign countries signed the visitors book at the park, coming from as far away as Russia. A couple traveling Highway 67 from St. Louis wrote, "Very fine, so nice we decided to stay in Newport." A couple from Canada that year wrote of the Highway 67 park, "You have the best all-round park in 7,000 miles of travel, this is a credit to your community."

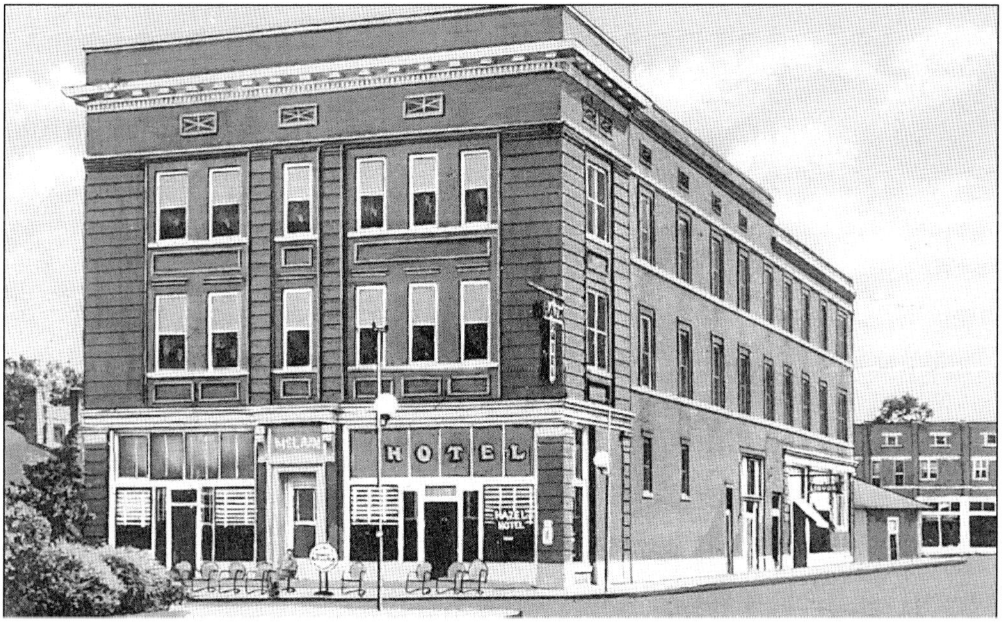

With the completion of Highway 67's paving in the late 1930s, motorists came through Newport in ever-greater numbers and were invariably drawn to Front Street. The hotel of choice in the 1940s was likely the Hazel Hotel with its coffee shop and banquet facilities. The hotel, built in 1905, was destroyed by a fire in 1961. All escaped without injuries, though some guests hurled their belongings out the windows while awaiting the fire trucks and rescue ladders.

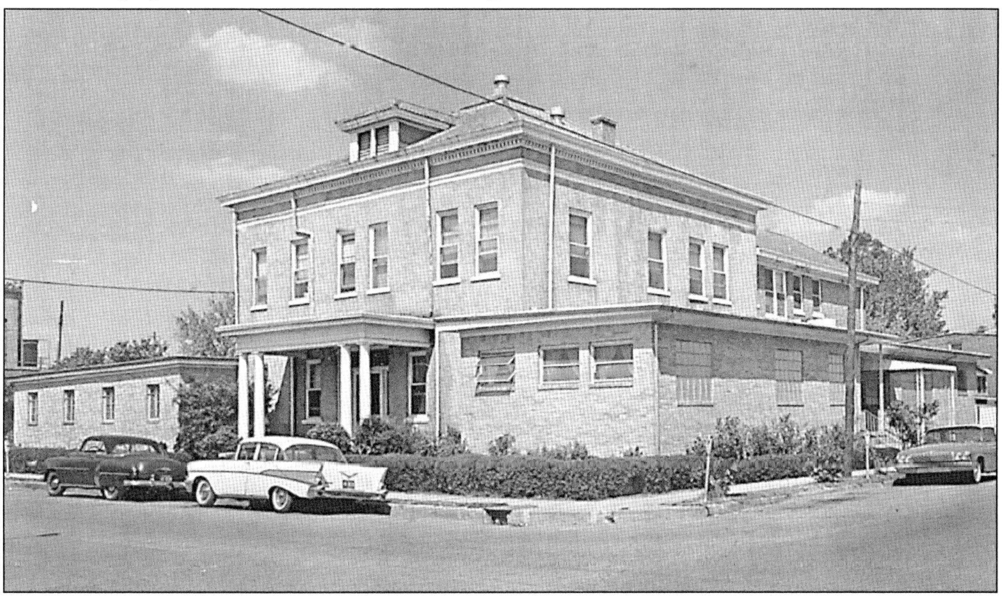

A member of the motoring public taken ill or injured on Highway 67 in the vicinity of Newport would have often been taken for treatment to the Newport Hospital and Clinic, located at Second and Laurel Streets. Built originally as the Elks Club in 1908, the building was bought in 1927 by Dr. A.M. Elton and Dr. M.L. Harris, who converted it into the Newport Sanitarium. Becoming the town's hospital, it operated in this unlikely building for 60 years before being replaced with a modern hospital. The building burned in the early 1990s and was razed.

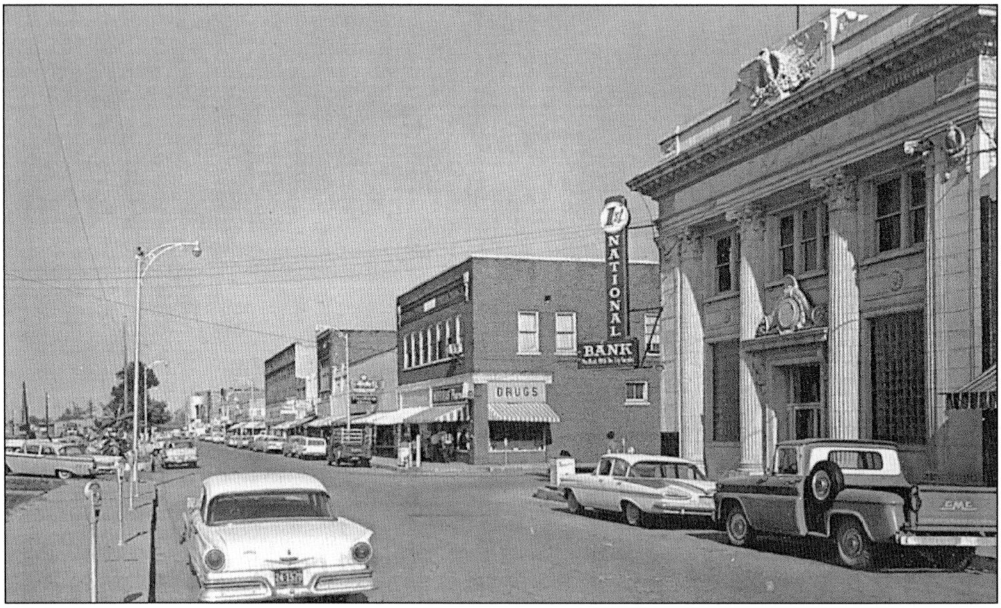

Travelers of U.S. 67 in the 1950s often made a turn off the highway and drove the few blocks onto Front Street, where Newport's business district was still located as it had been for decades. Many of the same buildings seen here are in the photo, taken 40 years earlier, at the top of page 36. The most striking structure on the street is the First National Bank building on the right, which was built in 1916. Today, the building is home to the John Minor Company, and most of the retailers have relocated out near the highway bypass shopping centers.

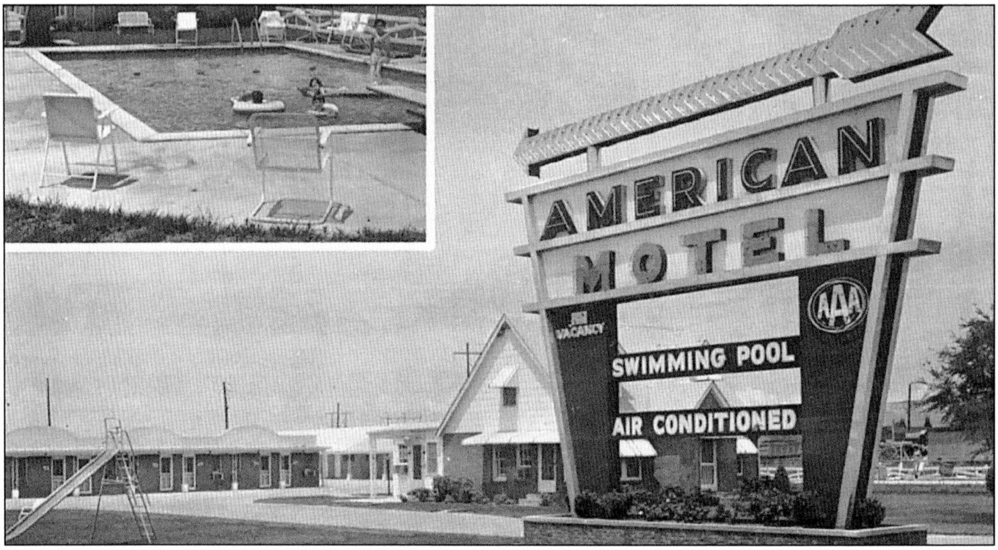

The nation's highway imagery of the 1940s and 1950s included the attention-getting signs of the developing motel industry trying to convince motorists to "STOP HERE." Such was that of the American Motel on Highway 67, on the edge of Newport, seen here in the early 1950s. Still in business after more than 50 years, the modern lodging establishment operates today as the Park Inn International. It must count on guests being drawn in by billboards or tour guides, since it is no longer visible from the more remote four-lane Highway 67 that now bypasses Newport.

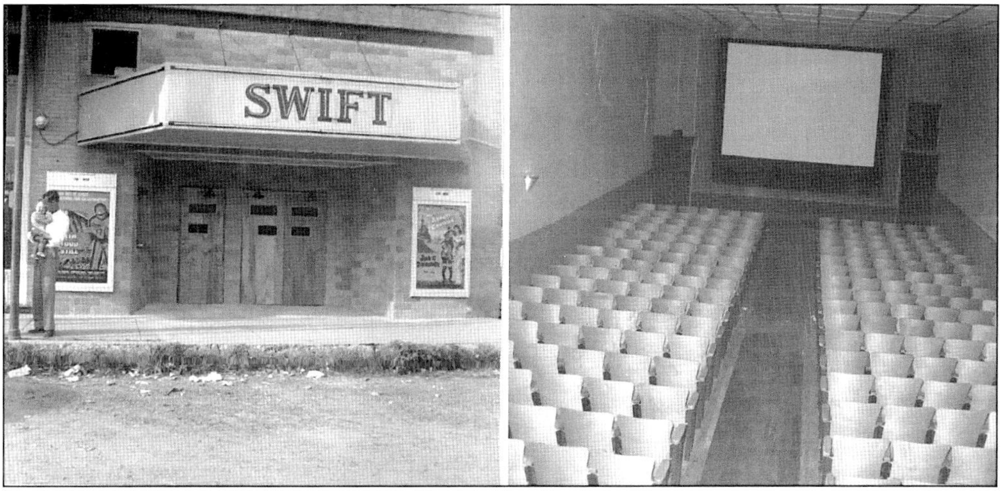

Travelers stopping over for the night in Newport might have taken in a movie at The Swift, a downtown classical movie house of the 1940s and 1950s. On the day in the 1950s when these photos were taken, a double feature was showing—*Jack and the Beanstalk*, starring Abbot and Costello, and *The Day the Earth Stood Still*. This theater is gone today, along with almost all of the nation's single-screen movie houses.

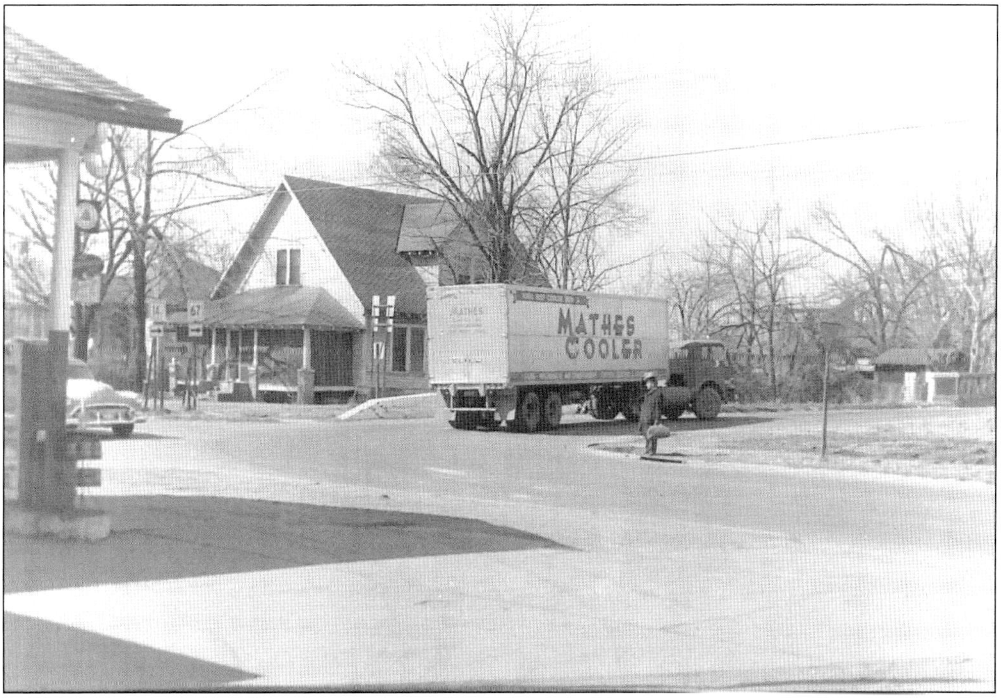

Today, a modern four-lane Highway 67 sees hundreds of 80,000-pound trucks per day pass around Newport. In the early 1950s, as seen above, the then-smaller trucks and other traffic came through town on a two-lane Highway 67, past residential areas and the gas station on the left before making the sharp turn onto the White River bridge, the corner of which is just visible to the right. The Highway 67 bridge opened in 1930; it was initially a toll bridge. A sign for Highway 67 beside the car to the left directs southbound traffic to the sharp turn onto the bridge, a few blocks from downtown Newport.

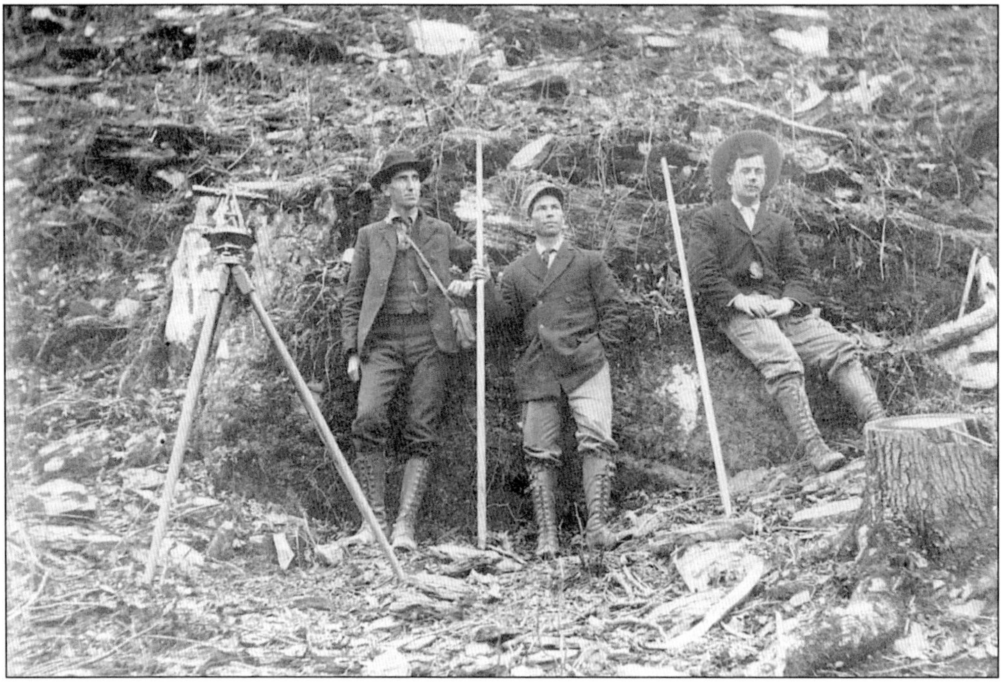

Travelers on Highway 67 leaving Newport drove through miles of farm land, where hardwood forests once stood, and then crossed into White County. The first route to cross the county had been the Southwest Trail almost 200 hundred years before, and it would be well into the 20th century before much in the way of improvements in ground transport across the county came to pass. In the above photo, a trio of surveyors in knee-high boots to guard against snakes paused for a photo while surveying for the construction of a wagon road in the northern part of the county. The photo below shows how rough the road was some 30 years before the paving of Highway 67 through White County. In order to pass the covered buggy, the vehicle to the left has run one wheel off the road.

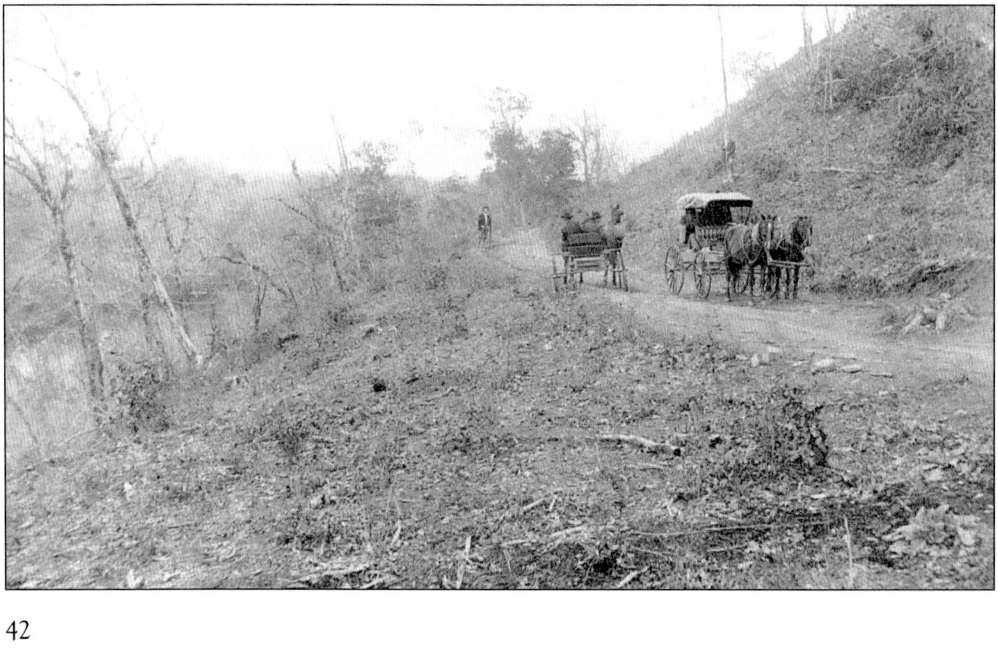

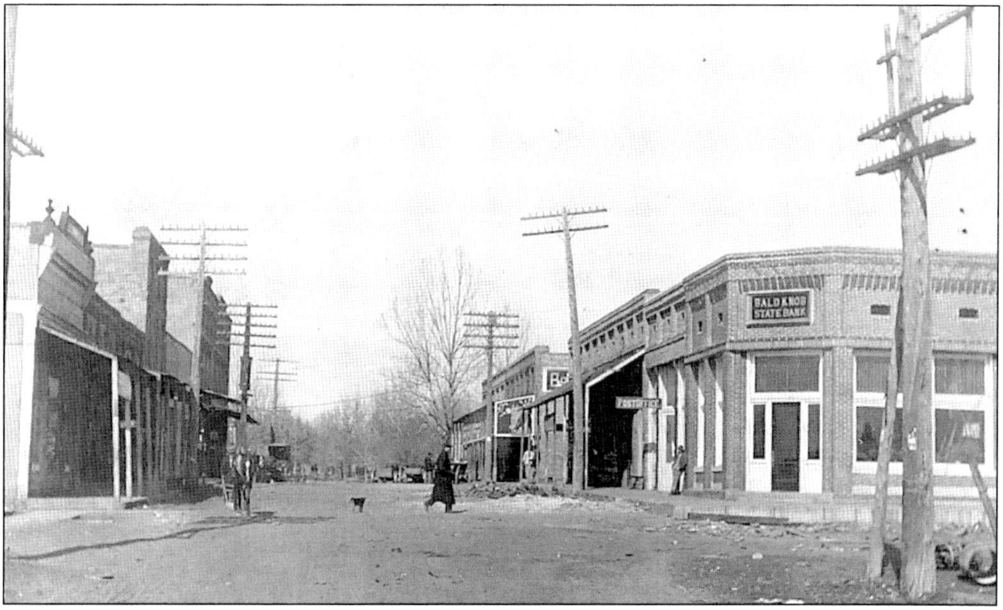

The first town of size to be found in the path of US 67 coming south into White County was Bald Knob, named for a rock outcropping that has long since been quarried away. Seen here in a view of Elm Street around 1905, Bald Knob was established in 1878 on the path of a railroad, the St. Louis, Iron Mountain & Southern, as were many towns in Arkansas. Today, much of the charming turn-of-the-century downtown area is intact and still doing business, even though Highway 67 has now been rerouted onto a four-lane road north of town. State Highway 367 does pass directly through the center of town, however.

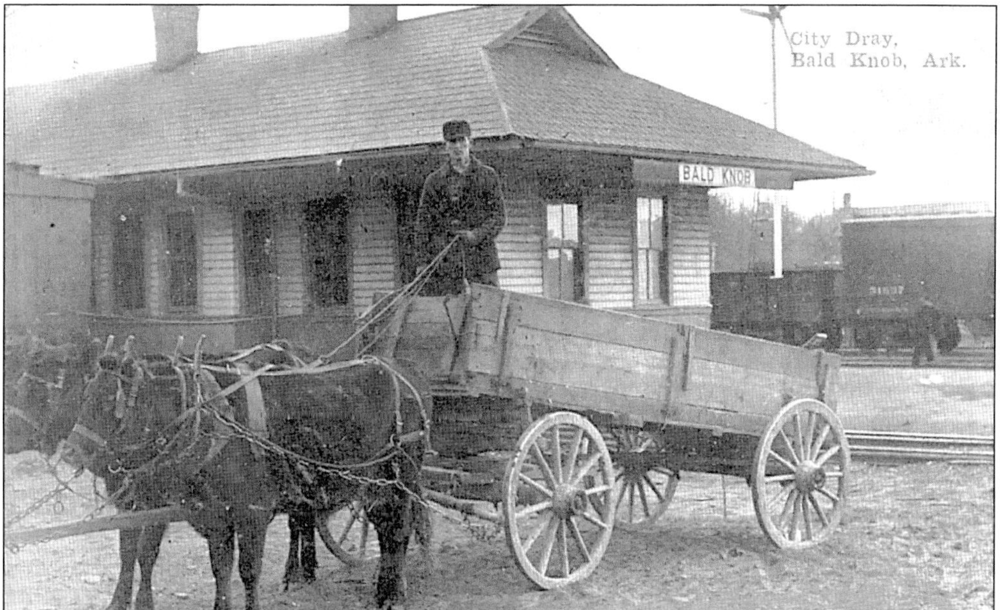

Before the roads improved, the economy of Bald Knob revolved greatly around the railroad. In the above 1911 postcard, a City Dray wagon was backed up to the tracks to load a delivery for one of the town's businesses. This service might be considered the UPS or FedEx of its day.

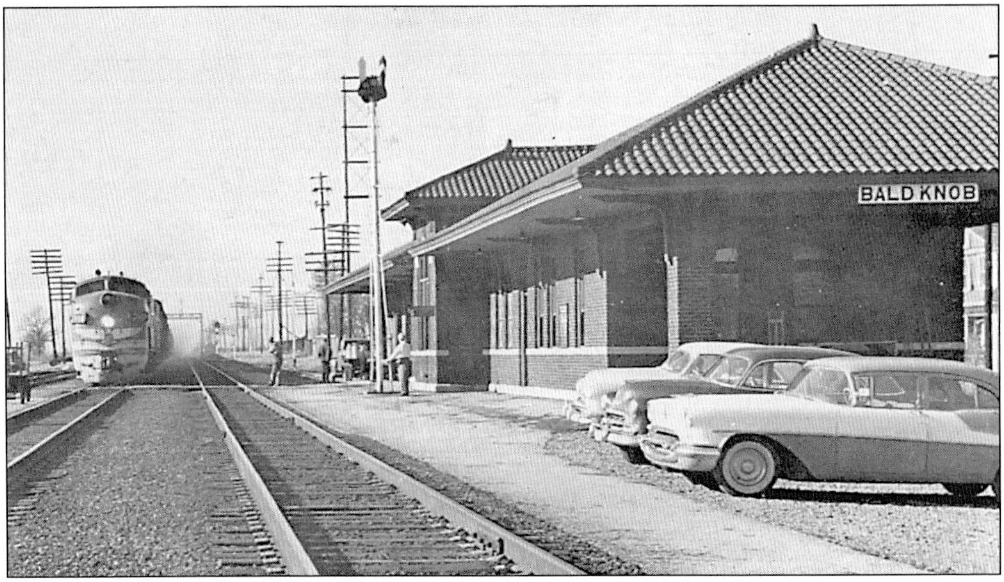

Shown in the *c.* 1957 postcard above, the era of train travel was drawing to a close as the public had begun, in ever-increasing numbers, to prefer the convenience of taking their cars out onto Highway 67. The long idle depot is today slated for restoration to house a museum and the Bald Knob Chamber of Commerce.

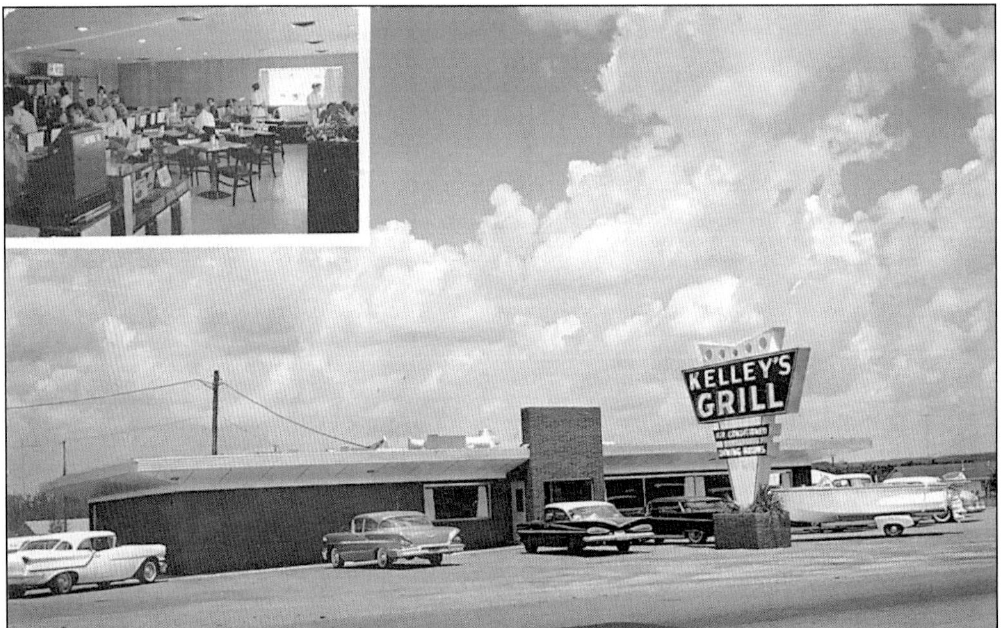

On the outskirts of Bald Knob, motorists on Highway 67 had several choices when in search of a meal. Among the most popular dining establishments was Kelley's Grill, seen here around 1957. The business boasted four dining rooms and air conditioning and played host to the local Rotary and Lions Club. "We ate breakfast here," is the penned message on the back of the postcard.

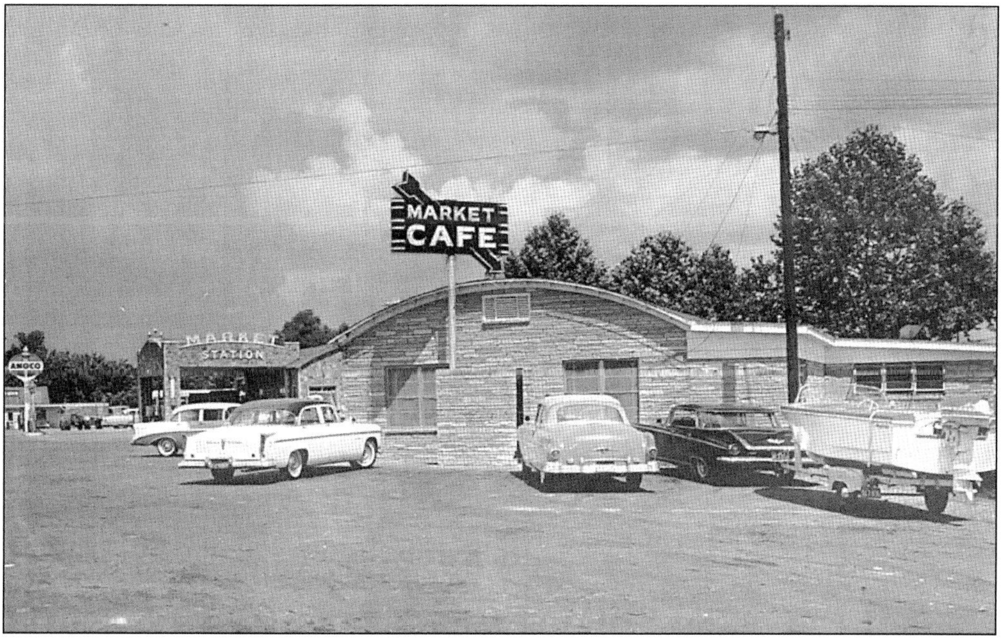

The boom in post-War World II traffic on Highway 67 inspired the building of the Market Cafe in 1946 at the point where Highways 67, 64, and 167 intersected. Roy Waller had operated a very successful Farmers' Market on the site for several years, capitalizing on Bald Knob's reputation as the "Strawberry Capital of the World." Waller thought the town needed a nice restaurant, and the product of his vision was said to have standing room only at certain times of the year, especially when the strawberry pickers were in town. "Just a good place to eat," is the motto printed on the back of both postcards. Today, the Farmers' Market is gone, but roadside stands abound during the strawberry season. The Market Cafe still serves hungry travelers who will leave the four-lane for the pleasure of a good meal.

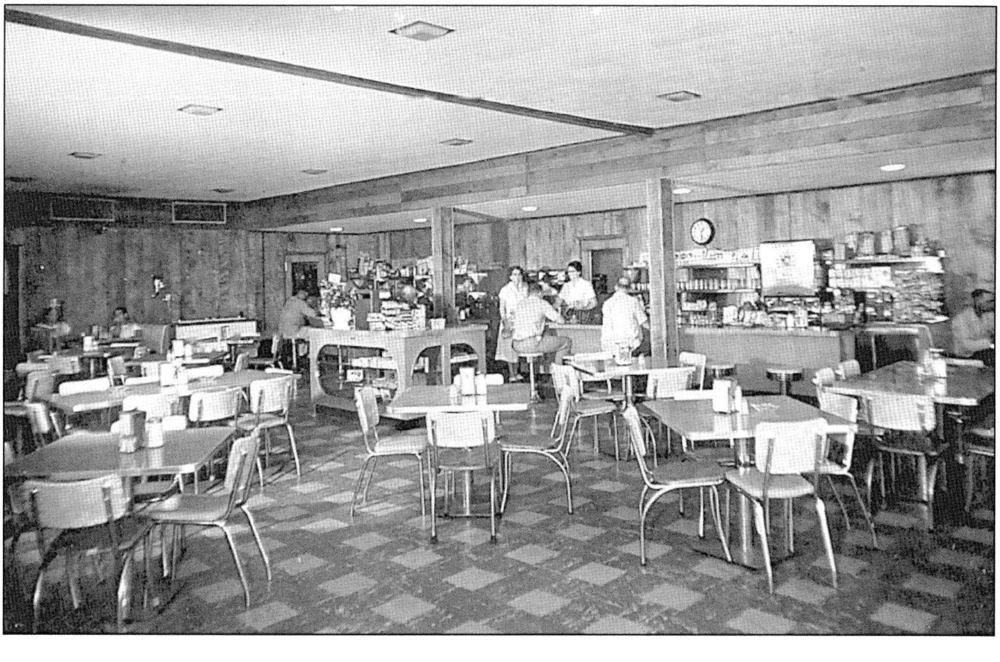

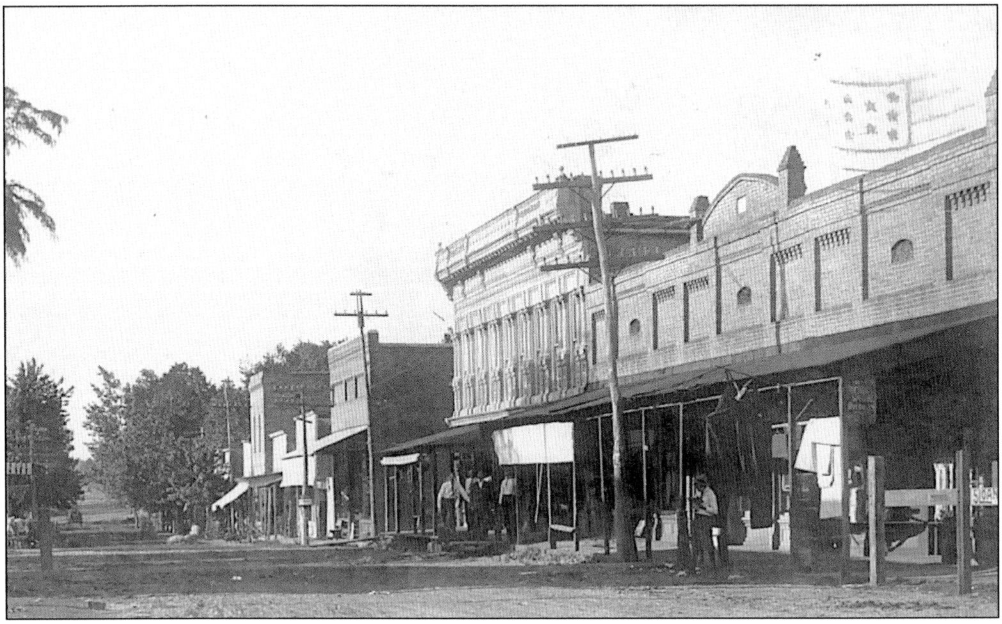

South of Bald Knob, travelers, for more than a century, have come through the small town of Judsonia, founded in 1840 under the name Prospect Bluff as a steamboat port on the Little Red River. The town was promoted heavily to northerners after the Civil War by Judson University, hence the town's name change to Judsonia in 1874. One of the results of that migration was a monument to the Grand Army of the Republic and a cemetery containing Union soldiers, a very rare thing in the South. The above *c.* 1910 photo captured the town's main street, which carried the route of the Lakes to the Gulf Highway by 1920 and then Highway 67 since the late 1920s.

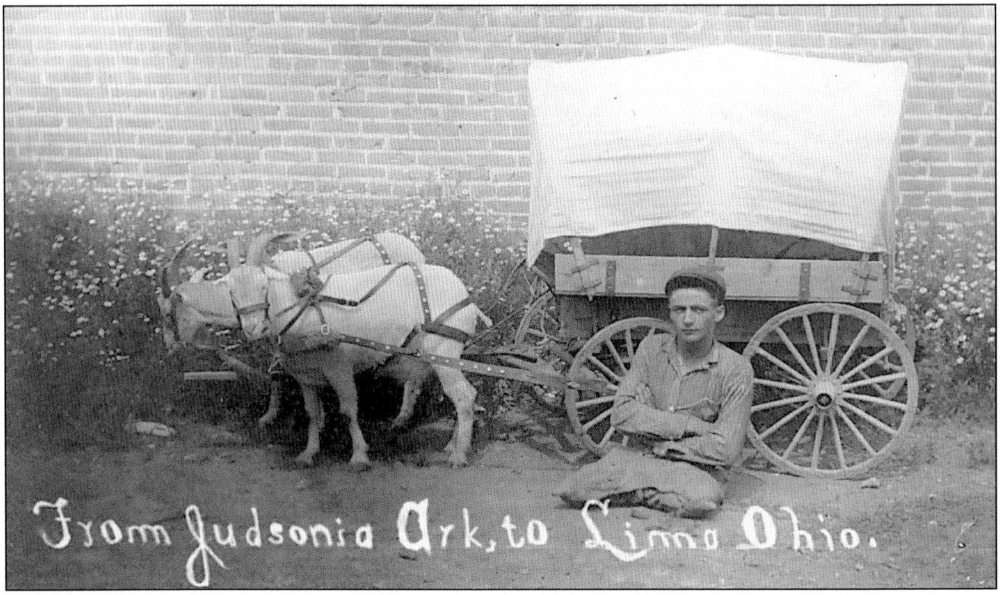

One of the most noticed travelers to roll into Judsonia on the dirt road leading into town was a legless man named Rose around 1915. Driving a small covered wagon pulled by a team of goats, Rose apparently traversed the country, selling postcards of himself to cover the expenses of his journey.

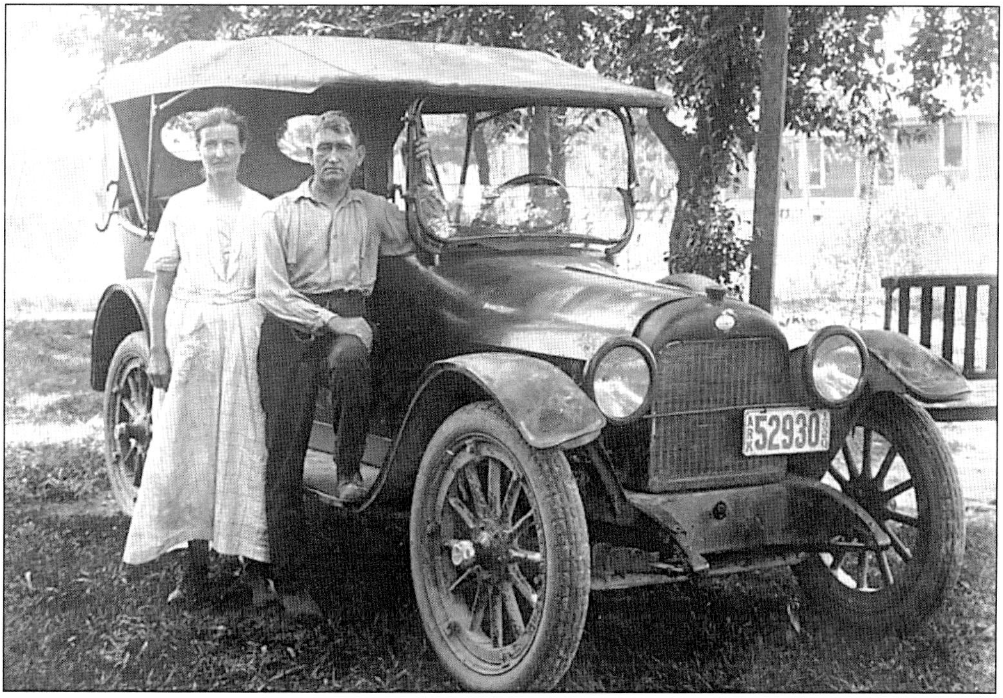

By 1920, the federally designated Lakes to the Gulf highway that passed through Judsonia was inducing local citizens to consider purchasing automobiles like the ones that were beginning to come through town in increasing numbers. One unidentified Judsonia couple posed with their car and its 1920 Arkansas license plate. It was at about this time that Will Rogers was quoted as saying, "We are the only nation in the world to go to the poorhouse in an automobile."

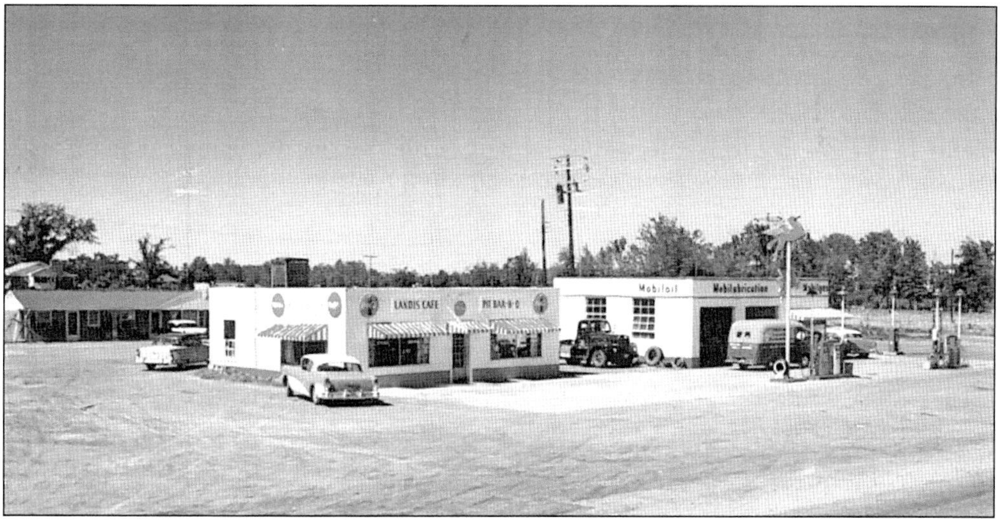

As the vehicles traveling Highway 67 through Judsonia changed over the years, so did the roadside services that the motorists depended upon. One of the versatile business ventures that tried to profit from meeting as many needs as possible was the Landis Motel, Cafe, and Mobil Station. "We Doze but Never Close—New and Modern," were the words on the back of the c. 1957 postcard. Though the name of the business has changed, the buildings still stand in the same location, now on State Highway 367 after U.S. 67 was rerouted onto a four-lane divided highway.

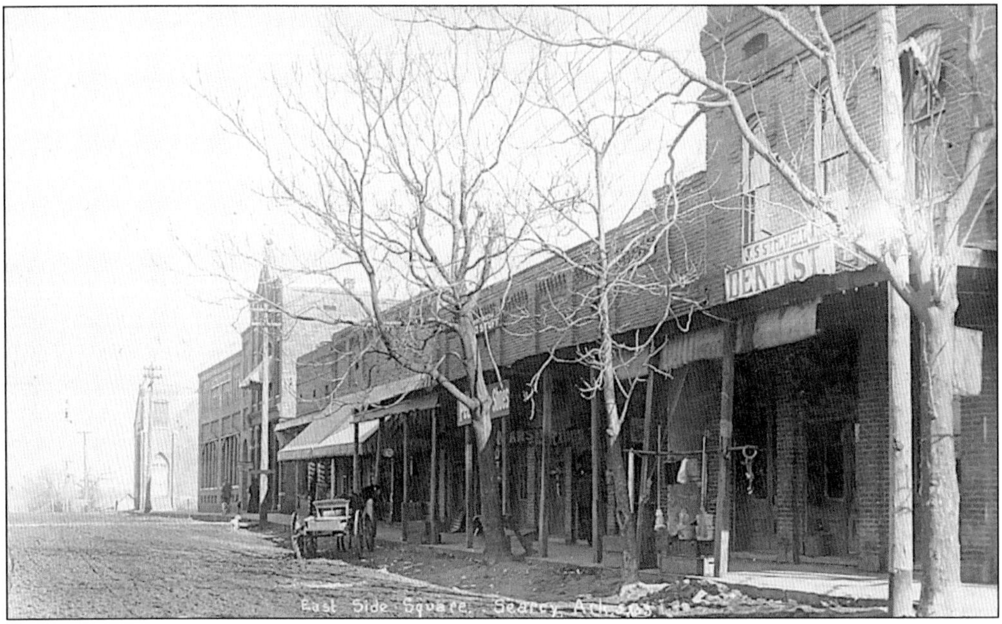

The White County seat of Searcy has been an important point on the path of Highway 67 since around 1830, when the town was called White Sulphur Springs for a spring deemed to have therapeutic values. The town was renamed Searcy to honor a territorial judge, Richard Searcy. The 1908 postcard above shows the east side of the classic courthouse square in the heart of the town that today has grown to some 15,000 residents. J.S. Stillwell's dental office is to the right on the rutted, dirt street. The postcard below offers a look at the early-20th-century ground transport system that was needed to handle the rough roads coming into Searcy. The four oxen have pulled a farmer's bale of cotton into town to be sold at market. In the background is the Presbyterian church.

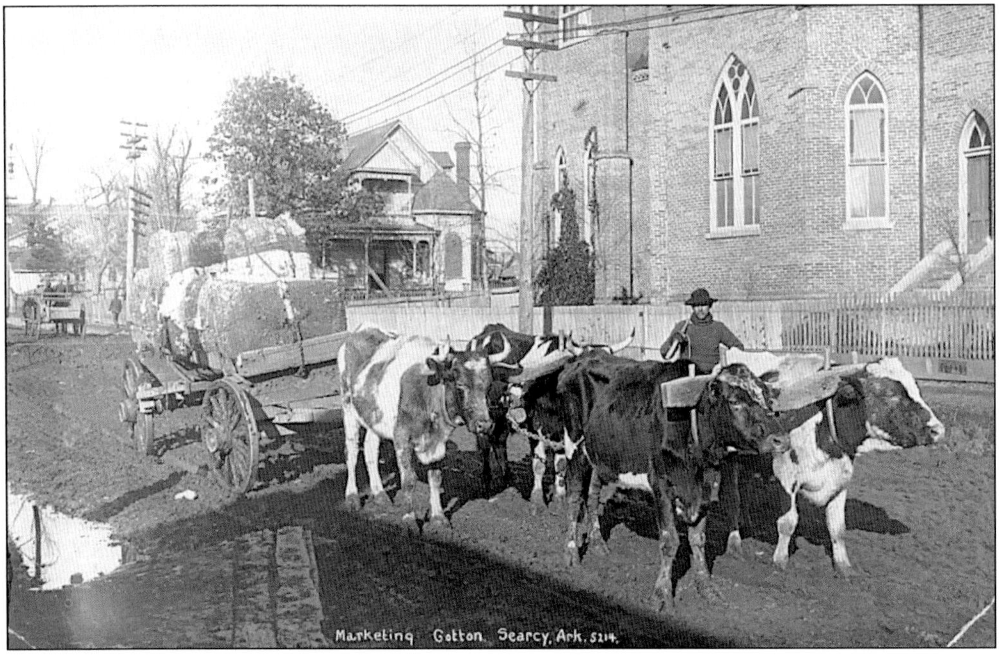

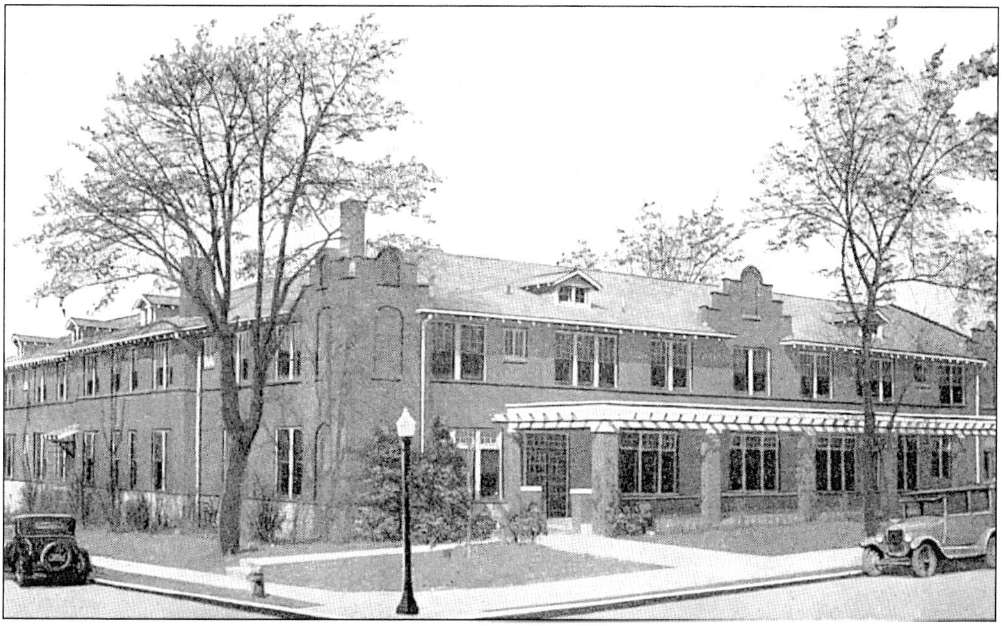

A notable traveler touring Arkansas in the 1920s wrote, "As the shades of night fall one can see traveling men and tourists, flocking to Searcy and the Mayfair Hotel. The excellent cuisine of the hotel accounts for this." The 50-room Mayfair was erected in 1924 on the corner of Spring and Center Streets, and over the years, it was "the" place to stay and to have special events in Searcy. The American Automobile Association listed the Mayfair in its publications because of its "culinary expertise, cordiality, and friendliness." Another writer of a travel magazine noted the hotel's "unforgettable grated sweet potato pudding." The postcard above was made c. 1930. As can be seen in the 1998 photograph below, the building still stands today, though it is no longer operated as a hotel. (Photo by Ray Hanley.)

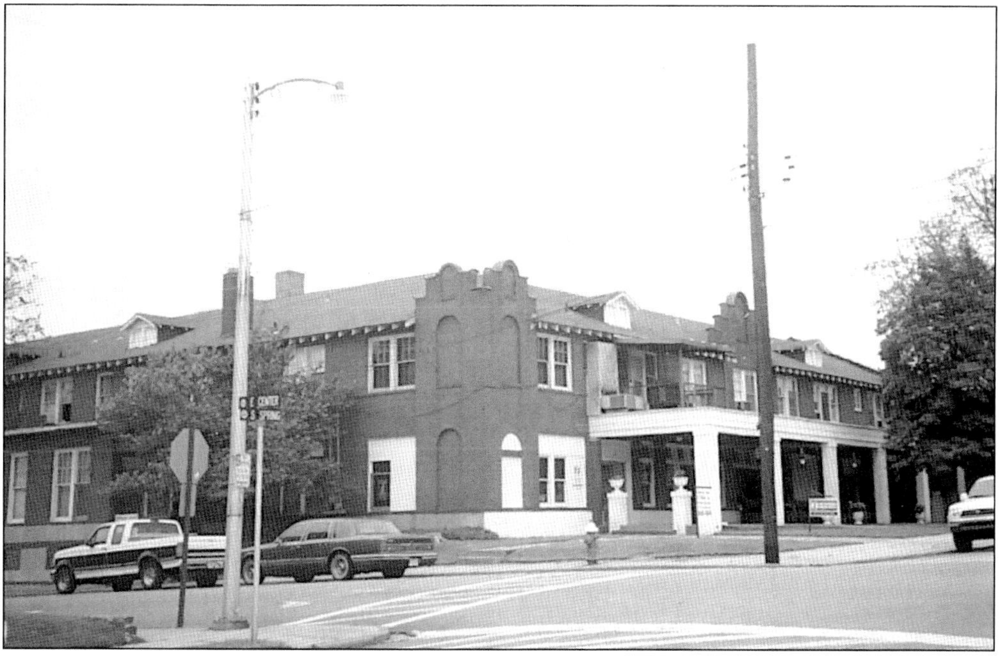

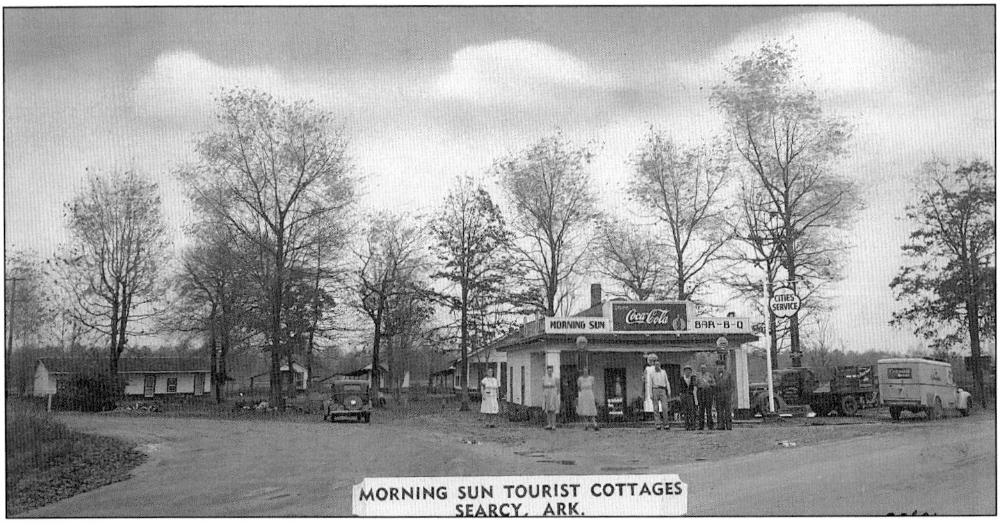

When the first tourist courts went up on the highway in White County in the 1930s, the crossroads community of Morning Sun, situated a little beyond the current location of the Searcy airport, was home to the Morning Sun Tourist Cottages. By the time this photo was taken around 1940, the business had added a barbecue menu as an additional service to motorists needing a bed for the night or a fill up by a uniformed attendant. To the right is the Colonial Bread truck making a delivery, and beside it stands a truck with a Falstaff beer sign, suggesting what might have been a popular drink with a barbecue sandwich. Today, the area is bypassed by the new highway, and the business is long gone.

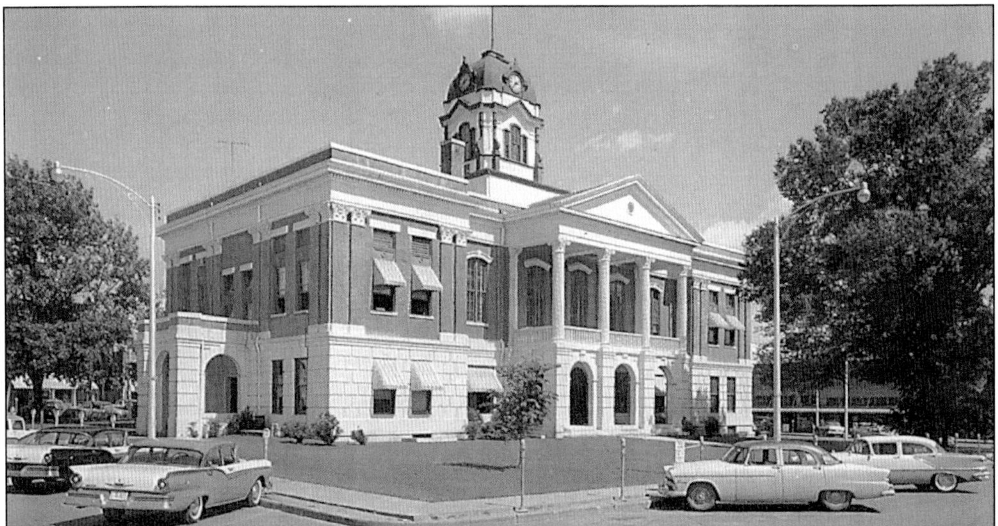

Sometime around 1940, Highway 67 was divided for a short distance below Judsonia. Highway 67 West routed motorists into downtown Searcy, then reconnected with Highway 67 East upon exiting the city. Motorists in the 1950s taking the western route entered a classical American small town, where the entire business district clustered around a courthouse square. The Georgian-style White County Courthouse above is among the state's most historic buildings; it was erected in 1870, and wings on either end were added in 1912. It is the oldest courthouse in the state that is still functioning as the seat of a county government and can be visited on Searcy's town square.

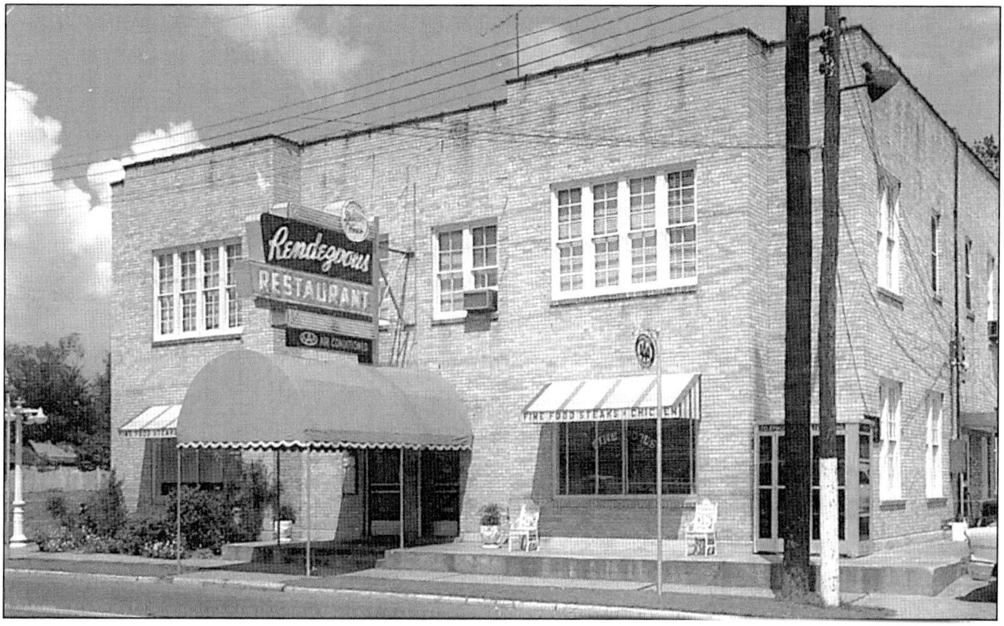

In 1945, as World War II was ending in the Pacific, Searcy turned out for local businessman E.C. Roberson's grand opening of his new restaurant. The building, seen here c. 1955, provided a new home for a favorite dining spot that had first opened in 1932. This modern version of the Rendezvous was located on the edge of downtown, directly on the path of Highway 67. For several years, the bus company had its depot in one section of the building. A public address system would call for the passengers before the bus pulled back onto the highway. The building still stands today but now provides space for office and commercial usage.

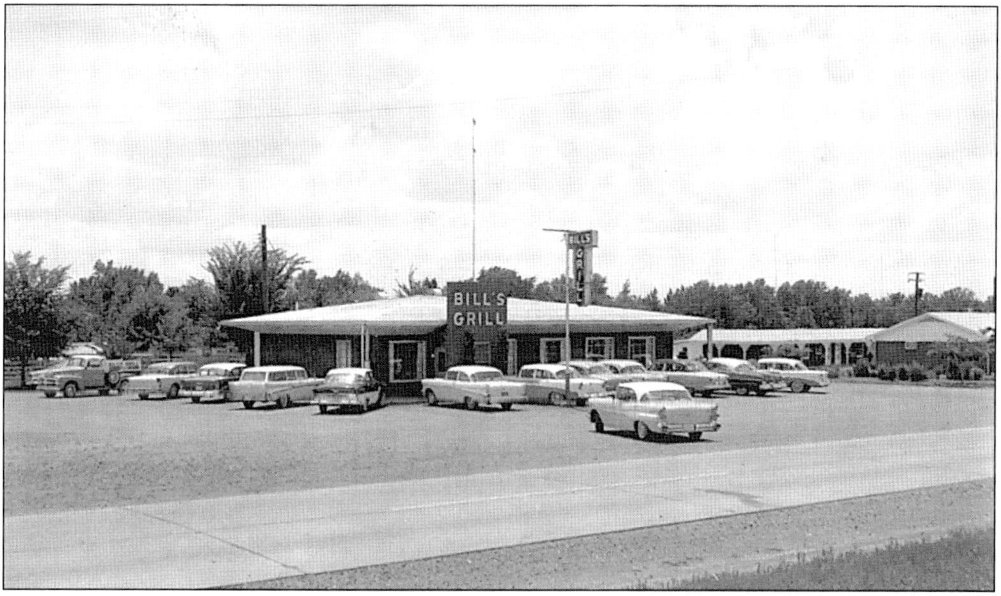

Among Searcy's popular dining offerings on Highway 67 was Bill's Grill, seen above around 1957. Its location on East Race Street caught the attention of motorists heading into town, and it advertised immediate seating for 150 people. The building still stands today but now houses a Chinese restaurant.

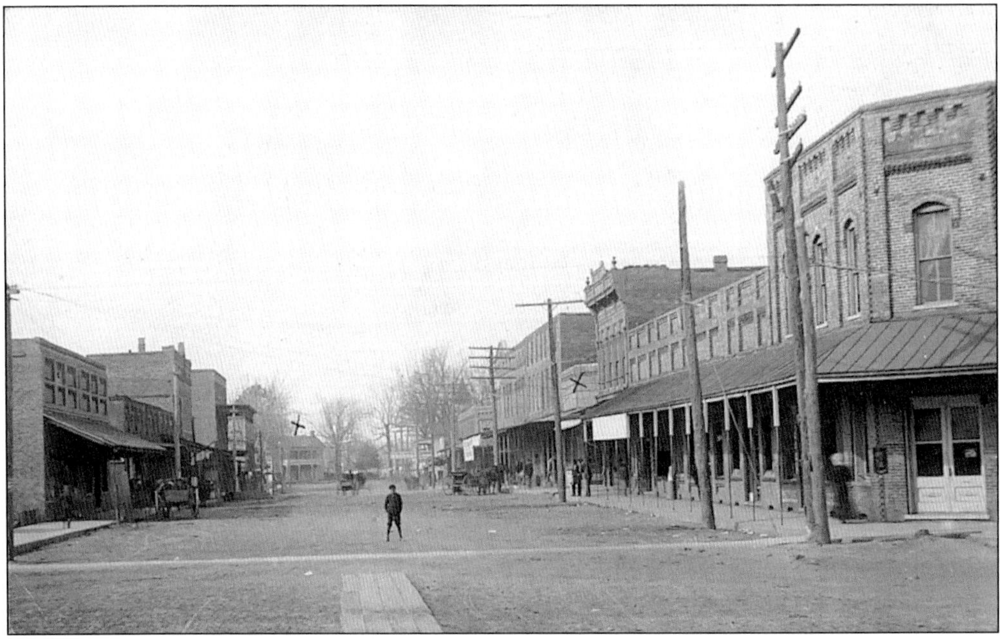

The traveler's last stop in White County has usually been Beebe, founded in 1872 and named for Roswell Beebe, the president of the Cairo & Fulton Railroad. Over the years, wagons and then automobiles made their way past the 1880s-era buildings, seen here in a 1910 view. The sender has marked with an "x" her house at the far end of the street, and her husband's place of work. Today, many of these buildings still survive, though the downtown area has been bypassed by the new freeway.

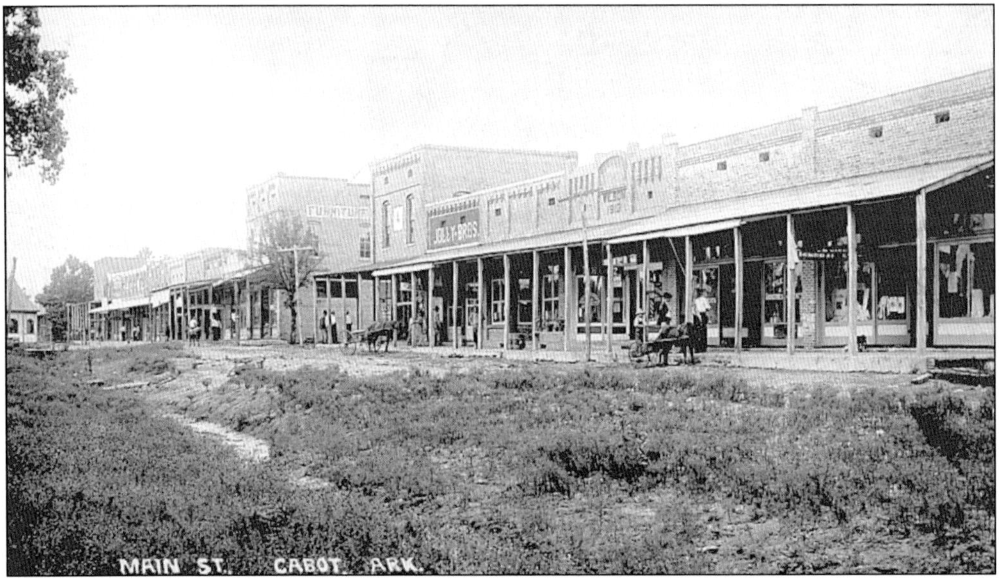

Highway 67 cut across the western end of Lonoke County, passing through the once very small town of Cabot. Before the coming of the first road improvements, this c. 1910 view found the town's Main Street lined with weeds and an open ditch. Today, the new interstate version of modern Highway 67 has made the little town a bedroom community for Little Rock, causing a population explosion.

Two

Pulaski County North Little Rock to Little Rock

Highway 67 and its predecessors, the Southwest Trail, the Military Road, and the federal highways, all passed through Pulaski County, as did almost all major roads in Arkansas. The county, home to the state capital of Little Rock, is almost exactly in the center of the state, and it is truly the crossroads of Arkansas.

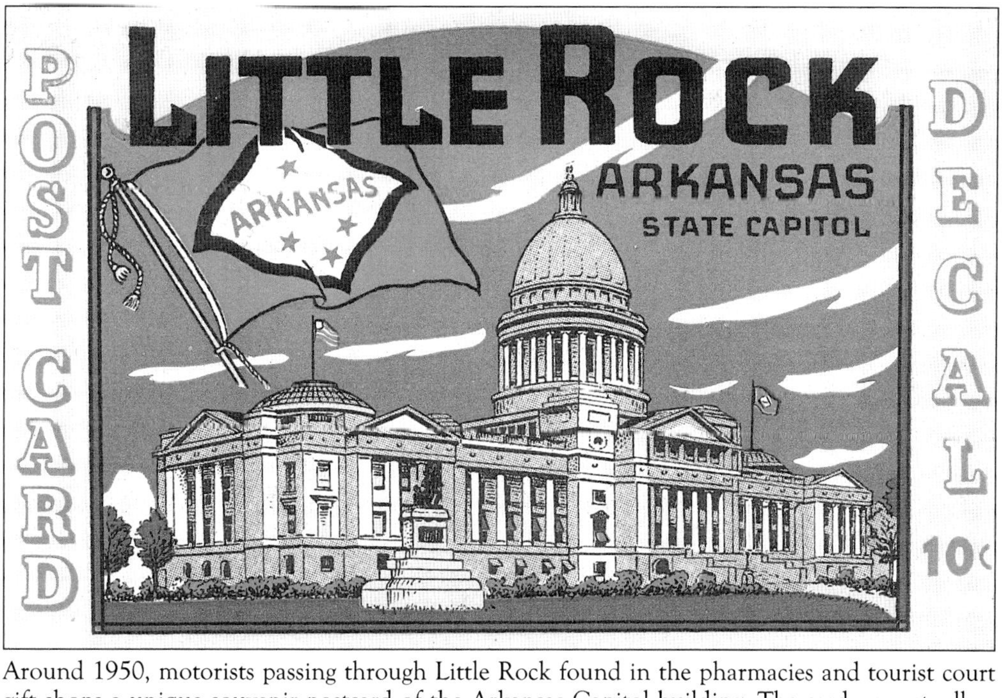

Around 1950, motorists passing through Little Rock found in the pharmacies and tourist court gift shops a unique souvenir postcard of the Arkansas Capitol building. The card was actually a decal; the image could be soaked in water, removed, and affixed to an automobile window.

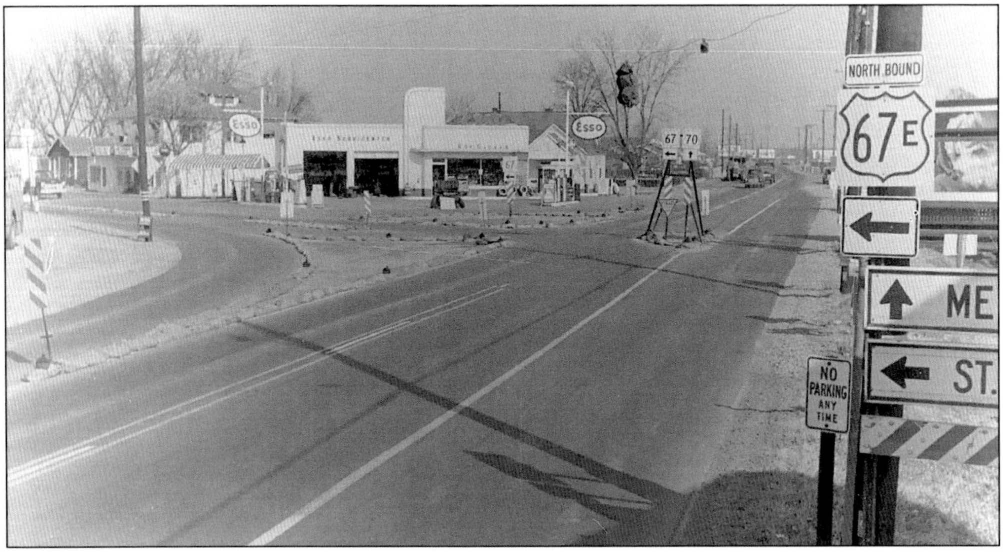

In the 1940s, Highway 67 was divided inside Pulaski County just below Jacksonville. Highway 67-West led into the city of North Little Rock on a fairly direct path, while 67-East met Highway 70, the Memphis Highway, at Protho Junction, seen here. Southbound traffic on 67-East, coming from the left in this photo, would slow down in front of the Esso station, turning left to go to Memphis or right to come into Little Rock. Today, Protho Junction still marks a major commercial crossroads on Interstate 40, where once there was only a two-lane blacktop road. (Courtesy of UCA Archives.)

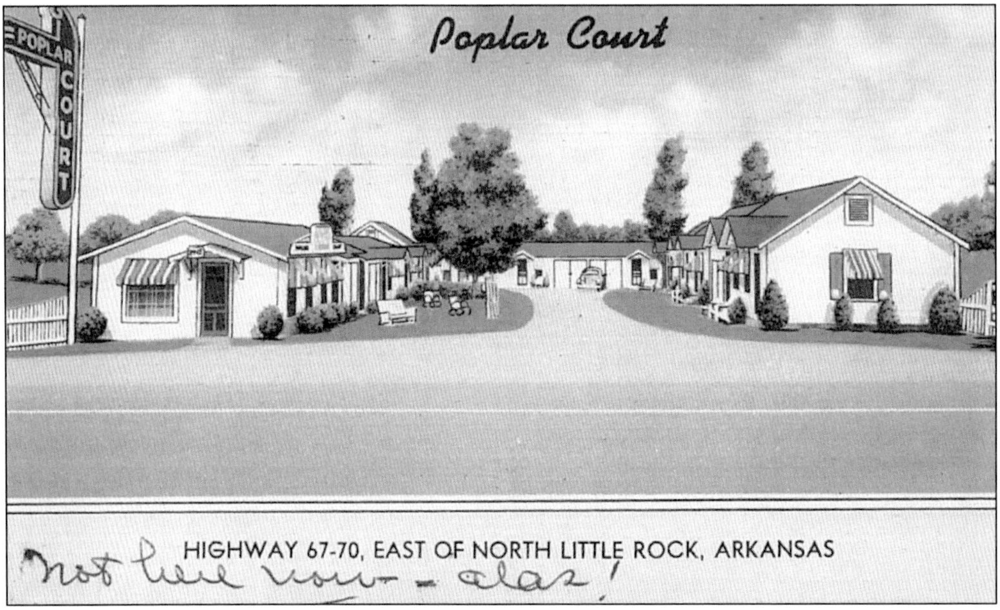

The few miles of shared blacktop between Highway 67-East and the Memphis Highway leading into North Little Rock saw the development of a number of tourist courts and other motorist support services. "Your inspection invited," was the claim on the back of a postcard of the Poplar Court. The card was mailed by a guest after leaving in 1952, and it has on it the words, "not here now–alas!" The court of 14 cottages is gone today, since Interstate 40 bypassed this section of highway in the early 1960s.

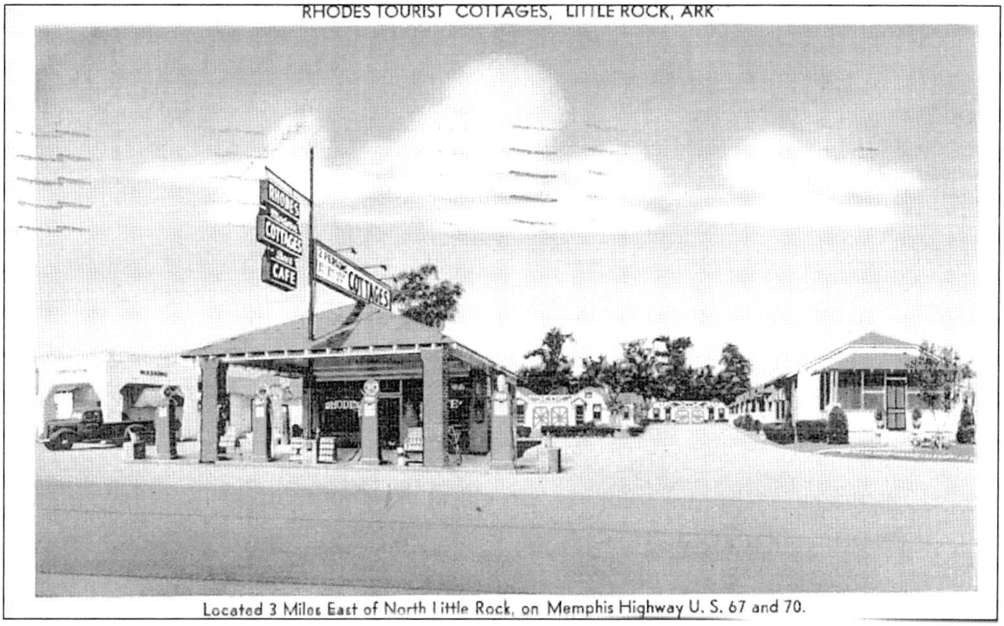

In the 1930s and 1940s, the concept of "chain" motels had not yet been visited upon the landscape, and Highway 67E offered many examples of the independent individuals who invested in small "mom & pop" courts. Mr. and Mrs. Jack Rhodes were operating the Rhodes Tourist Cottages in 1939 when a guest mailed the card above with the notation, "We are having a swell trip." The Rhodes offered 23 cottages, each with a garage, a bell for room service, radios, ceiling fans, a cafe on the premises, and an auto repair facility that promised "car service of all kinds while you sleep." By the early 1950s, as seen below, Mr. and Mrs. Rhodes had replaced their 1930s cottages with 40 "Fedder Refrigerated Air-Conditioned units." "This is one of the finest courts in Arkansas," boasted the proud owners on the back of the card they gave free to their guests.

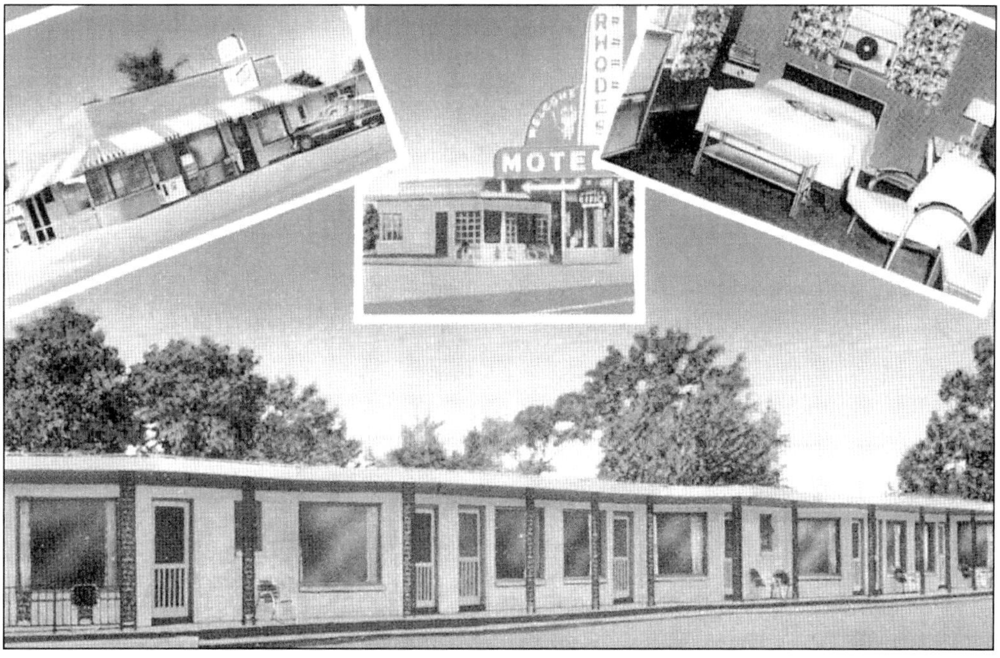

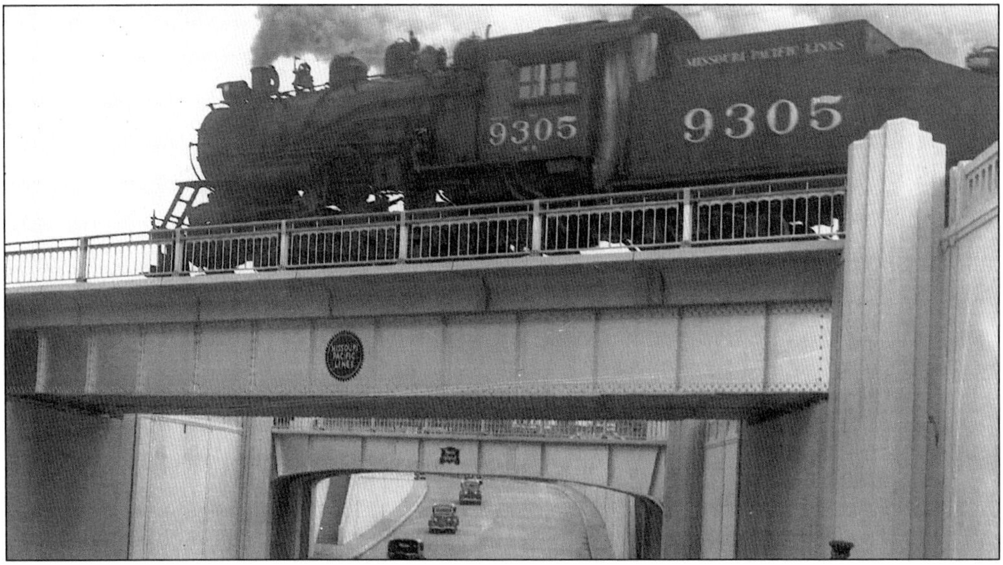

Approaching downtown North Little Rock, where Locust Street crossed Highway 67-East in the early 1940s, motorists would have seen, but perhaps not recognized, a visual representation of the ending of one era and the beginning of another. Over the next decade, the ever-increasing flood of automobiles would put a virtual end to passenger rail travel in Arkansas. (Courtesy of UCA Archives.)

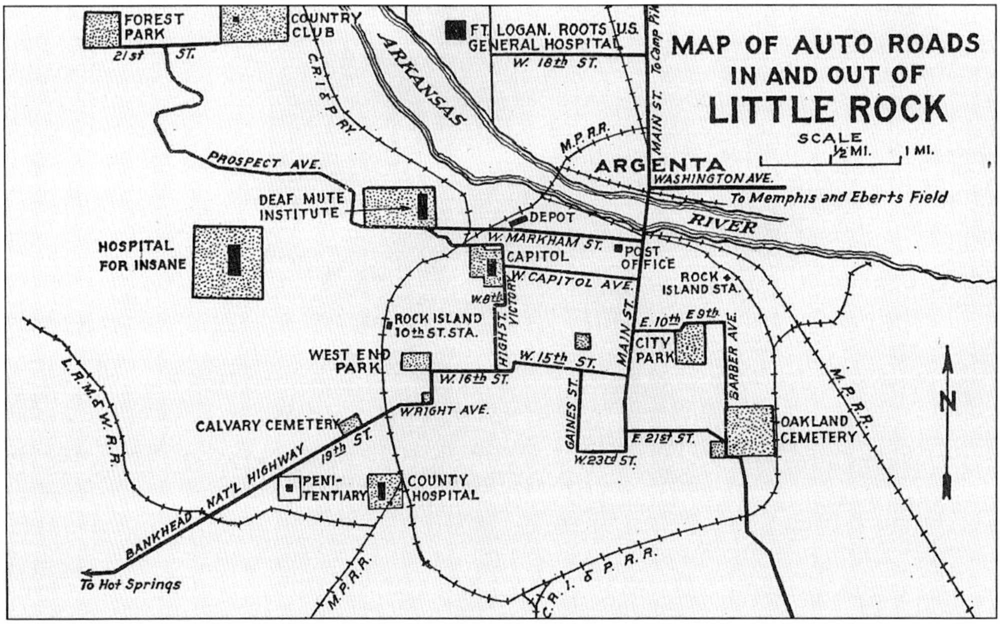

Before Highway 67's designation around 1930, the Lakes to the Gulf Highway came from northeast Arkansas and joined the Bankhead Highway that led into southwest Arkansas. In 1920, at the time the above map was made, there was only one non-railroad bridge connecting North Little Rock and Little Rock. Travelers coming from the east or northeast crossed the Main Street bridge, as shown on the map, and drove over the Arkansas River onto Little Rock's Main Street. A turn down Fifteenth Street to reach Sixteenth and Wright Avenue would lead out to the Bankhead Highway and points southwest.

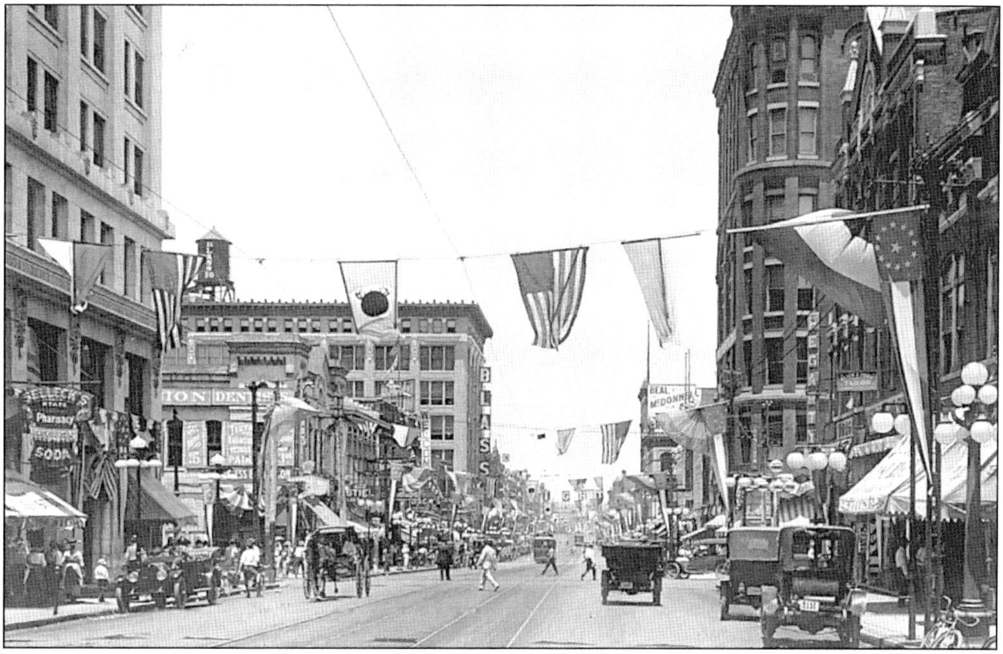

Travelers in the early 1920s crossing the Main Street bridge, seen on the map above, would have rolled onto a scene in Little Rock similar to the one seen here—streetcars crowded by the increasing numbers of automobiles, numerous bicycles, and an occasional horse and wagon still occupying the street. In the center of the photo, at the corner of Main and Capitol Avenue are the offices of Union Dentists, which advertised "teeth extracted without pain."

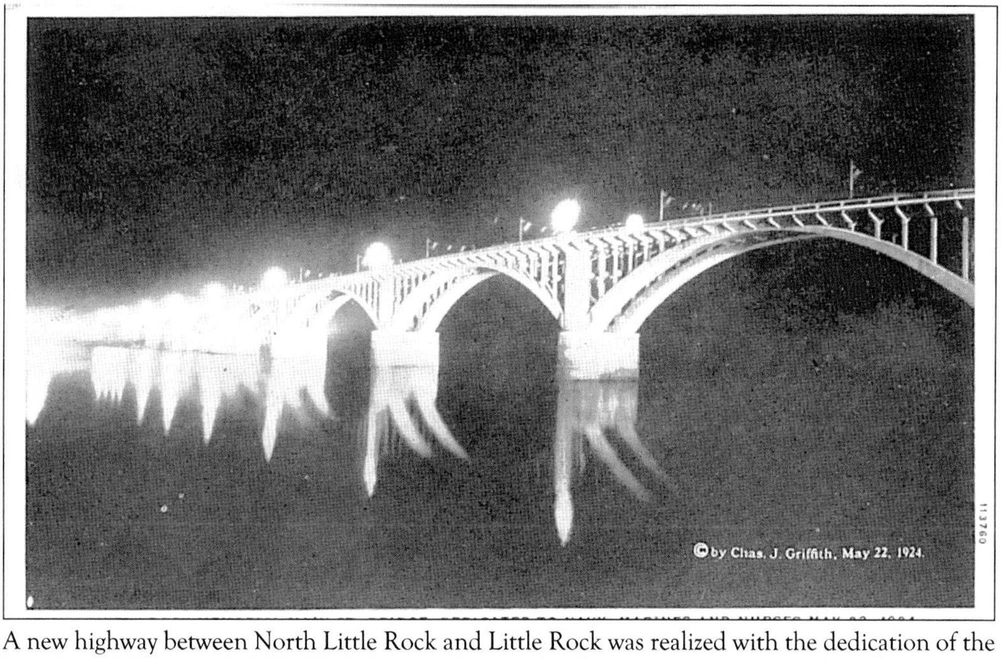

A new highway between North Little Rock and Little Rock was realized with the dedication of the Broadway bridge in 1924. Traffic had crossed the bridge for a year before it was officially dedicated to Navy personnel, Marines, and nurses of the American Armed Forces who, six years before, had provided decisive help to win World War I.

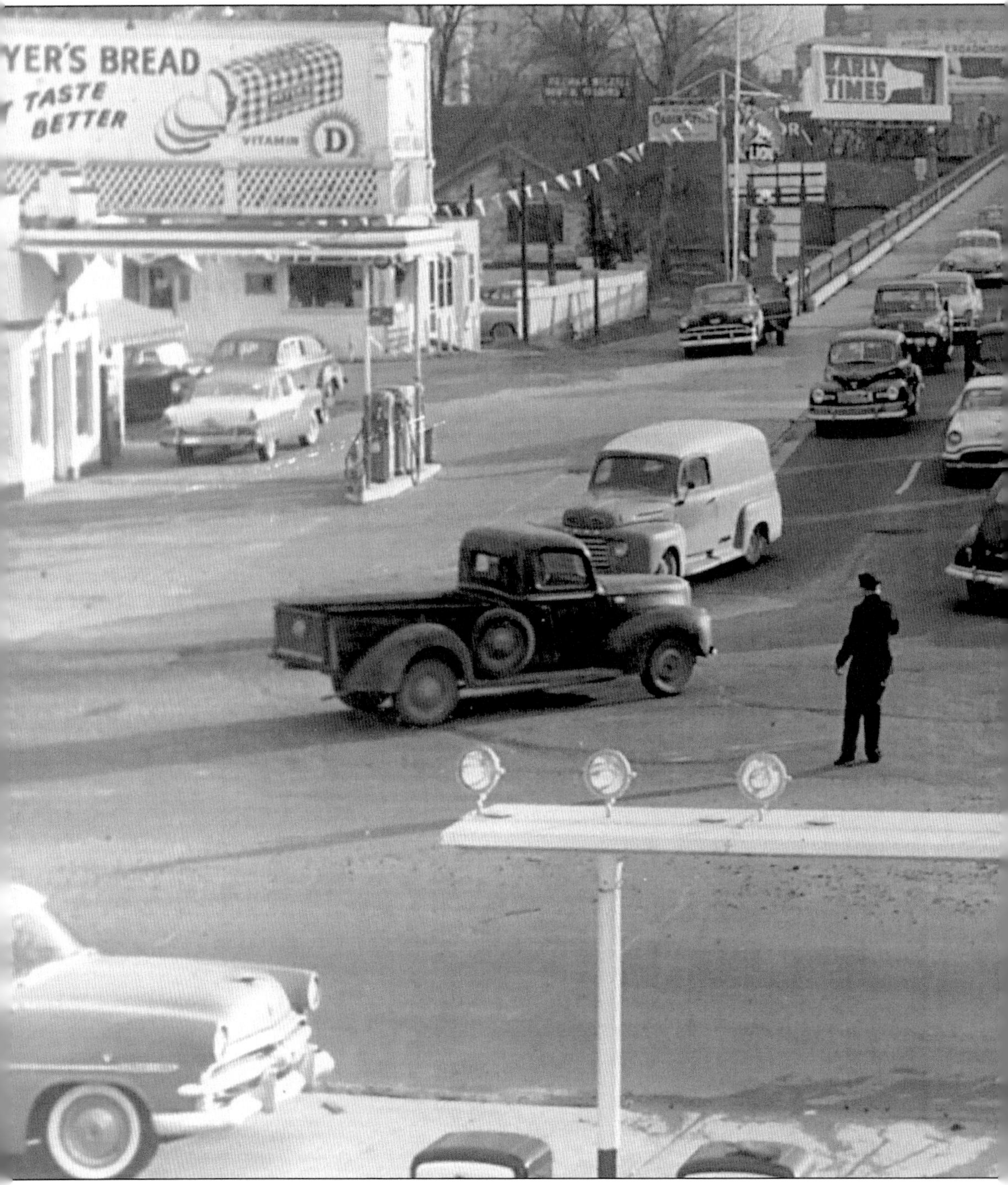

By 1955, the traffic on Highway 67 crossing the Broadway bridge into Little Rock was bumper-to-bumper and required the services of the policeman in the foreground to direct the flow. Today, most traffic crosses the Arkansas River on the Interstate 30 bridge, located a few blocks downstream of the Broadway bridge, and not a trace remains of the gas stations seen here flanking the intersection. The station on the left has been razed, and today, a commemorative

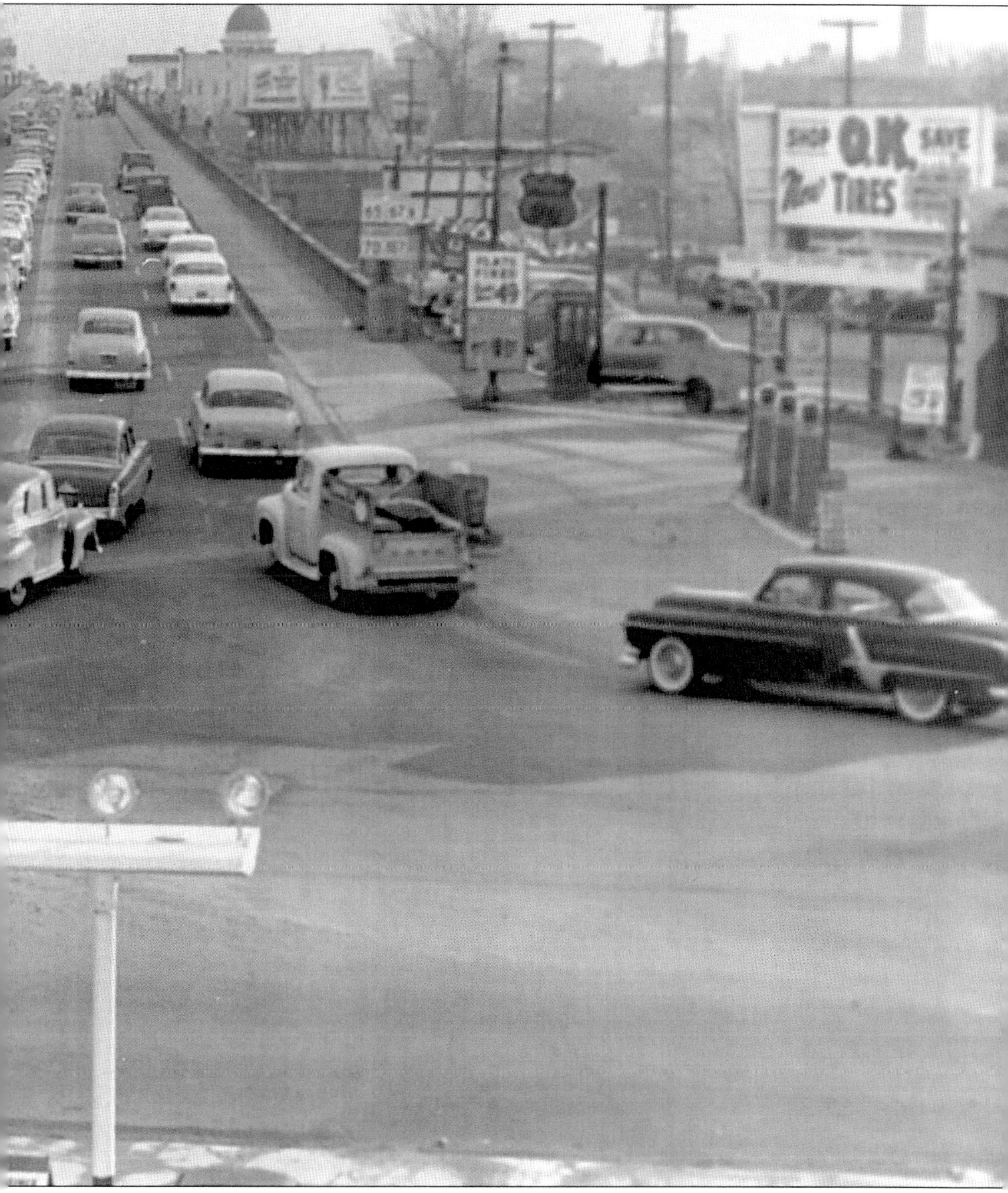

Sesquicentennial Sundial adorned with stones from around the world occupies the site. The landmark is the work of North Little Rock civic activist Audrey Burtram Stanley. The domed building seen in the distance on the right side of the bridge is Little Rock's city hall. Also evident are several billboards, advertising such products as Meyer's Bread and Early Times Whiskey.

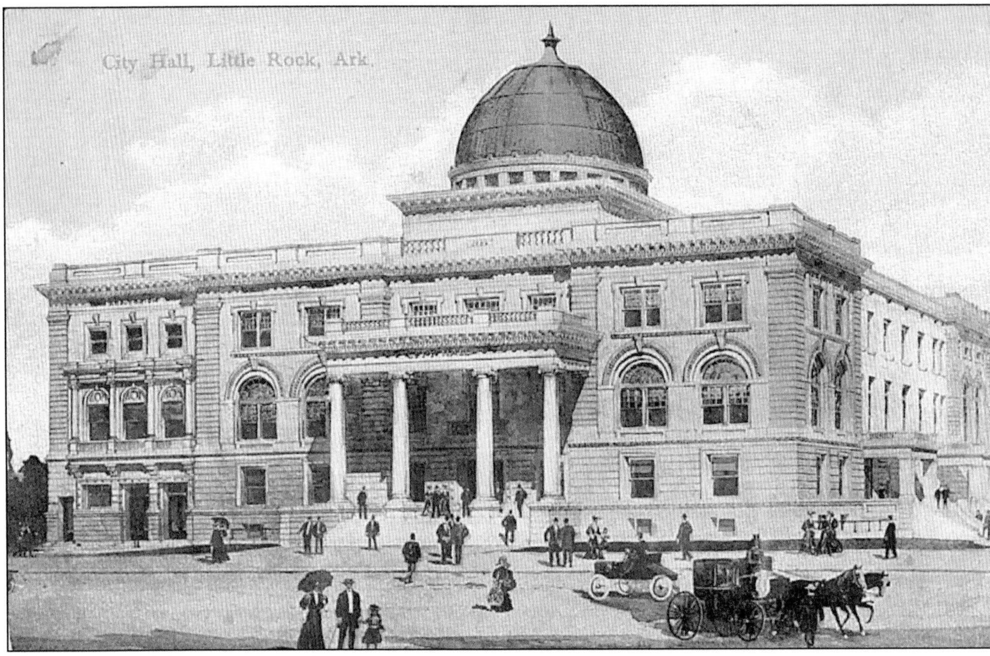

Little Rock City Hall was a landmark that caught the eye of those Highway 67 motorists crossing the Broadway bridge. The city hall, located just off the end of the bridge facing Markham Street, was erected in 1908, about the time the above postcard was made. The photo below, c. 1958, was taken looking across Broadway just before it goes over the bridge. A notable difference between the two images is the absence of a dome—Little Rock voters elected, by postcard, to remove the deteriorating dome rather than to expend the funds to fix it in 1958. The Gulf Station across from the city hall was in a prime location to catch traffic entering Little Rock on Highway 67. (Photo courtesy of Arkansas History Commission.)

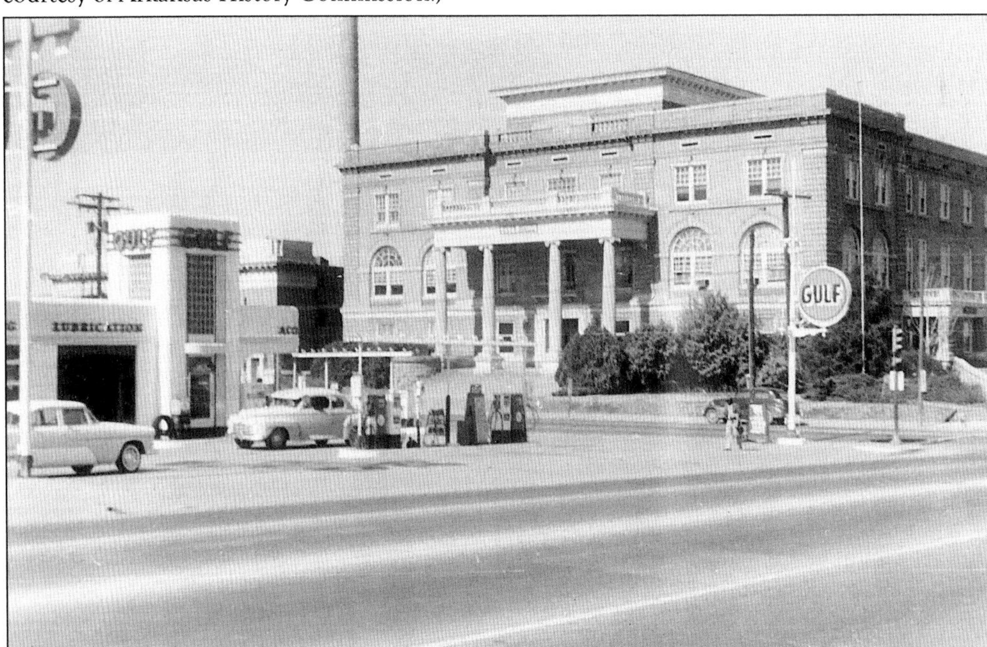

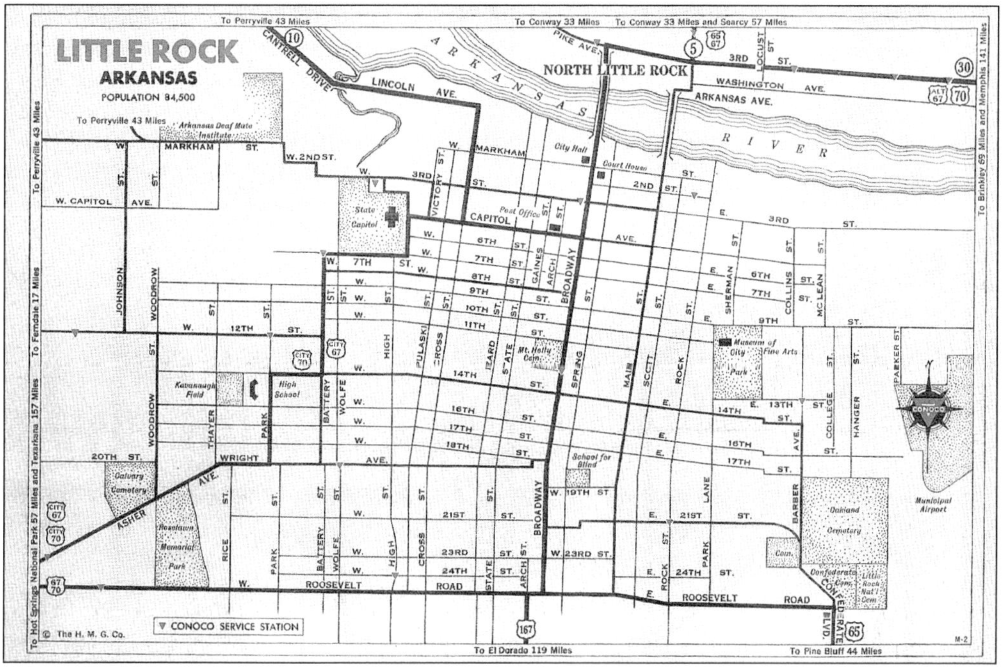

This c. 1940 map, when compared to the 1920 map on page 54, shows how the traffic pattern through Little Rock changed with Highway 67 going over the Broadway bridge. Broadway replaced Main Street as the major artery for through traffic, with most drivers proceeding to Roosevelt Road for a right turn that led out of town past another large number of tourist courts and restaurants. A secondary artery feeding into Highway 67 from downtown came from Wright Avenue, designated as City Route 67 and 70 (on the lower left). Today, Interstate 30 crosses the river and runs between City Park and Oakland Cemetery, on the right in this map.

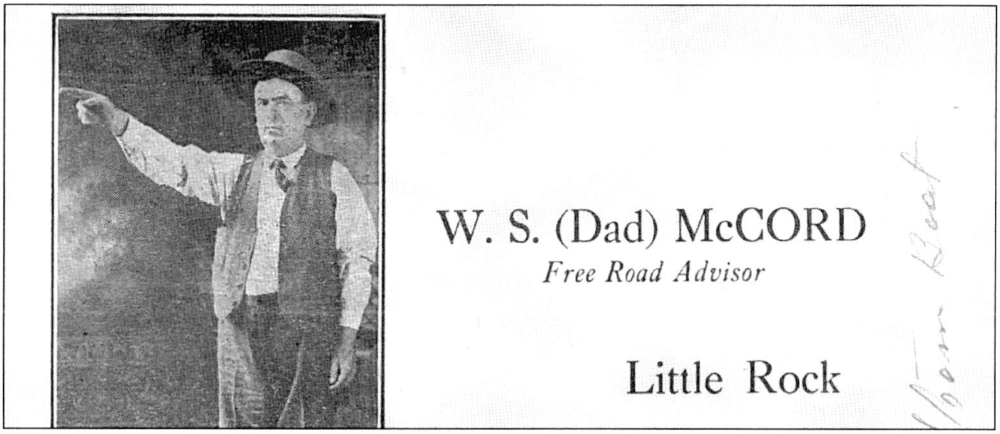

Around 1930, Gay Oil, one of the service stations at Third and Broadway, gave customers these advice cards, preserving the words of W.S. "Dad" McCord. "Dad's Creed" on the back included such proverbs as the following: "Don't keep the alabaster boxes of your love and tenderness sealed up until your friends are dead"; "I would rather have a plain coffin without a flower, a funeral without a eulogy, than a life without the sweetness of love and sympathy"; "Post-mortem kindness does not cheer the burdened spirit. Flowers on the coffin cast no fragrance back over the weary way"; and "The faults of our brothers we write upon the sand; their virtues upon the tablets of love and memory."

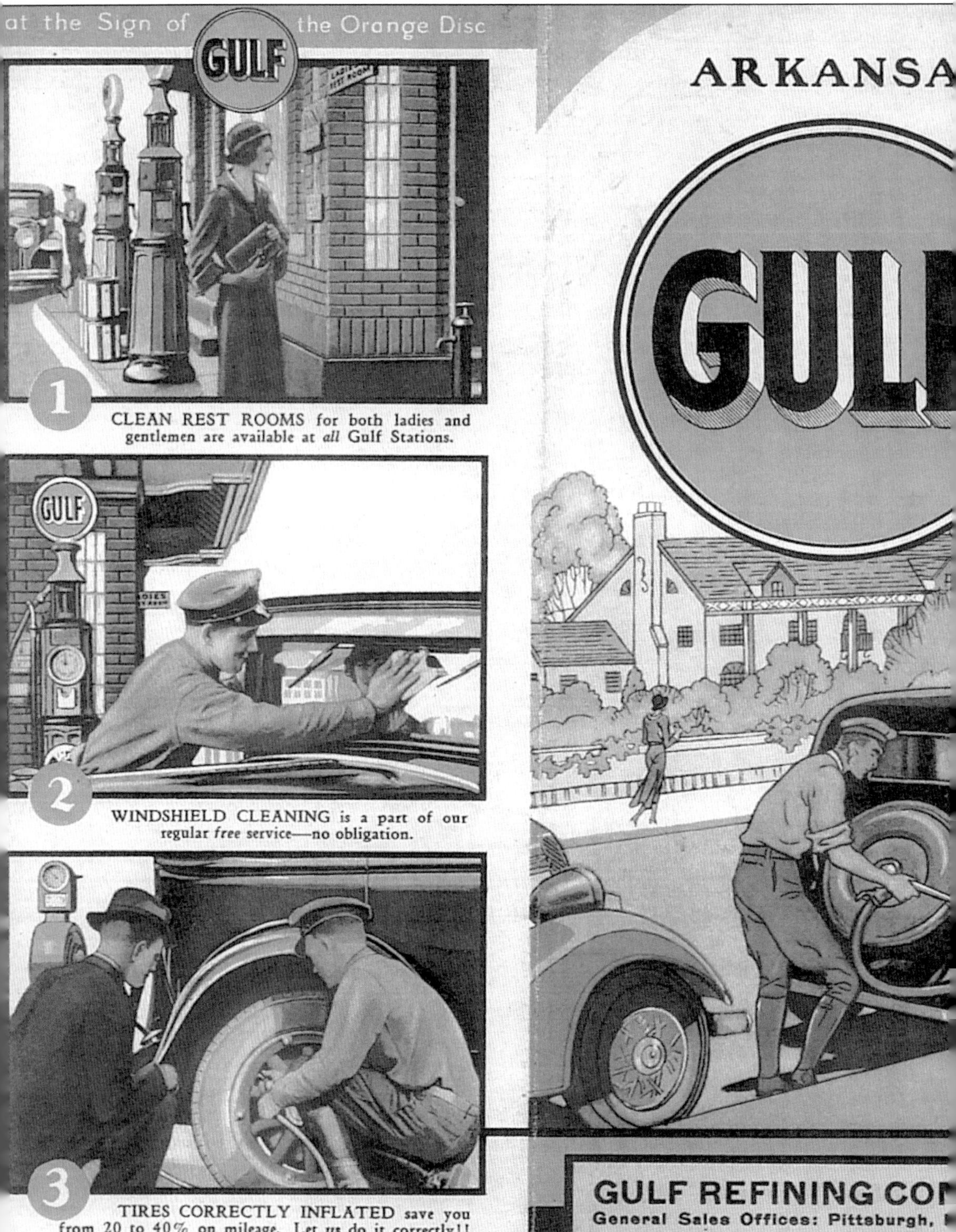
at the Sign of GULF the Orange Disc
CLEAN REST ROOMS for both ladies and gentlemen are available at *all* Gulf Stations.
WINDSHIELD CLEANING is a part of our regular *free* service—no obligation.
TIRES CORRECTLY INFLATED save you from 20 to 40% on mileage. Let *us* do it correctly!!
ARKANSA
GUL
GULF REFINING CO
General Sales Offices: Pittsburgh,

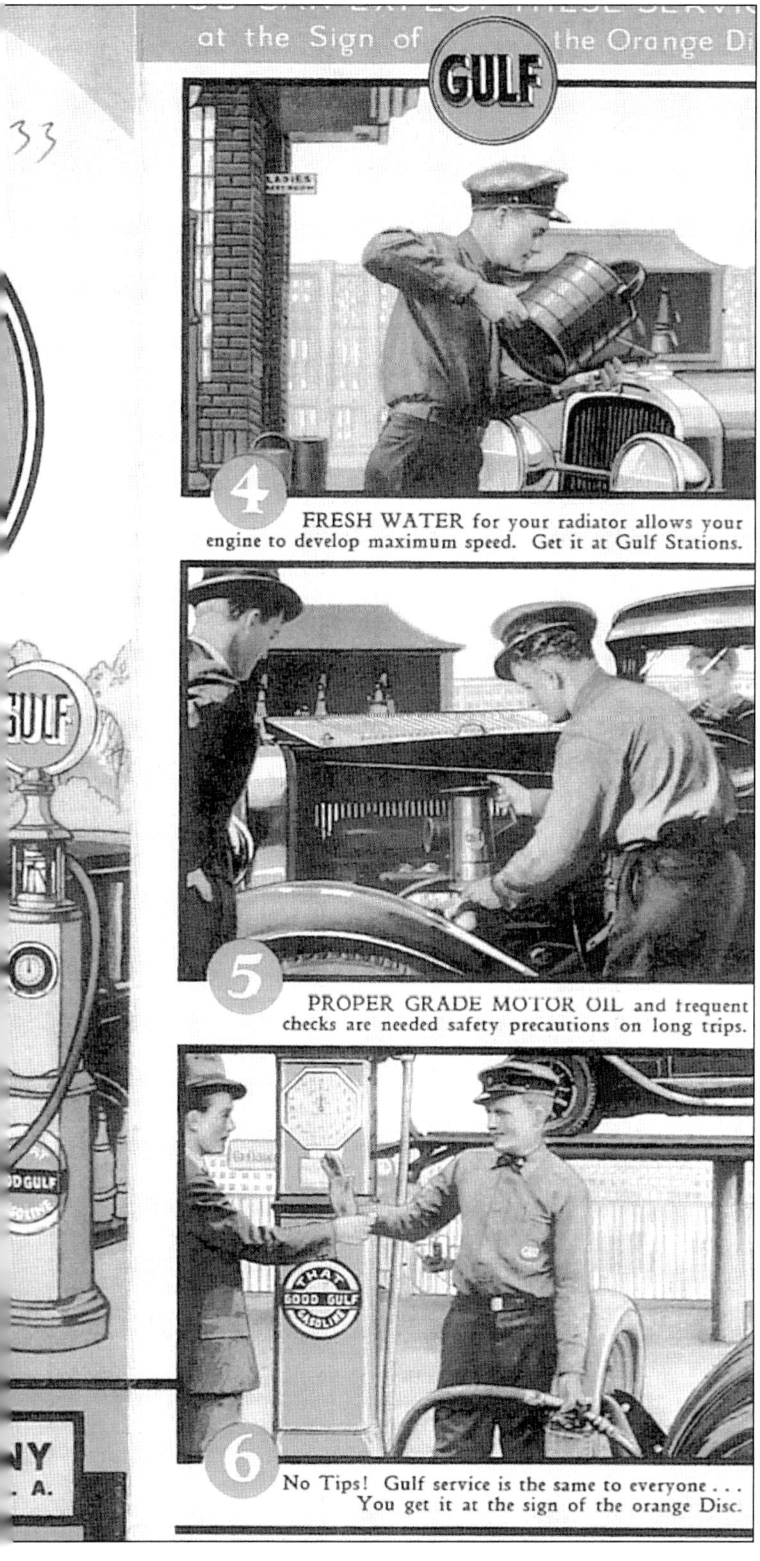

Gas stations such as the Gulf Station at the foot of the Broadway bridge offered full service–the term "self service" was unknown until recent years. The oil companies, seeking brand loyalty and visibility, gave away maps, including this one of Arkansas. The outside of this c. 1933 map offered a number of car care tips, promoted all the attention the uniformed Gulf attendant gave, and made clear in the last panel "No tips! Gulf Service is the same to everyone . . . You get it at the sign of the Orange Disc." Panel #1 promises clean restrooms for both ladies and gentlemen, while panel #4 advises, "Fresh water for your radiator allows your engine to develop maximum speed."

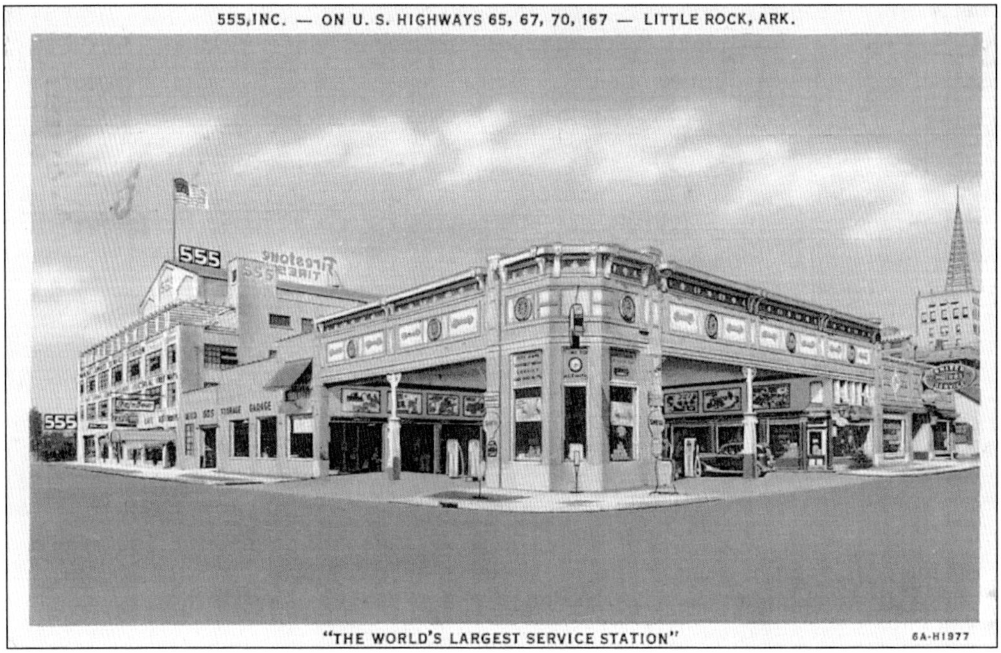

The competition to claim bragging rights as Broadway/Highway 67's largest gas station was won, without question, by the 555, Inc. at Third and Broadway. From its opening around 1925, not long after the new bridge started bringing highway traffic down Broadway, the 555 had laid solid claim to being "the world's largest service station," as it declared in the above 1945 card. The placement of a Model T automobile on the roof of the structure was an engineering marvel to many who craned their necks to look at the rooftop car. The back of the postcard below offered customers of the station, perhaps while their car was being serviced, a choice of messages to send home. A choice between "Town is full of good looking girls" and "No better lookers than you" was left to the motorist, but two adages about the 555 came pre-checked.

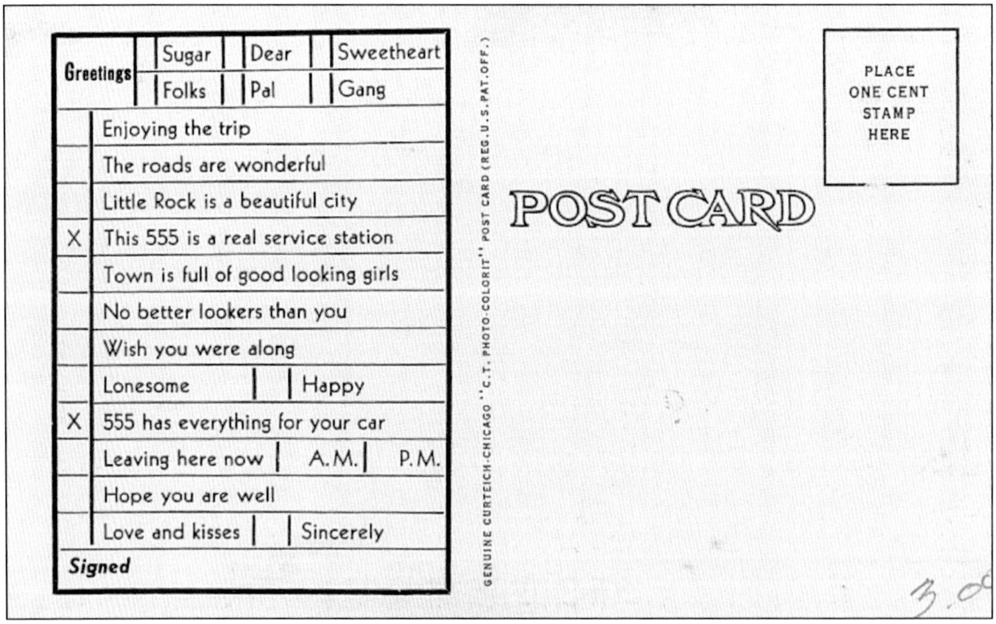

Greetings Sugar | Dear | Sweetheart | Folks | Pal | Gang

	Enjoying the trip
	The roads are wonderful
	Little Rock is a beautiful city
X	This 555 is a real service station
	Town is full of good looking girls
	No better lookers than you
	Wish you were along
	Lonesome | Happy
X	555 has everything for your car
	Leaving here now | A.M. | P.M.
	Hope you are well
	Love and kisses | Sincerely

Signed

GENUINE CURTEICH-CHICAGO "C.T. PHOTO-COLORIT" POST CARD (REG. U.S. PAT. OFF.)

POST CARD

PLACE ONE CENT STAMP HERE

3.00

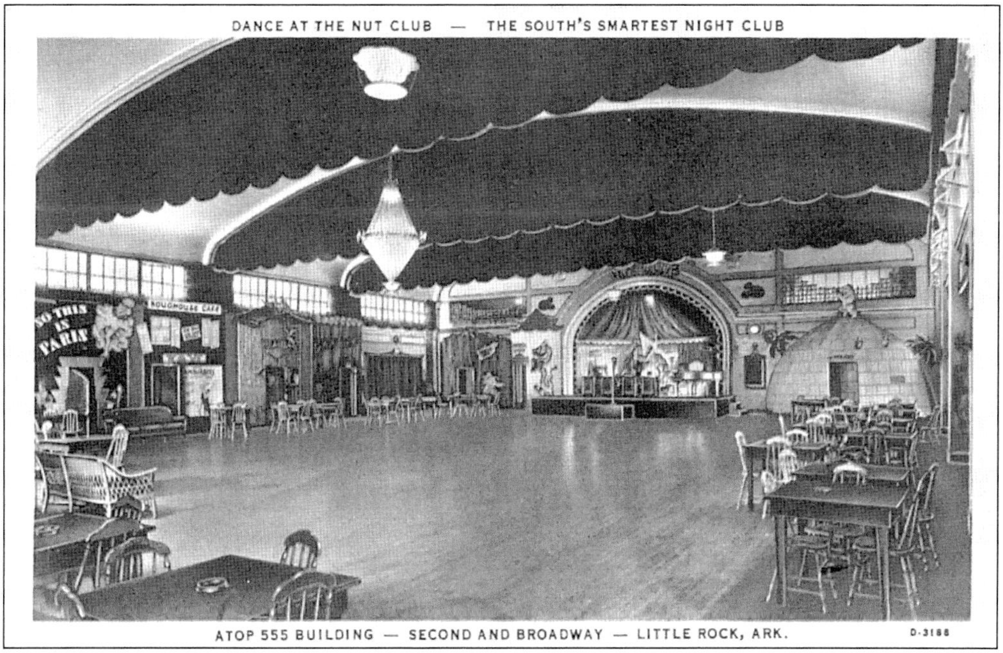

The 555 had not only the state's, if not the nation's, largest gas station, but its top floor was home to what, for a time, was Little Rock's premier night spot. The Rainbow Garden, the nightclub atop the building, was home to The Nut Club, promoted in this card as "The gayest place in Little Rock . . . The largest dance floor . . . Beer and good things to eat . . . Tuesday Bargain Nite—Gentlemen 40 cents, Ladies Free . . . Saturday—Whoopee Nite 40 Cents per person . . . Music by Frankie Littlefield and his 10 piece band." The 555 is gone today, and the building survives as office space.

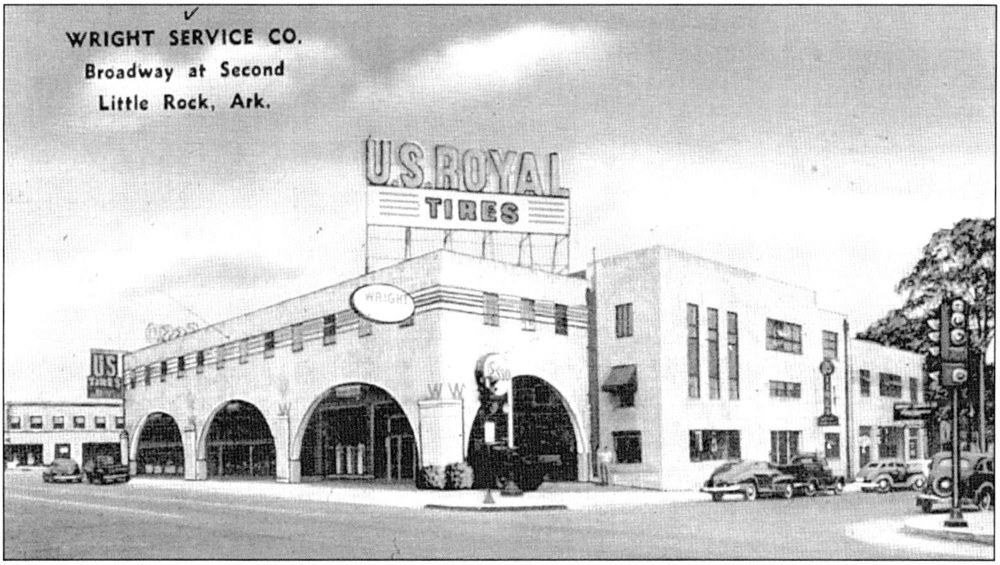

The closest competitor to the 555 in terms of size and volume of business was the Wright Service Company at Second and Broadway, prominently selling U.S. Royal Tires and Esso gasoline. The adage on the back of the card is "Service the Wright Way." The service station closed with the coming of Interstate 30 several blocks to the east, but the building still survives as commercial and office space.

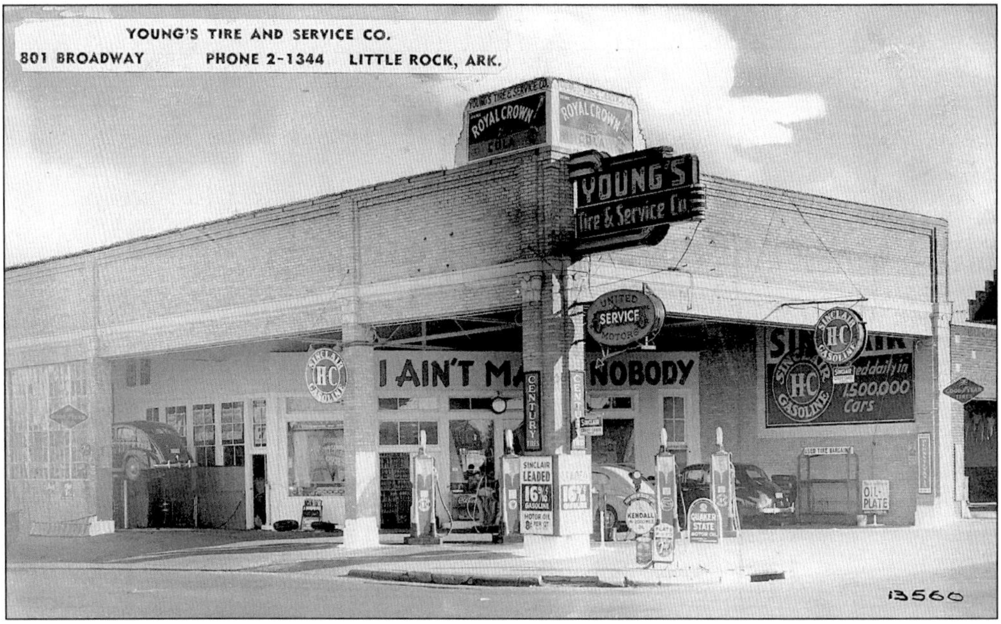

The first few blocks of Broadway south of the river bridge were dominated by gas stations and related support services for the thousands of vehicles using Highway 67 each week. One of these, pictured here *c.* 1940, was Young's Tire and Service Co. at 801 Broadway, which sold Sinclair gas for 16.9¢ per gallon and motor oil for 8¢ per quart. The sign across the door of the station reads, "I Ain't Mad At Anybody," thought to be a pledge of forgiveness for people who bought gas on credit during the Depression and who failed to pay. Mr. Young wanted these people back as customers.

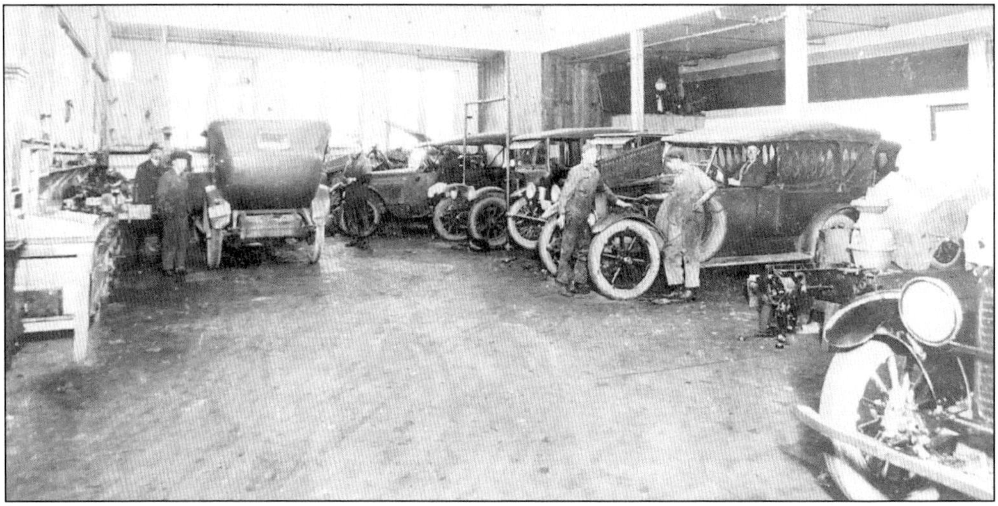

In the 1920s, vehicles passing through Little Rock in need of serious repairs might have ended up in the service department of the Little Rock Motor Car Company on Capitol Avenue, a few blocks off of Broadway/67. An indication of how comparatively simple the mechanics of automobiles were in the 1920s can be found in the following advice offered on one oil company map of Arkansas: "If you run out of oil, pour water into the crank case until the oil in the bottom rises to a point where the crank shaft will splash it. You can run thirty miles additional without endangering the engine." (Courtesy of Arkansas History Commission.)

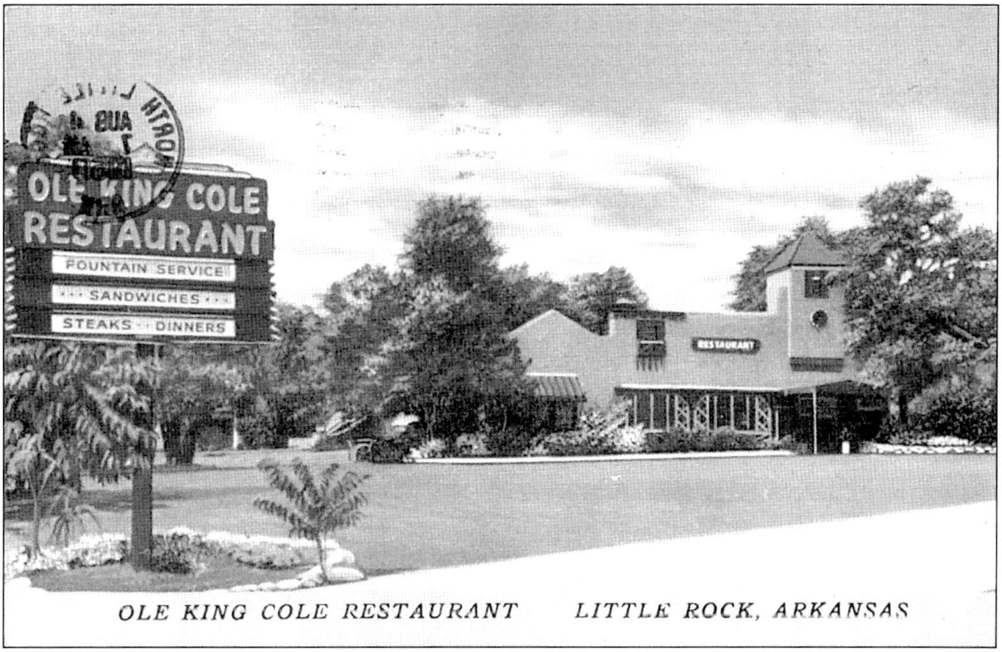

Once past the gauntlet of gas stations on the lower part of Broadway/67 heading south, motorists would have been tempted by an array of dining establishments, most of which printed their own postcards. One of the best known was the Ole King Cole Restaurant, seen here *c.* 1945. From its start at Fifth and Broadway in the 1920s, Ole King Cole offered curb service and some of the best hot fudge sundaes in town. For a serious sit-down meal inside, the eggplant casserole was often a top selection. The building is gone today, though memories of its delicious cooking remain for a few local seniors.

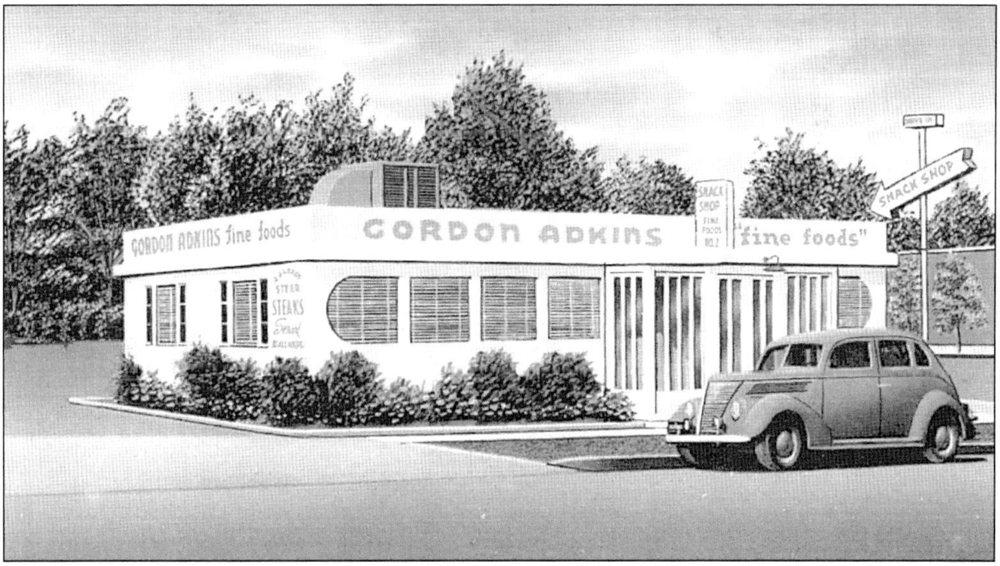

"Quick Service and Air Conditioned" was Gordon Adkins' claim to patrons of his diner located at Tenth and Broadway. Built sometime around 1940 and pictured here *c.* 1950, Adkins's typified the roadside diner of the era—a plain, functional structure with parking spaces and a basic menu. The building is gone today.

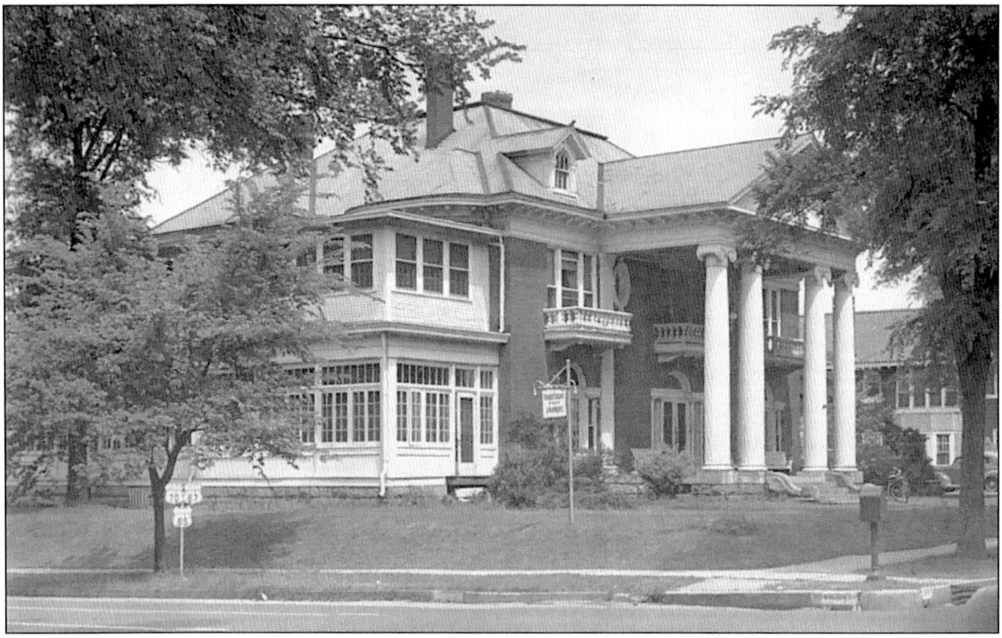

Proceeding down Broadway, tourists had a choice at the corner of Eighteenth Street—they could turn onto Business 67/70, which, by way of Wright Avenue, would later rejoin Highway 67, or they could stay on the regular 67 down Broadway to Roosevelt Road. Some stopped at Garm's Tourist Home at the corner of Eighteenth and Broadway, where kitchenette apartments with a private bath rented for $2.50 per night. One could sleep for just $2 with a shared bath down the hall. In the misguided urban renewal/clean-up of the 1960s, this wonderful home was torn down.

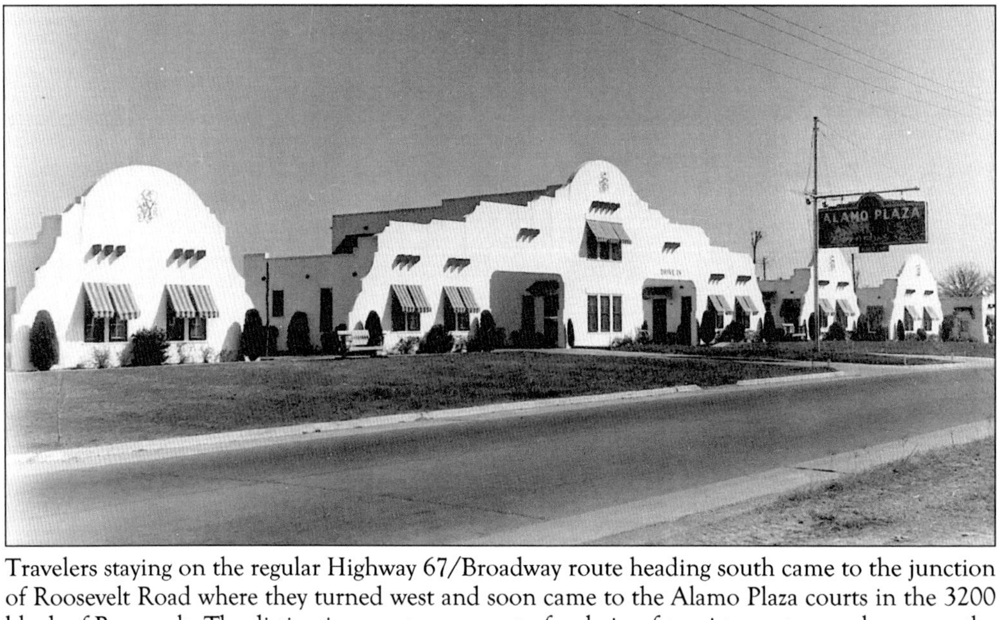

Travelers staying on the regular Highway 67/Broadway route heading south came to the junction of Roosevelt Road where they turned west and soon came to the Alamo Plaza courts in the 3200 block of Roosevelt. The distinctive courts were part of a chain of tourist courts popular across the southwestern United States. The buildings were razed years ago, and a McDonald's is located on the site today.

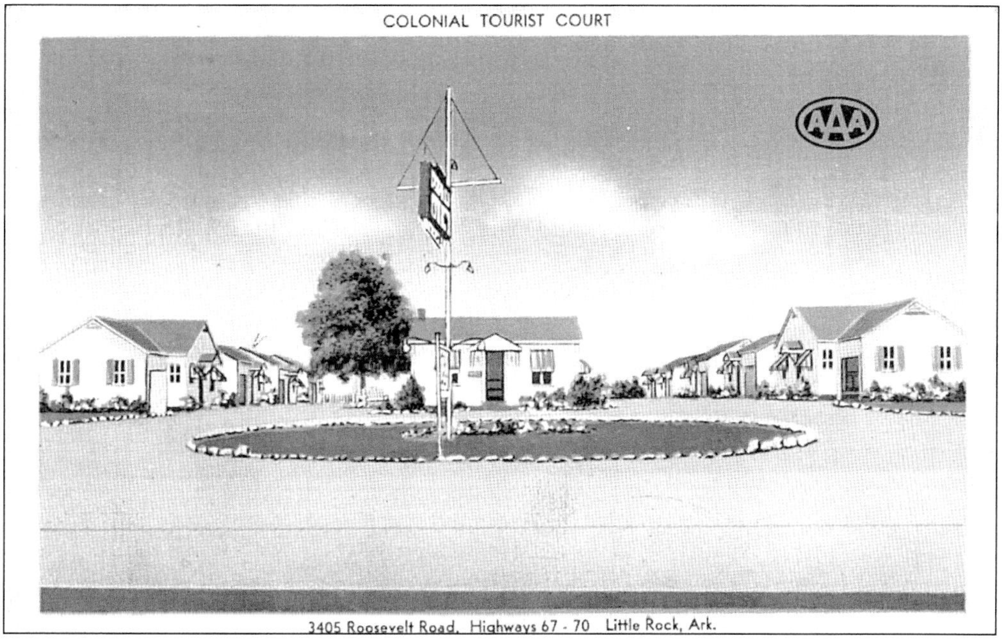

Beginning in the 1930s, travelers on Highway 67 frequented the Colonial Tourist Court at 3405 Roosevelt. "11 separate cottages on 3 acres of beautifully landscaped hill, cottages with kitchenette for those who like to cook, inner spring mattresses, garages," proclaimed the back of the 1941 postcard above. Below is evidence of the business's prosperity, for by 1954, the Colonial Tourist Court had expanded its 11 cottages to 40 units, and it was using air-conditioned rooms as a draw. The air conditioning was especially important to the guest who mailed this card home to Illinois with the comments, "We are in Little Rock, have our cabins for night. It is terrible hot. They told us at a filling station it was 110 degrees. Our cabins are cool, everything is dry." The cottages were later remodeled into a more typical motel style; today some of the buildings still stand but no longer serve as a motel on the route long ago bypassed by Interstate 30.

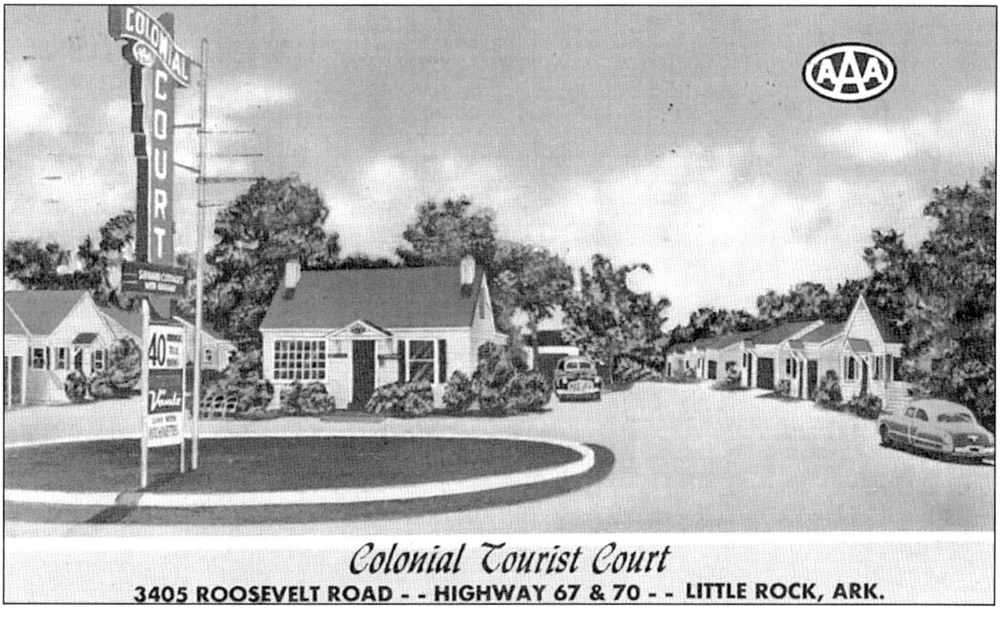

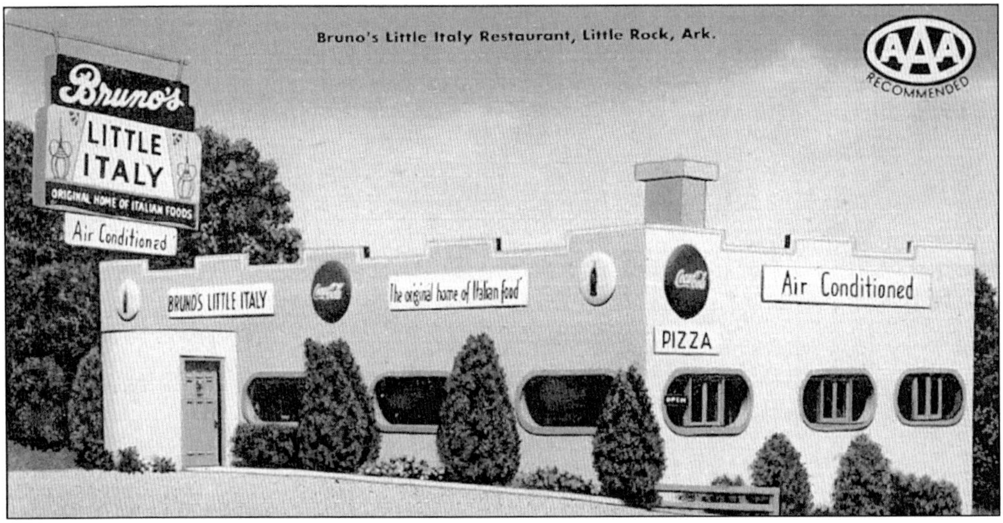

Just down Roosevelt Road from the Alamo Plaza was Bruno's Little Italy, the best-known Italian eatery in Arkansas. The restaurant had its origins in 1903 when Gennaro, Nicolo, and Vincenzo Bruno arrived in New York from Naples, Italy. The trio induced their brother, Giovanni, to join them in New York and begin a restaurant there. As fate would have it, years later, Giovanni's son Vincent "Jimmy" Bruno was stationed during World War II at Camp Robinson in North Little Rock, where he had served both as a chef and a USO entertainer. After a stint in Chicago plying the culinary skills learned from his father, Jimmy left the Windy City, in part because of the threat of organized crime, and came back to Little Rock. In 1949, he opened an Italian eatery at 3400 West Roosevelt, and for the next 29 years, it was among the favorites of Little Rock. At one point, Bruno's was classified as 99th among American's 12,000 most popular restaurants in Darnell's *Guide to Good Eating in the South.*

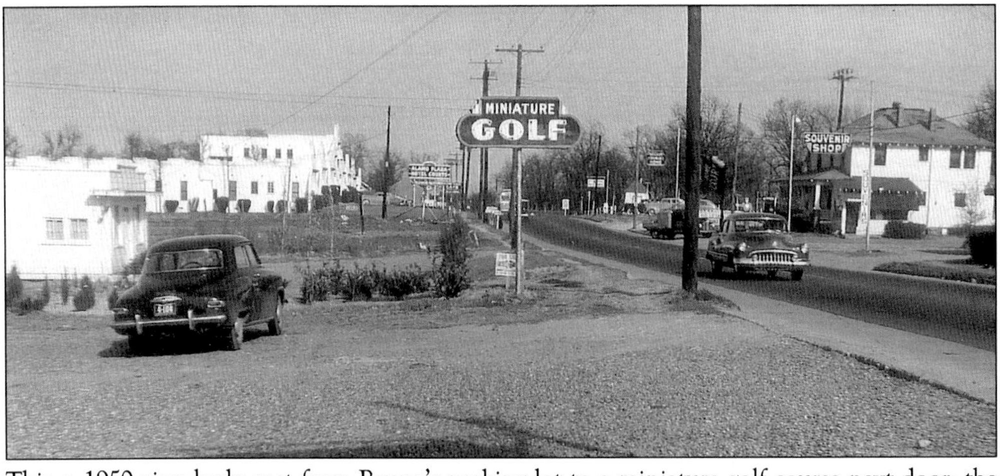

This *c.* 1950 view looks east from Bruno's parking lot to a miniature golf course next door; the Alamo Plaza is in the distance. The Bruno's menu of the early 1950s offered tenderloin tips with mushrooms for $3.50, the priciest item available; lobster tails in butter sauce for $2.75; and "round the world" pizza for $1.50. Coffee and Bulgarian buttermilk were a dime, Budweiser and Miller beer were 35¢, and a Heineken was 50¢. Desserts included two demitasse for 40¢. Bruno's was sold long ago and relocated to west Little Rock, following the changing demographics of the city. The building still stands on the Roosevelt Road site, but today it is vacant and painted bright blue. (Courtesy of Gio Bruno, son of Jimmy Bruno.)

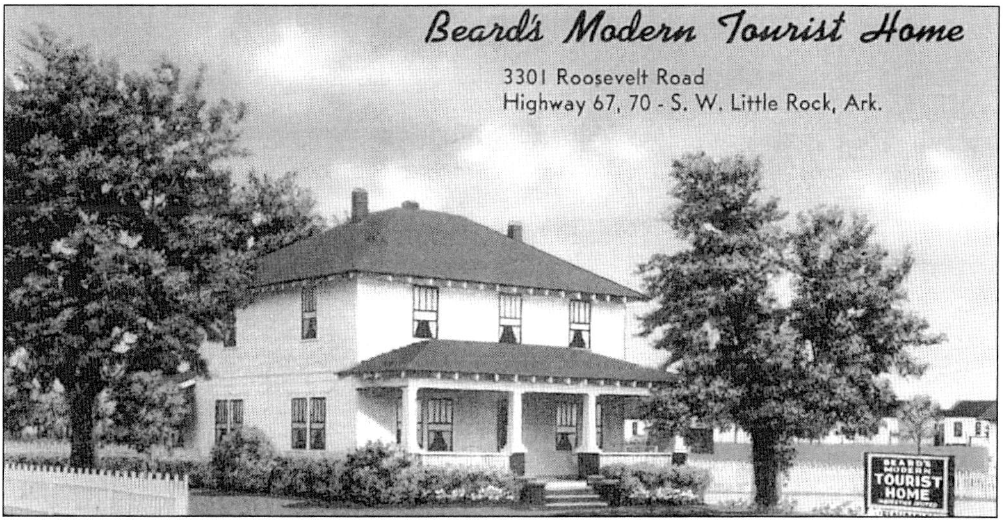

Across Roosevelt Road, on the right side of the photo on the bottom of page 70, is Beard's Modern Tourist Home, an example of lodging before the tourist courts began to grow in number. The above card, c. 1940, was produced by Mrs. Genie Harris, the manager of Beard's, for guests to mail home. "This home is arranged and furnished for your comfort." The two-story frame house, across the street from the Alamo Plaza, offered a less-expensive alternative to the "fancy" tourist court. The home is gone today, and a brick commercial building is on the site.

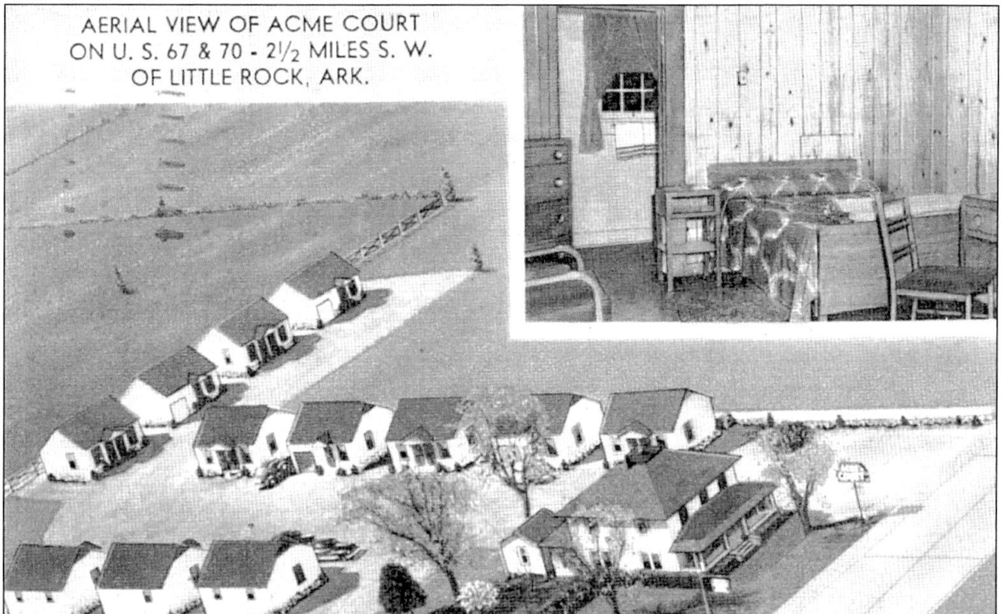

Some time in the late 1940s, Beard's Tourist Home expanded to become the Acme Court. This aerial view shows that 27 cabins had been built in an "L"-shaped layout behind the original Beard's building that faces out onto Roosevelt. "Grandpa & Grandma-We have been having a nice trip so far" is the 1949 message back to Iowa. "Simmons furniture, $3 for 2 people, $5.00 and $6.00 for 4 people, B.G. Beard, owner" is Mr. Beard's ad on the back of the card. A decade later, the lawn was paved over, most of the cabins were removed, and a two-story "modern" motel was built that is still in business today.

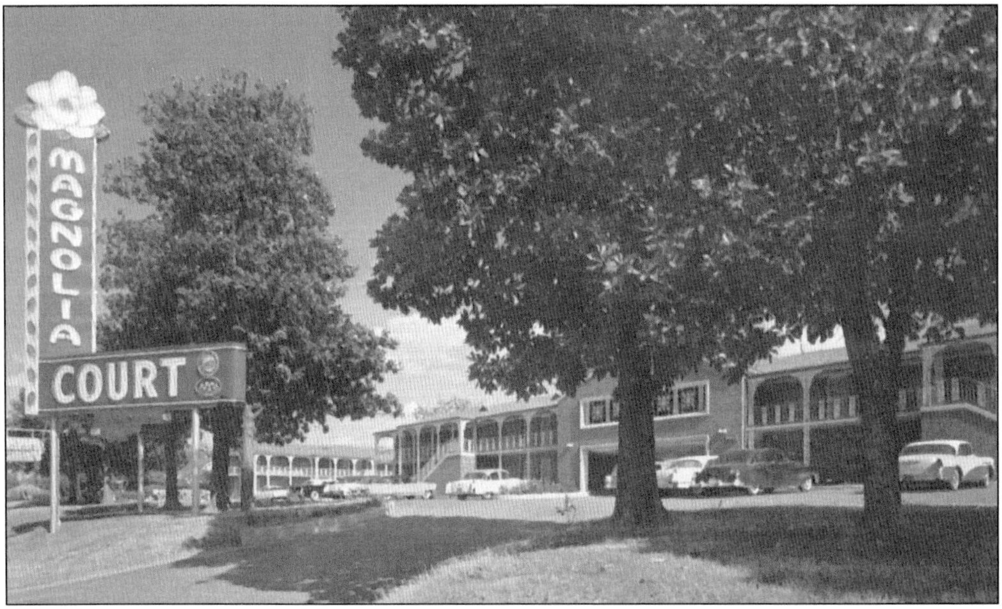

In the early 1950s, an ever-increasing flow of traffic on Highway 67 led to the building of even more tourist courts on Roosevelt Road and Asher Avenue. The largest of these was the Magnolia Court, which had 122 rooms and was located at 3601 Roosevelt. Features that attracted guests included 24-hour room service, a swimming pool, and a location "only three miles from downtown." The Magnolia still stands but no longer serves as a motel. It has been used as a residential care facility for the elderly and handicapped in recent years.

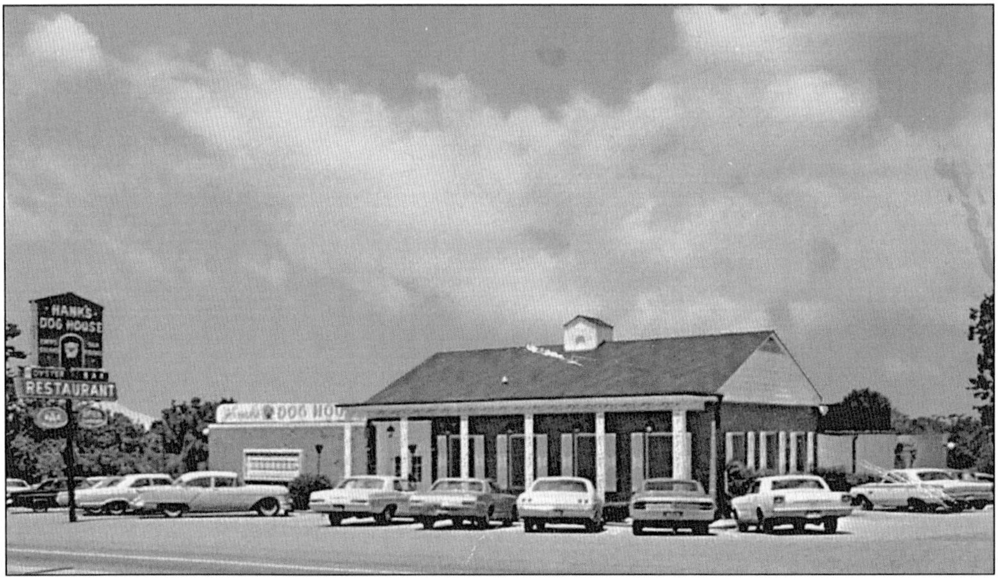

Across the road from the Magnolia was one of the most popular eating places in Little Rock during the 1950s—Hank's Dog House. Aged steaks, live Maine lobsters, and the city's only "Oyster Bar" drew both travelers and locals to sample the fine food Hank's put on the table. The large restaurant held five banquet rooms and had a seating capacity of up to 350 patrons. Like many of the businesses that once served motorists on the now-bypassed highway, Hank's is no more.

Highway 67/Roosevelt Road merged with Wright Avenue/City Route 67, which then sent a combined stream of traffic on down the Asher Avenue leg of the highway. Motorists who had taken the City Route had their choice of automobile services, including this very unusual gas station located on Bishop Street just off Wright Avenue. A woman poses with her baby, while an attendant from the mushroom-shaped station services her car. The station was razed decades ago. (Courtesy of Arkansas History Commission.)

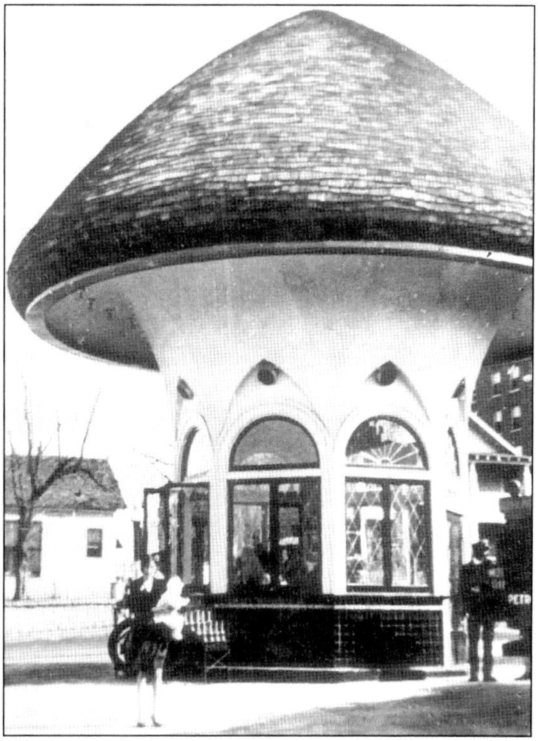

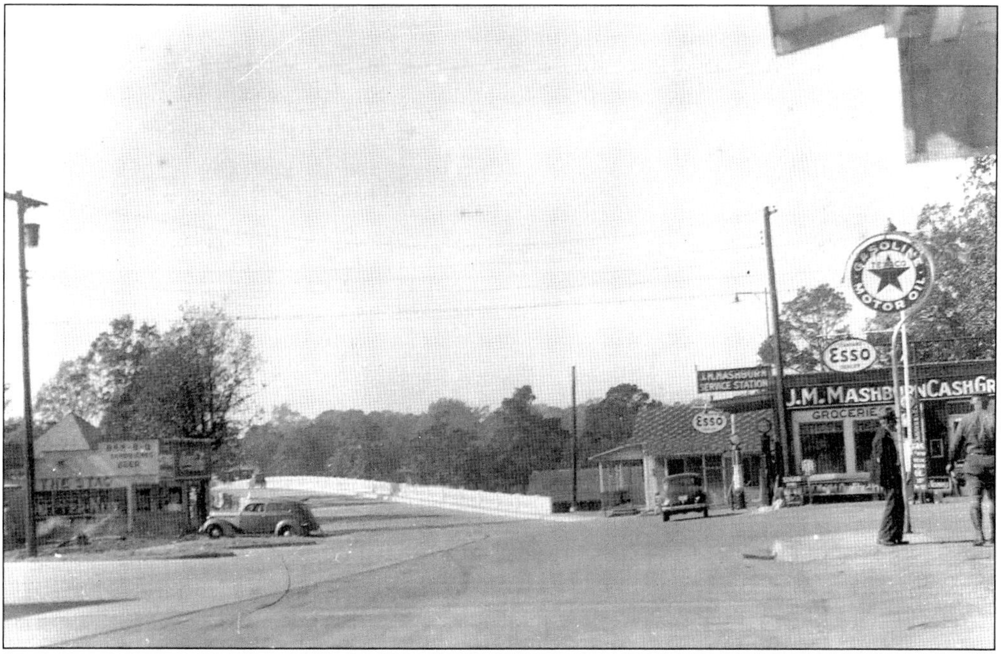

A few blocks before City Route 67/Wright Avenue and Asher Avenue met, a westbound motorist approaching the Missouri Pacific Railroad overpass might have stopped at J.M. Mashburn's Cash Grocery and Esso Station. Just up from it, on the right, is a Texaco station with a uniformed attendant visible. If the traveler was hungry, across the road to the left was a barbecue stand offering beer. The bridge is still there today, but the businesses are all gone. (Courtesy of UCA Archives.)

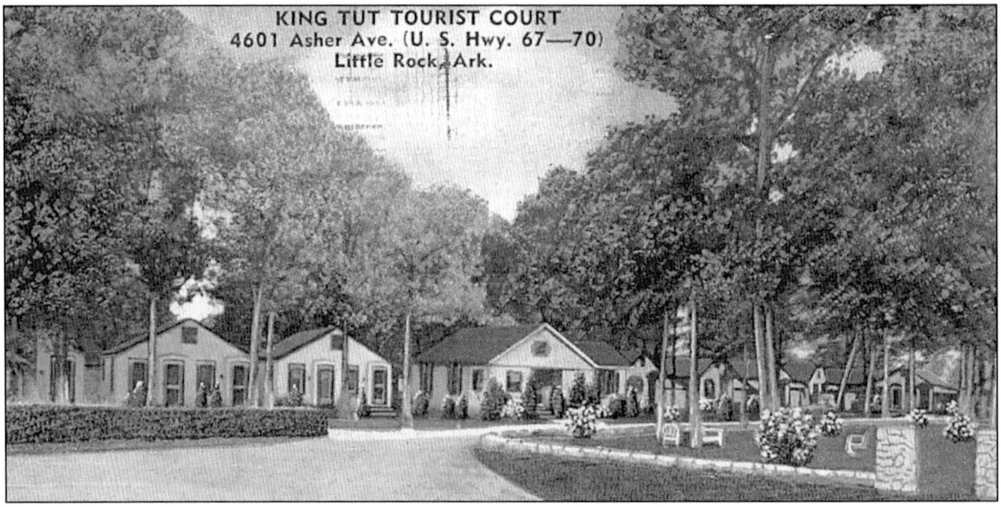

Once Roosevelt Road and City Route 67/Wright Avenue merged to form Asher Avenue, motorists heading west passed through another long stretch of motels and eateries. Among these was the strangely named King Tut Tourist Court at 4601 Asher. "Dear Kids, We are in one of these cabins to-nite, car works good, loads of love," read a mother's penned note home to Michigan in 1954. The King Tut opened in the late 1930s; room rates were $1 to $2 into the 1940s when it advertised "sleep in comfort and safety without extravagance." The shady, park-like grounds and "popular priced" cafe on the premises were all draws to motorists on Highway 67. The King Tut is gone today.

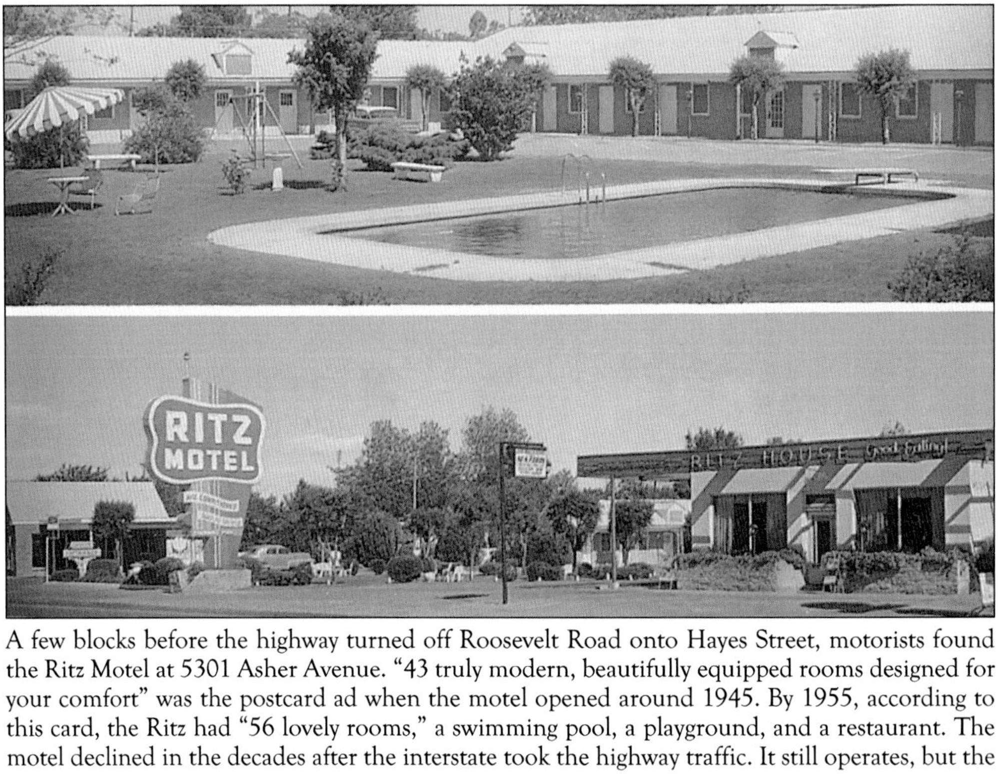

A few blocks before the highway turned off Roosevelt Road onto Hayes Street, motorists found the Ritz Motel at 5301 Asher Avenue. "43 truly modern, beautifully equipped rooms designed for your comfort" was the postcard ad when the motel opened around 1945. By 1955, according to this card, the Ritz had "56 lovely rooms," a swimming pool, a playground, and a restaurant. The motel declined in the decades after the interstate took the highway traffic. It still operates, but the pool is filled in and the restaurant has been converted into a liquor store.

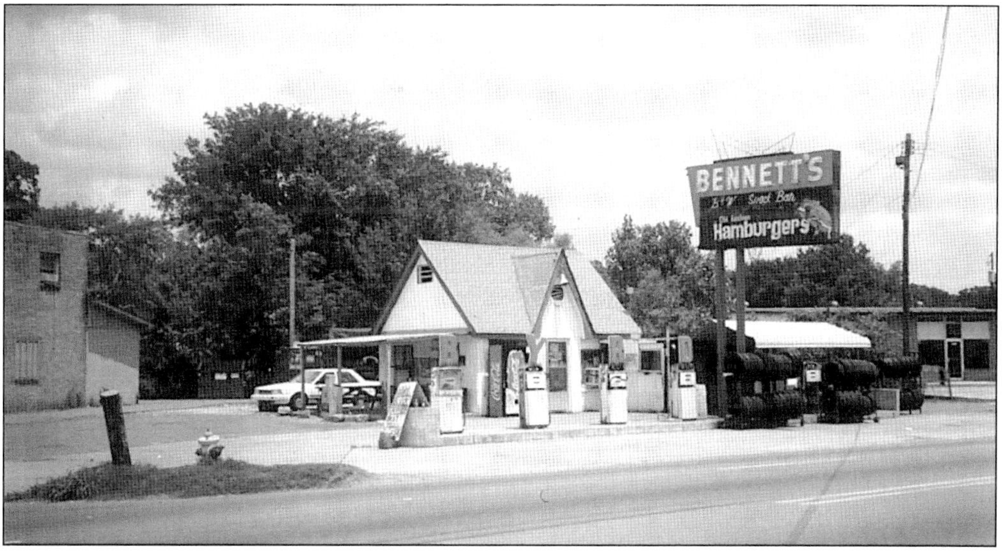

The coming of Interstate 30 almost four decades ago took the highway traffic away from Asher Avenue/Highway 67, so that most of the original roadside enterprises the traffic once supported are today gone without a trace. Yet, here and there along the avenue, if one looks, may be found remnants that survived to serve other uses. The above building was a gas station that began sometime around 1940, and a decade or so later, Bennett's Hamburgers was added. The large letters atop each vintage pump spell out "BYRD"—perhaps the name of an oil company or a past owner. The many years since the pumps served gas is evident from the price per gallon—57¢. Another surprising remnant is found behind the still-operating Acme Court. Resembling an abandoned movie set, weeds poking through asphalt, the boarded up cabins seen in the 1940s aerial view on page 71 are still standing, though unused for many years. (1999 photos by Ray Hanley.)

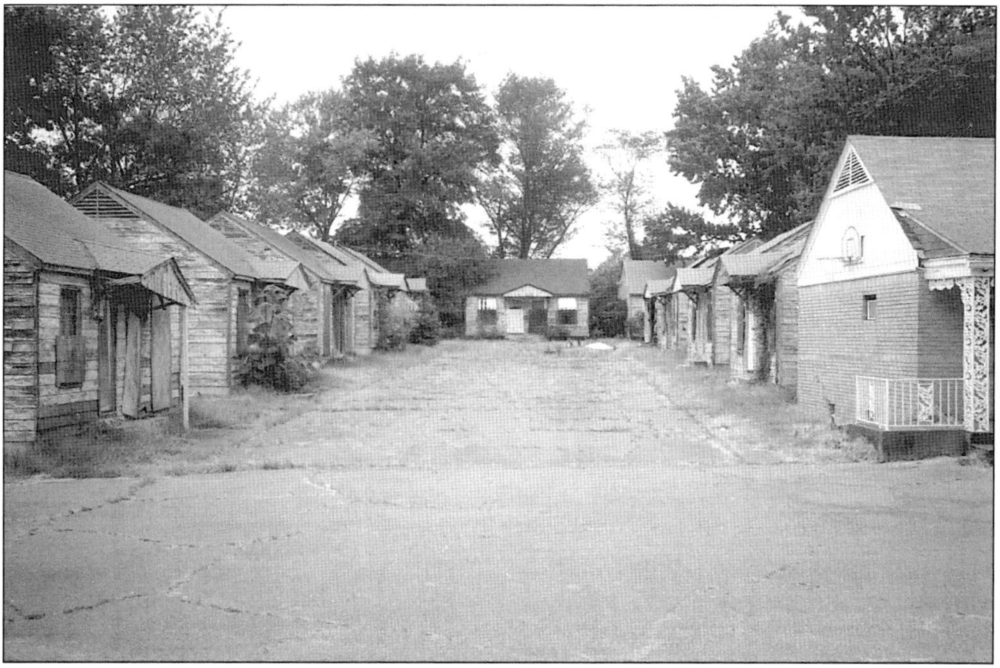

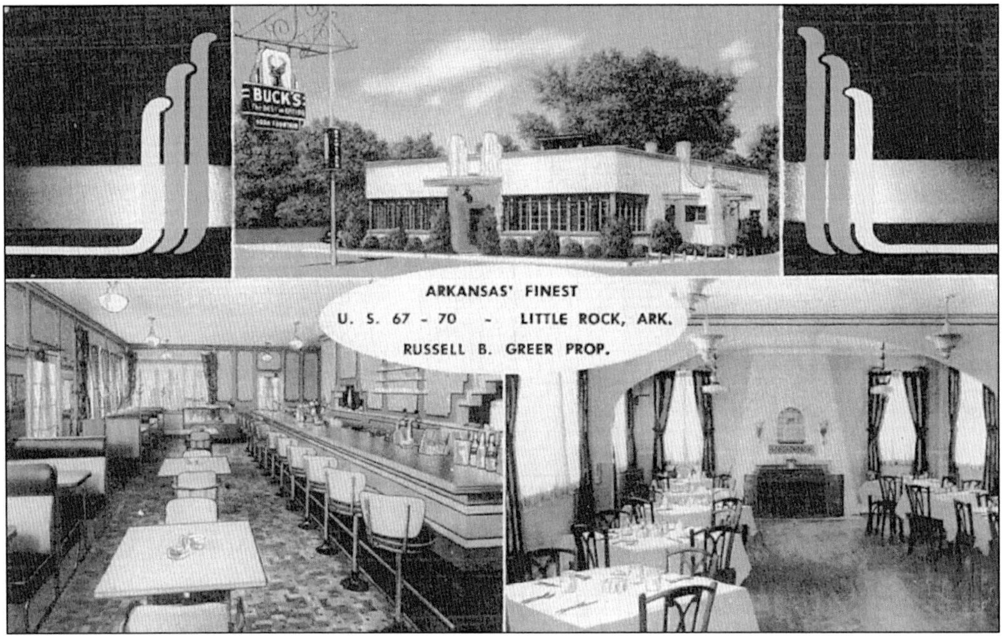

Across from the site of the Ritz was one of Highway 67's nicest dining spots—Buck's Restaurant. "The best in eating, famed for steaks and chicken dinners, private parties a speciality [sic]." The restaurant had both a casual section with a counter and booths but, as shown in this *c.* 1940 image, also a very upscale section with draped windows where diners could watch the traffic or dine by candlelight. Buck's has been gone for many years.

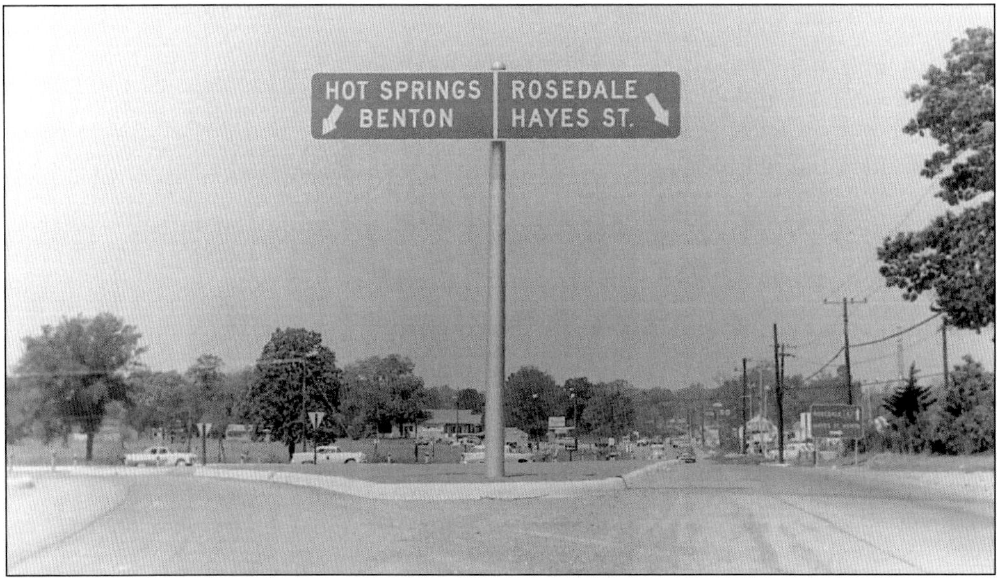

The intersection of Asher Avenue and Hayes Street (today University Avenue) has changed dramatically since these two photos were taken some 40 years ago. The above view would have met the motorist stopping to follow Highway 67 to the left toward Benton. Today, the field to the left is home to K-Mart, a strip mall, and an assortment of fast food restaurants. In fact, this entire area, bypassed when I-30 came through, is now built up with many commercial enterprises. In 1955, there was not even a traffic light.

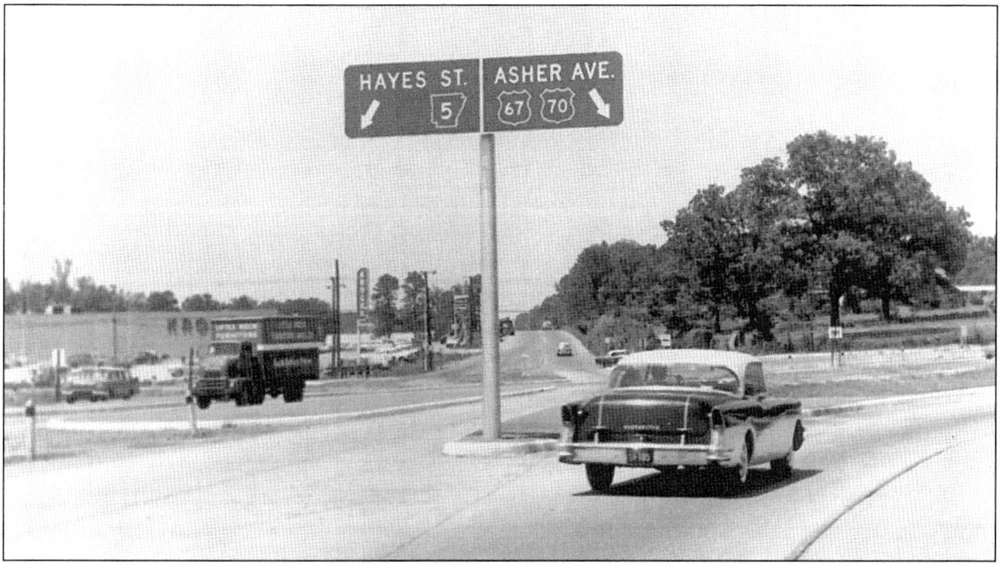

The 1957 Buick is preparing to turn onto Asher Avenue/Highway 67 north, the route covered on the last few pages. The tree-covered hill to the right is today paved and home to a shopping center erected in the early 1960s. Today, University Avenue goes straight on what was then Hayes Street. The Kroger store on the left is gone, but at that time, it occupied what is considered Little Rock's first shopping center, the Town and Country.

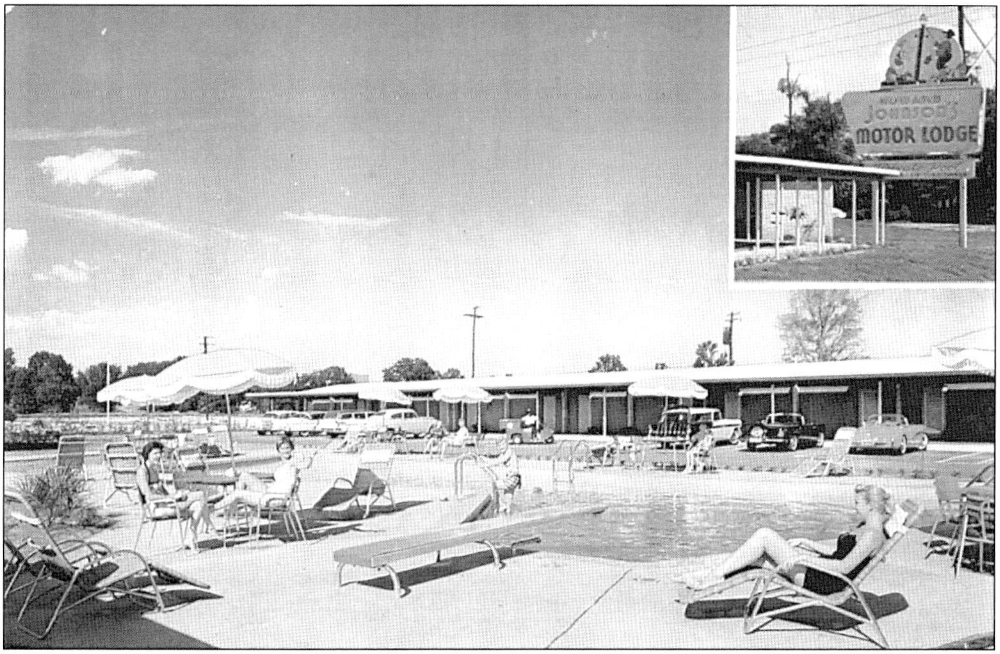

A turn off Asher Avenue onto the Hayes Street section of Highway 67 would have taken drivers immediately passed Howard Johnson's Motor Lodge in the mid-1950s. Its 72 units and swimming pool had drawn these ladies and a host of vintage-era automobiles off the highway on a sunny day around 1955. With the bypassing of highway traffic onto I-30, the motel declined over the years and was razed in 1997. Today, a McDonald's and Texaco mark the site where these ladies once swam.

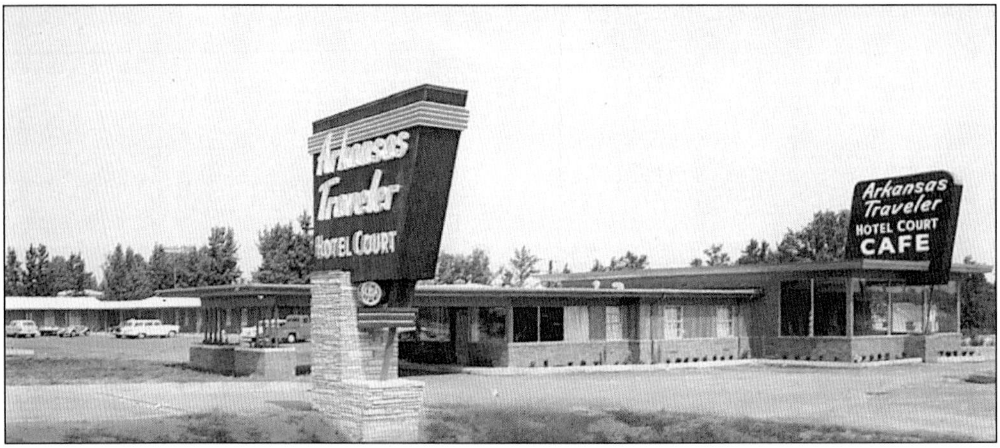

The Arkansas Traveler Hotel Court and Cafe was built around 1950 on the section of Highway 67 known today as South University Avenue. The court, which took its name from the Arkansas traveler of folklore, was affiliated with the emerging Best Western group of motels. Pictured here c. 1955, the Arkansas Traveler is still in business today, as Budget Inn, and is located across from Little Rock Dodge.

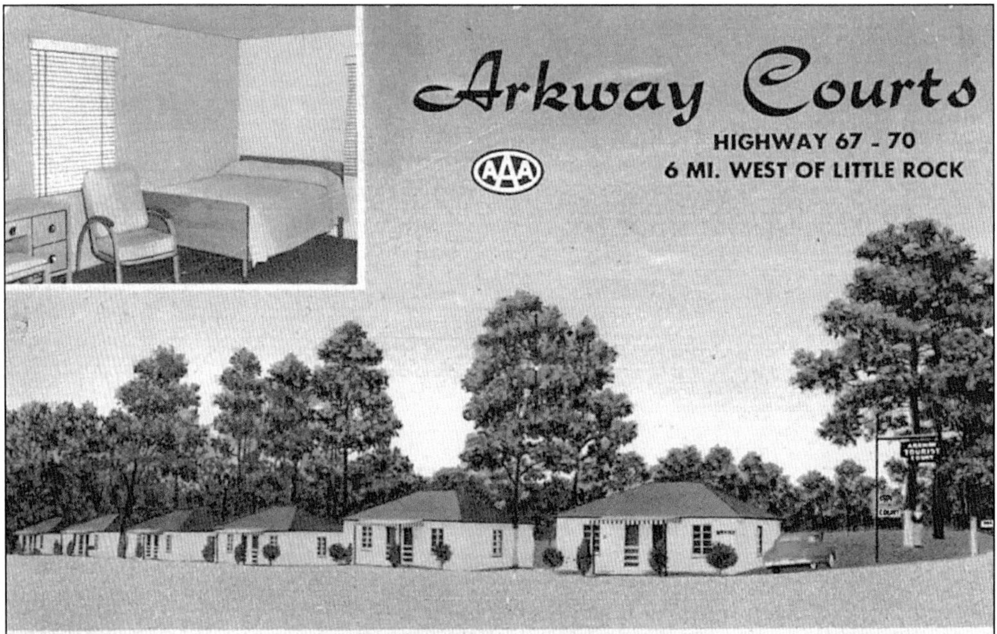

Six miles south of Little Rock heading for Benton, Highway 67 motorists' last chance for a room in Pulaski County may have been the Arkway Court, which was built around 1940. "12 modern courts—complete with Simmons Modern Furniture and tile bath" were the published features. The traditional court was apparently razed in the acquisition of right-of-way for Interstate 30 in the late 1950s.

Three

SALINE COUNTY TO MILLER COUNTY

BENTON TO TEXARKANA

Today, the 20 miles of highway that now form Interstate 30 between Little Rock and Benton, leading from Pulaski County into Saline County, is the most heavily traveled in the state. In the development of Highway 67, this stretch seemed to get the most attention and work from early in the century. From Benton, Highway 67 was less vigorously developed as it wound through the wooded countryside of southwest Arkansas, passing through downtown Malvern and Arkadelphia.

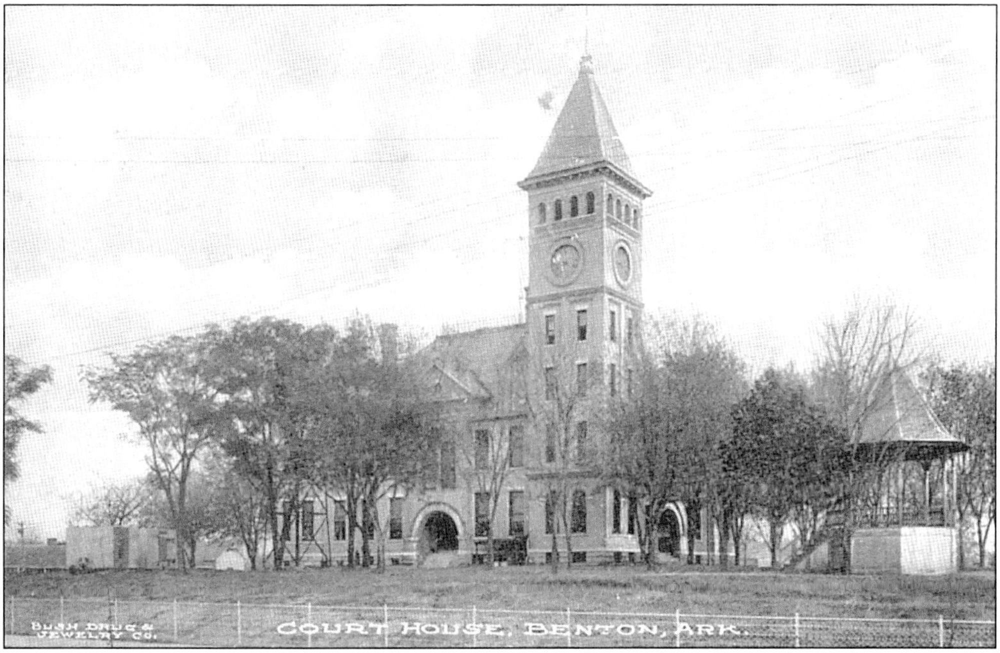

The Saline County Courthouse in Benton, with its tower defining the skyline of the town, has been a landmark for travelers since its construction in 1902. Among the movies set around this classical southern courthouse has been *White Lightning* with Burt Reynolds. Even today the building's clock tower may be seen from miles away, as motorists descend a hill on Interstate 30 south of Benton.

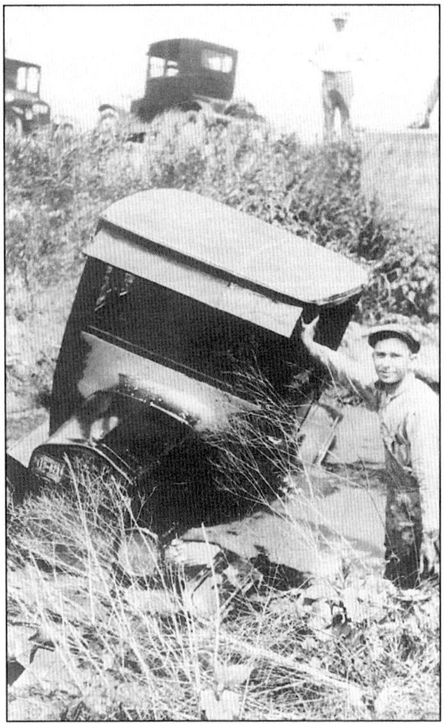

For much of the period from the 1920s and into the 1950s, engineers complained that the 20-mile stretch of highway between Little Rock and Benton was the most dangerous in the state. The national Bankhead Highway was the road's designation in the 1920s, before it became Highway 67. Although paved from Little Rock until just below Benton where the gravel resumed, wrecks were fairly common due to relatively greater traffic volume. These men were photographed studying how to extradite this Model T from a rain-swollen ditch around 1925. (Photo courtesy of Arkansas History Commission.)

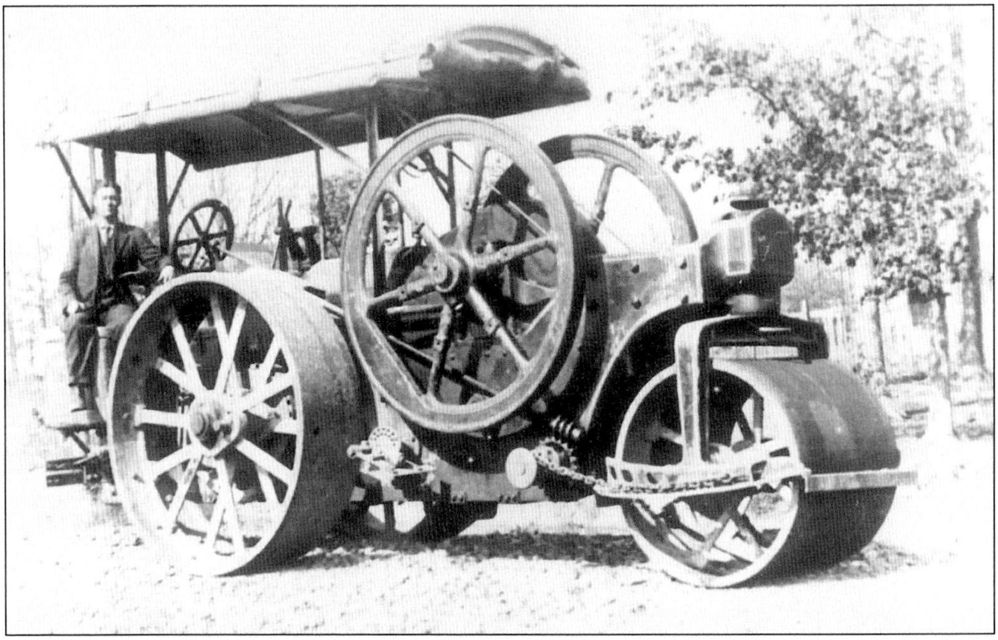

For a decade, the only paved sections of the Bankhead Highway and, later, Highway 67, were the sections leading into and out of Little Rock. The work was slow, complicated by fragmented financing, local politics, and floods. Progress was also dependent in large part upon the developing industry of construction and heavy equipment. The first paving of the road between Little Rock and Benton was done with equipment such as this early steamroller, which compressed the dirt and rocks to a point where concrete slab could be spread. (Courtesy of Arkansas History Commission.)

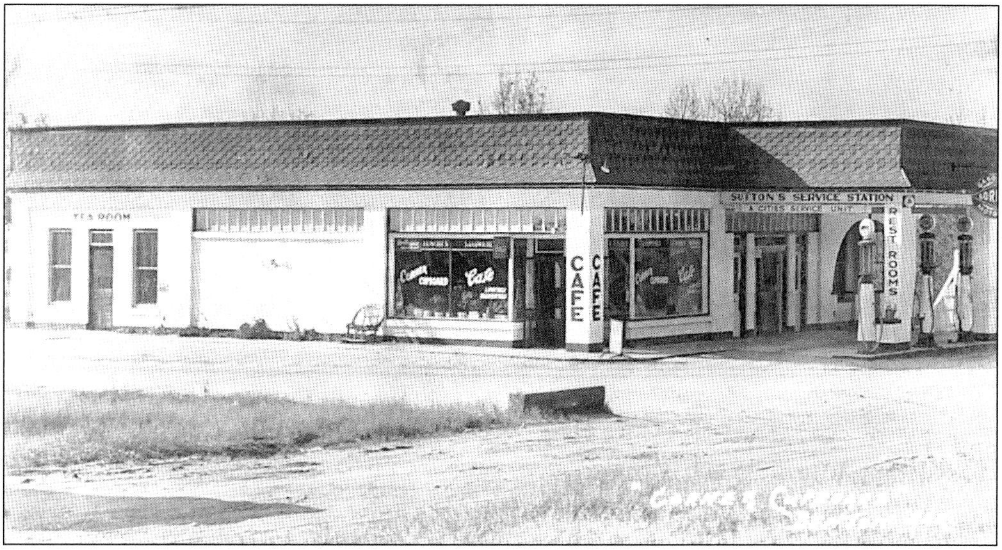

Highway 67 travelers who did venture down the highway to Benton in the early 1930s would have patronized the Corner Cupboard and Sutton's Service Station, which sold Cities gasoline. A prominent sign by the gas pumps reads "Rest Rooms," a convenience gas stations have promoted for decades. The business had not only a cafe at the front corner of the building but also a tea room with its own entrance toward the back. The business was reportedly destroyed in a 1936 tornado.

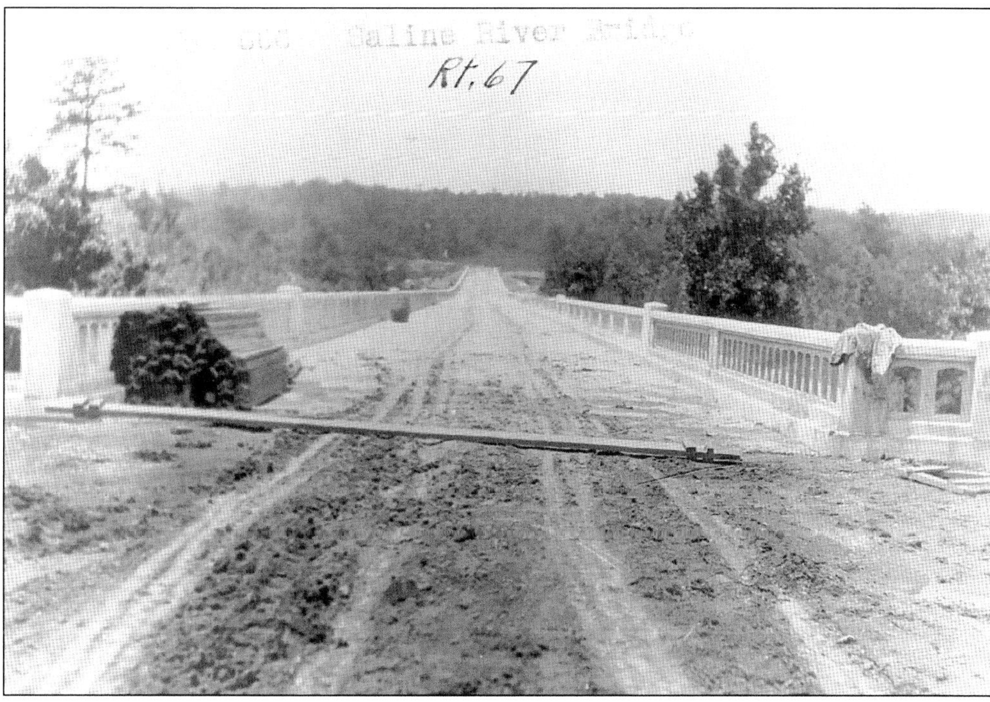

One of the barriers to early automobile traffic through Benton was the Saline River, which remains one of the very few free-flowing, un-dammed streams in the state. State and local officials were proud of this new concrete, two-lane bridge that was nearing completion across the river just below Benton around 1930. The road was yet to be paved beyond Benton, but the new bridge boosted confidence that Highway 67 would continue to improve.

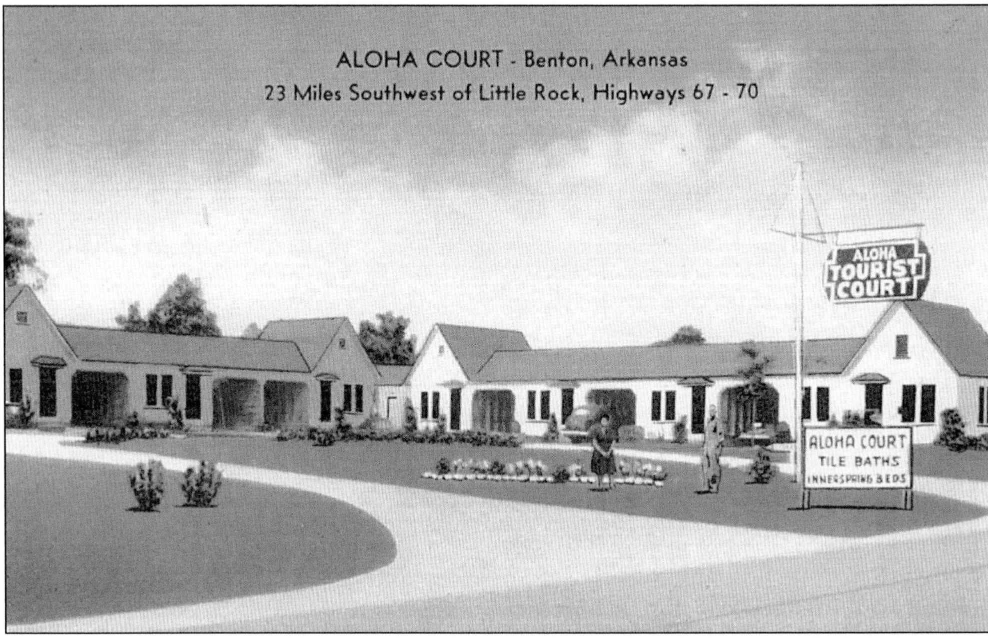

"REST HERE FOR THE REST OF YOUR LIFE" was the slogan on the back of this *c.* 1945 postcard of the Aloha Court on Highway 67 in Benton. "The Aloha Court offers comfort without extravagance, tile baths, ceiling, attic or table fans at no extra cost; specially constructed innerspring mattresses, a garage for every room, and unsurpassed physical and moral cleanliness." The latter claim raises unanswered questions decades later as to what the owner of the court meant.

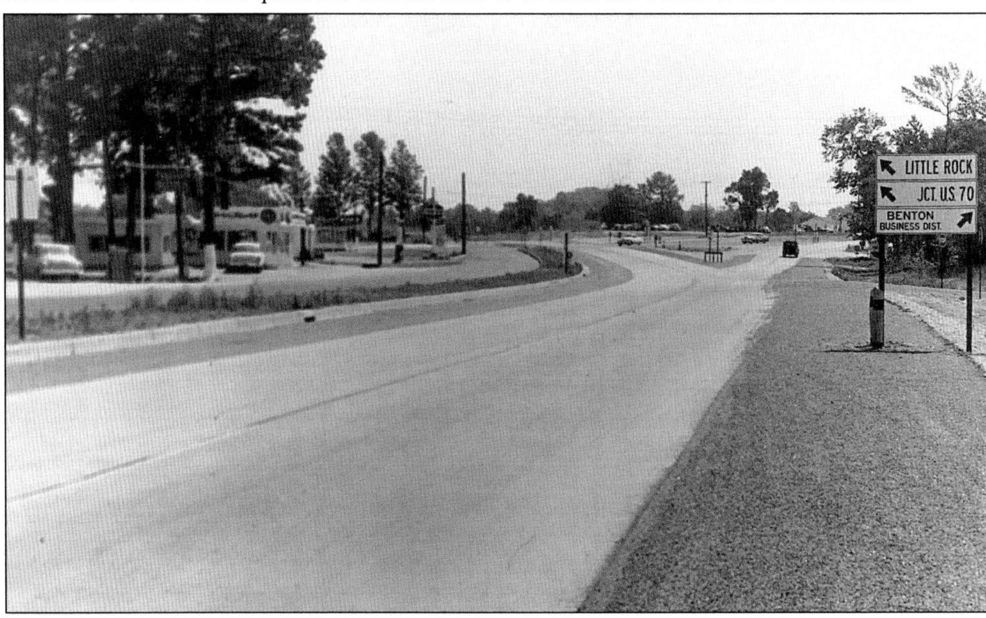

Where today four lanes of Interstate 30 are jammed with thousands of vehicles a day, in the early 1950s there was a narrow, two-lane road with comparatively little traffic. Highway 67 motorists heading east toward Little Rock could have turned right into downtown Benton or to the left for the 20-mile trip to Little Rock. Highway 67 and Highway 70 shared a common path from North Little Rock to below Benton, where 70 veered off to Hot Springs. (Courtesy of UCA Archives.)

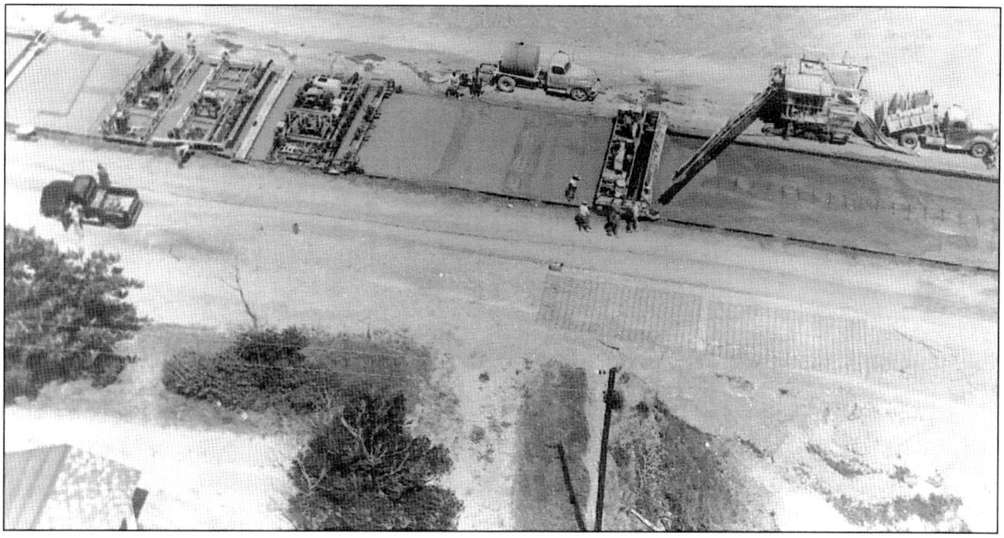

In the early 1940s, Highway 67/70 between Little Rock and Benton was targeted by the state as the beginning point of a modern highway system for Arkansas. In what was to be commonly called the "New Benton Highway," a 200-foot right-of-way was purchased, and two lanes of engineered slab pavement were laid with 10-foot blacktop shoulders. The extra right-of-way allowed for the future planned expansion to four lanes. The concept of the federal interstate system was yet to emerge from the Eisenhower administration, which began in 1953. (Courtesy of UCA Archives.)

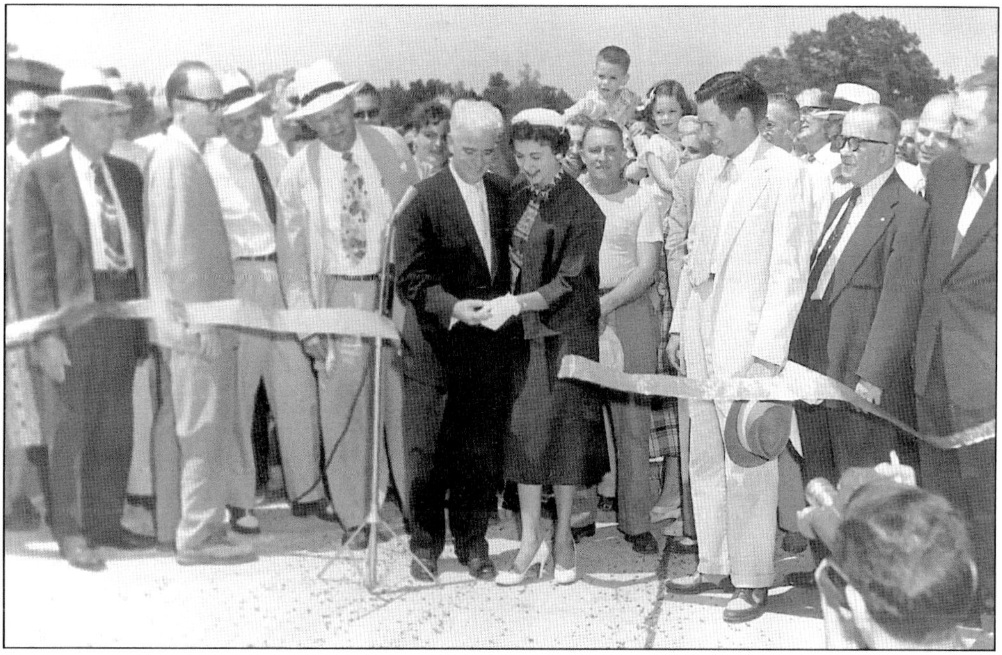

Politicians, for decades, have used highway improvements as a backdrop for speeches and campaign promises. Such was the case with Gov. Francis Cherry, who came out onto the new and improved 20-mile section of Highway 67 linking Little Rock and Benton. Governor Cherry had been defeated a week earlier for a second term by political unknown Orval Faubus, but he kept his date with members of the Highway Commission to cut the ribbon opening the section that had cost almost $200,000 per mile and had been in the works since 1944. (Courtesy of UCA Archives.)

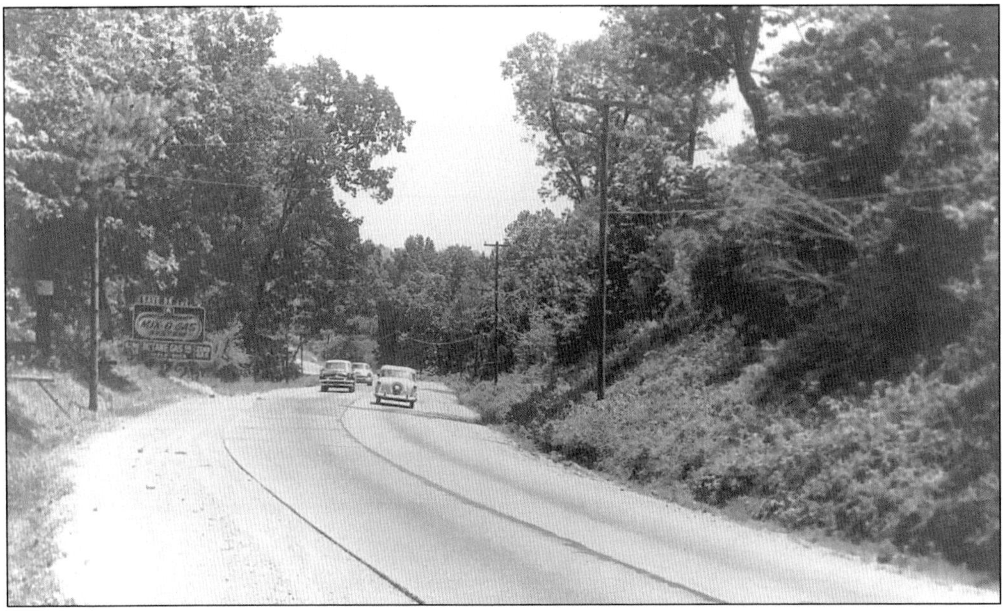

While the stretch of Highway 67 between Little Rock and Benton had been modernized, the road below Benton retained much of its narrow "country road" feel, as seen from this driver's view between Benton and Malvern around 1955. The billboard in the shade of the trees to the left advertised "Mix-O-Gas High Octane." (Courtesy of UCA Archives.)

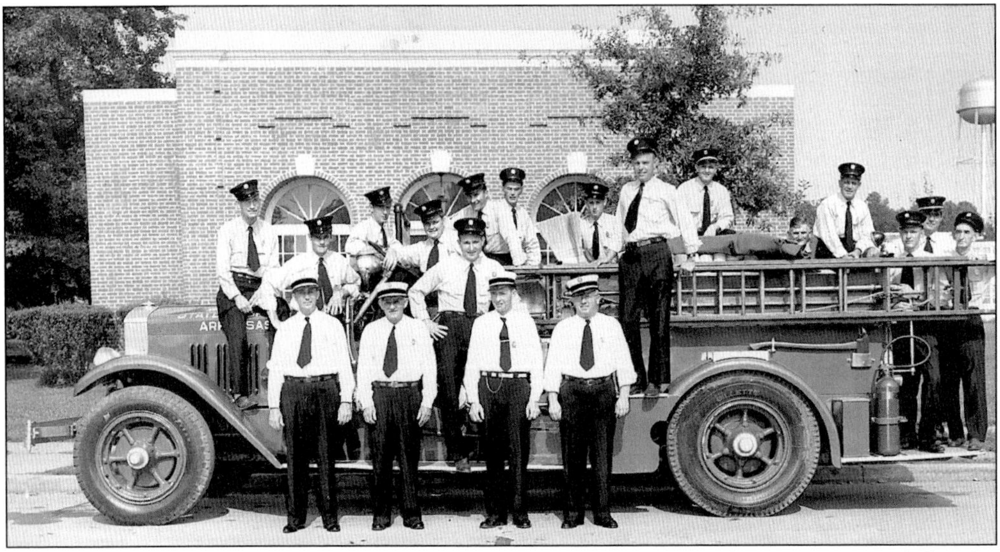

Motorists along the stretch of Highway 67 seen above, *c.* 1950, might have encountered this fire truck from the Benton State Hospital. The psychiatric hospital was relocated from Little Rock to a 500-acre tract in Saline County between Benton and Malvern in the 1930s. It is labeled as the "Insane Hospital" on the map on page 56. With the hospital's extensive frontage on Highway 67, drivers had a clear view of the facility and sometimes of some of its hundreds of patients. During World War II, Arkansas governor Homer Adkins made the trip down Highway 67 for a tour of the hospital. It is said that while walking on the grounds he introduced himself to a patient, saying, "Hi, I'm Homer Adkins, the governor." The patient put his arm around the governor and said, "That's ok, buddy, when I first got here, I thought I was Winston Churchill."

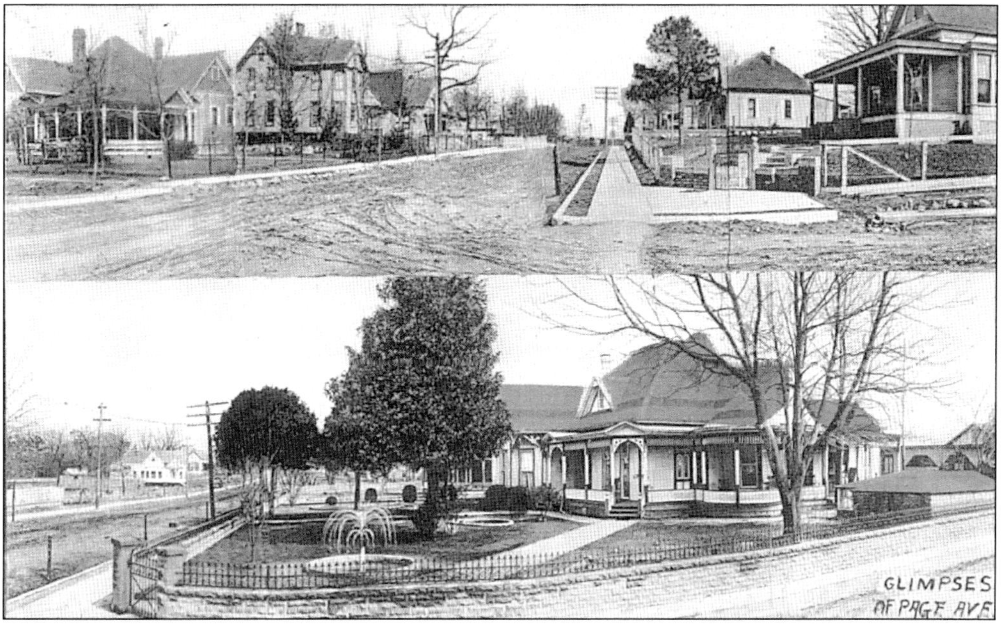

Continuing on a wandering southwestern course from Benton, the path of Highway 67 crossed into Hot Spring County, entering the county seat of Malvern. The highway, beginning as a dirt track, was relocated in the 1920s to come down East Page Avenue as it approached downtown. The card above, mailed in 1909, shows the street when it was lined with the finest homes in the city. "Many thanks for your card. I am glad you will exchange views," wrote A.E. Sweeny, who was swapping postcards with a young man in New York. By the 1950s, the grand homes were giving way to a commercial strip along the busy Highway 67.

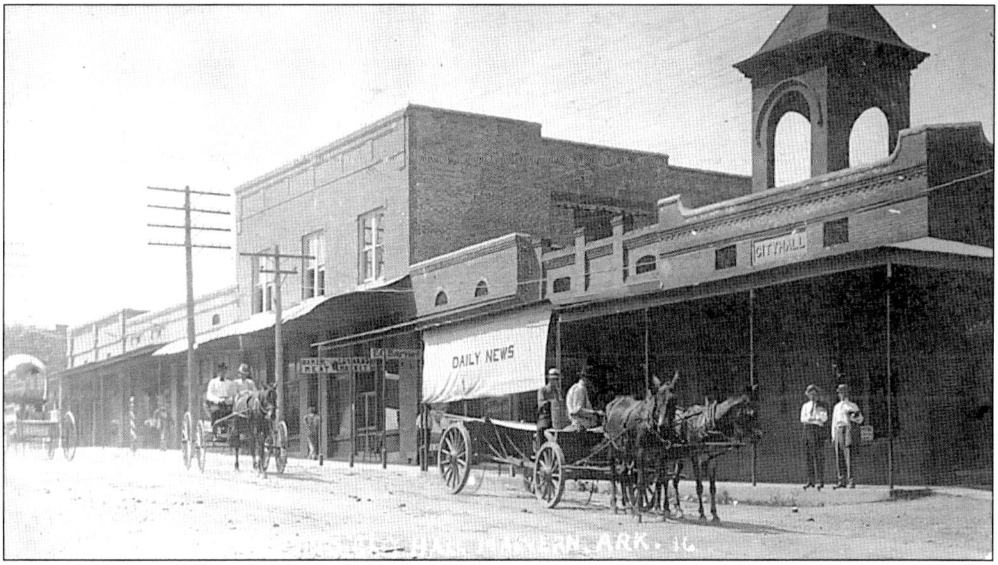

Malvern was named, it is thought, for Malvern Hill, Virginia, because someone from there thought it reminded them of their old home. Laid out by the Cairo & Fulton Railroad in 1873, the town grew as a lumber and brick manufacturing center. The first road through the area had crossed the Ouachita River at nearby Rockport, but when the automobile road was laid out around 1915, it crossed Main Street near where these wagons were rolling down the dirt street around 1900.

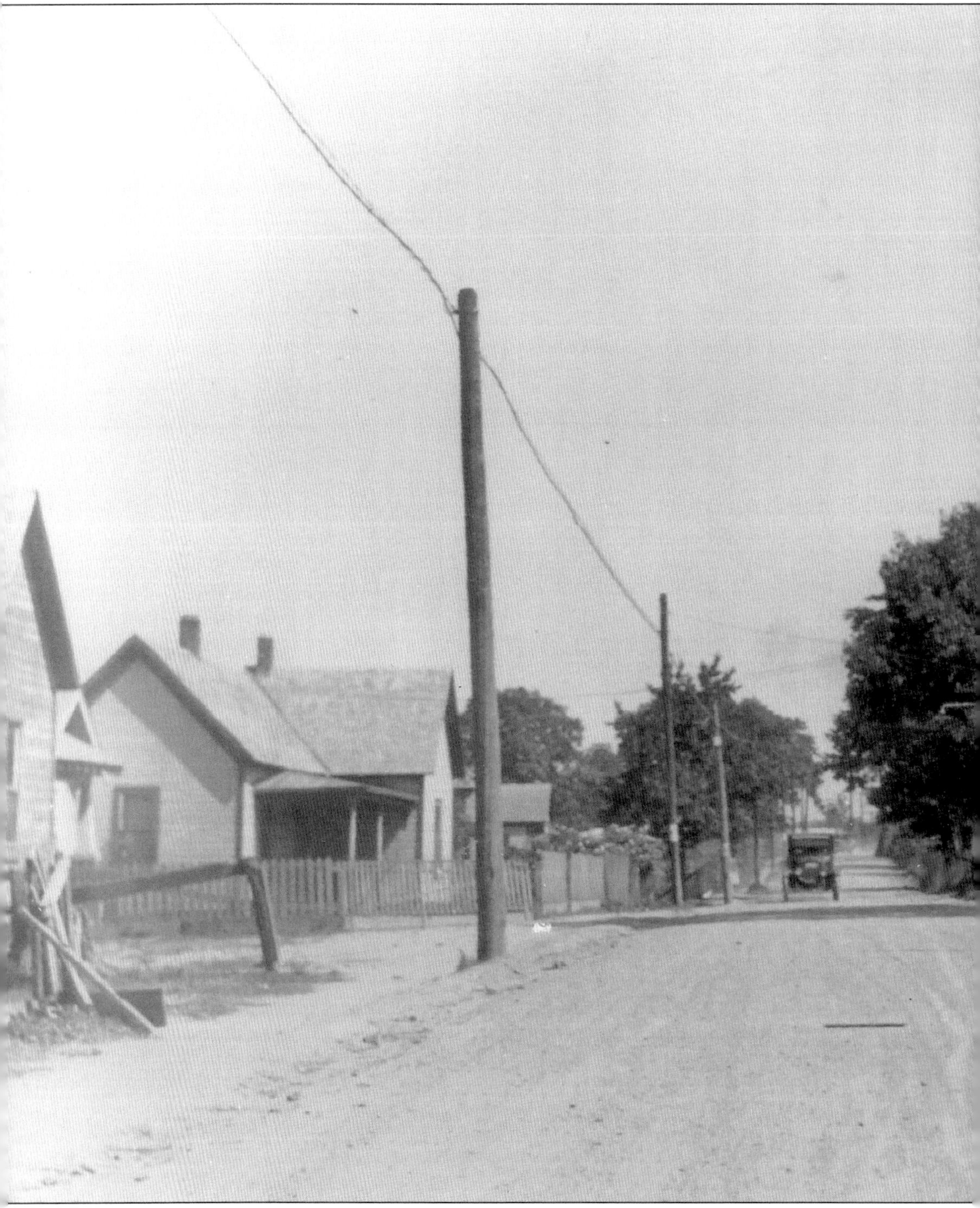

Malvern was in the path of the still unpaved, but improving Highway 67 when this photo was made around 1928. The photo is thought to be of the west side of town, with the motorist coming down the dusty road on what is now Stanley Street, heading for Main Street. The photo captured an early Highway 67 sign, and just beyond it is C.W. Ray's Feed & Groceries and "Standard"

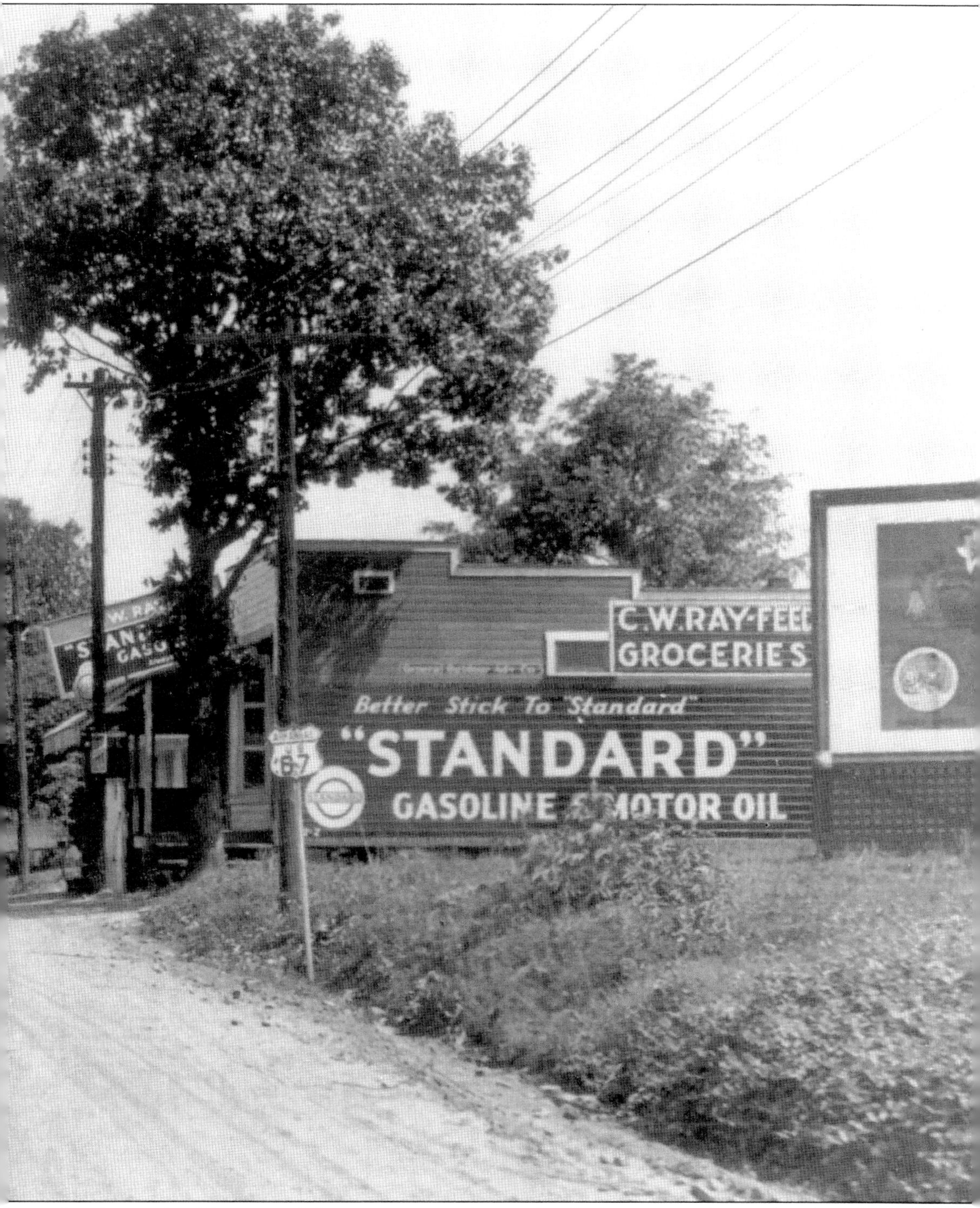

Gasoline outlet. The gravity-fed pumps were on the porch, which was quite close to the edge of the road; a car simply pulled over by the porch so Mr. Ray could pump the gas and check the oil, all for less than 10¢ per gallon. The billboard to the right features a boy kicking a ball, promoting an unidentified product. (Photo courtesy UCA Archives.)

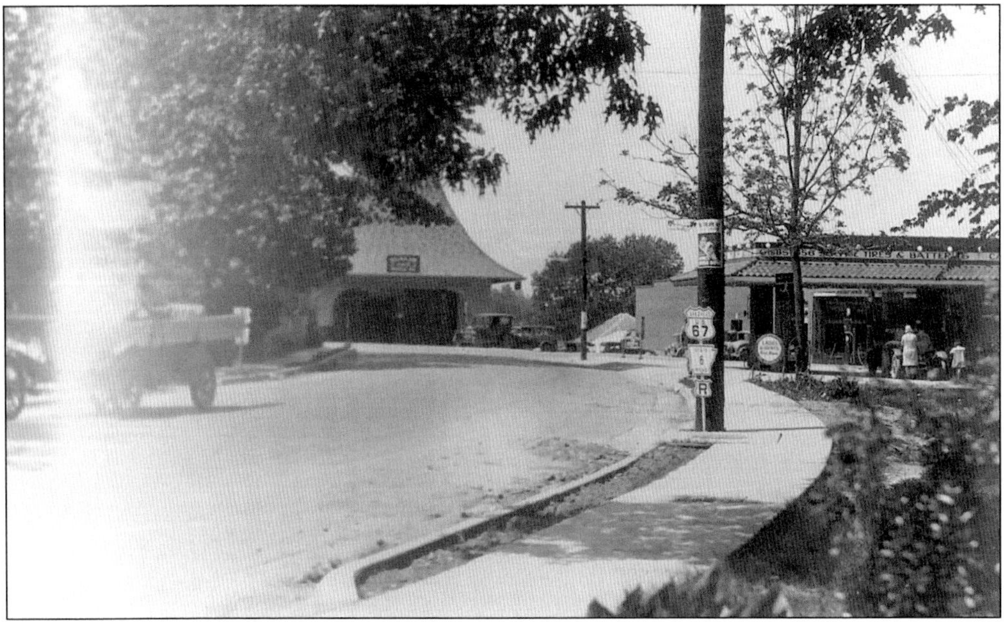

Approaching Malvern's Main Street around 1930, a motorist would have seen the sign on the pole for U.S. Highway 67 and State Road 6 (today's Highway 270). The road was not yet paved, but concrete curbs and sidewalks were fairly recent improvements. The drivers passing through town on dusty 67 had a choice of two gas stations at this intersection. Gibson's, to the right, had a round sign on the curb reading, "Ladies and Gent's Restrooms." The building with the high roof is also a gas station, though of undetermined brand. This intersection has been reconfigured to more conventional right angles since this early photo was taken.

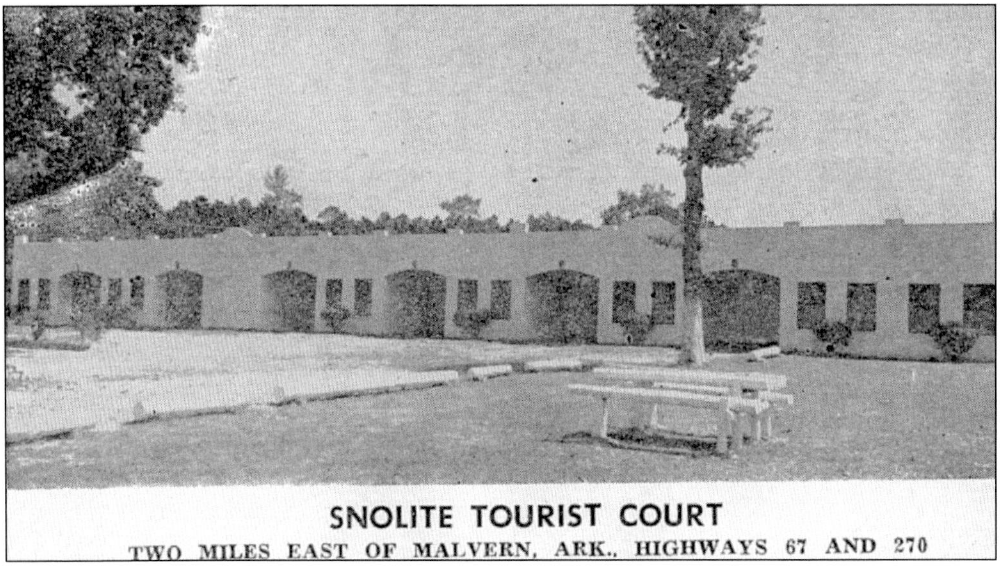

By 1940, Highway 67 was paved through Malvern, and as the volume of traffic flowing down the road between St. Louis and Texas increased, the number of tourist courts increased to keep pace. The Snolite Tourist Court on Highway 67, east of Malvern, in the community of Pearla, opened in the late 1930s and had the popular feature of the day—garage parking for each room. The Snolite is gone today, razed sometime in the 1960s.

"Cafe and Play Garden in connection, Beauty Rest Mattresses on Every Bed," as well as a very large swimming pool were features billed on this postcard to make the Aqua stand out from the competition. The motel was remodeled and converted into attractive apartments in the mid-1990s, minus the swimming pool with slides.

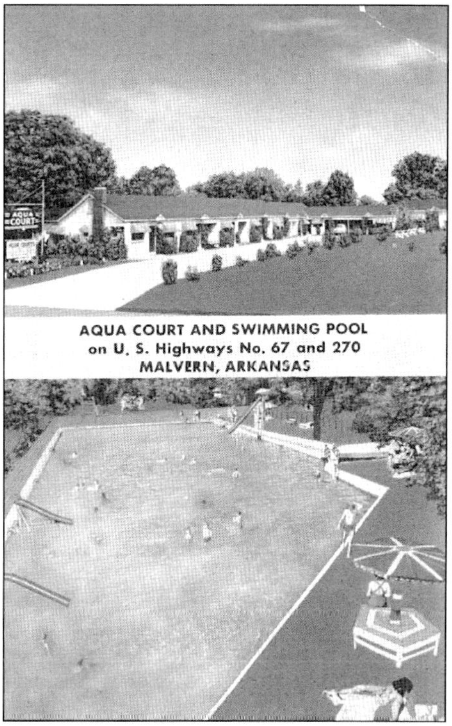

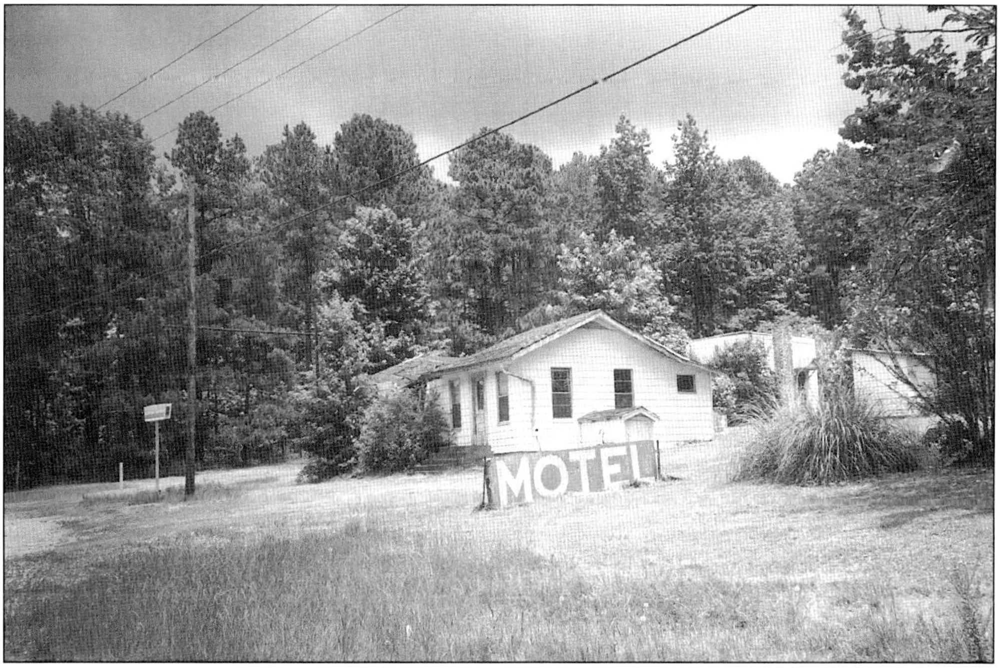

Most of the family-owned tourist courts and motels that once dotted Highway 67 on either side of Malvern are rapidly slipping away, the traffic having shifted more than 30 years ago to Interstate 30 several miles north, bypassing Malvern and old 67. The photo above shows what little remains of one of the small Highway 67 courts that was once owned by a family named Frolik and located just east of the city—a grounded rusty sign and overgrown cabins. (1999 photo by Ray Hanley.)

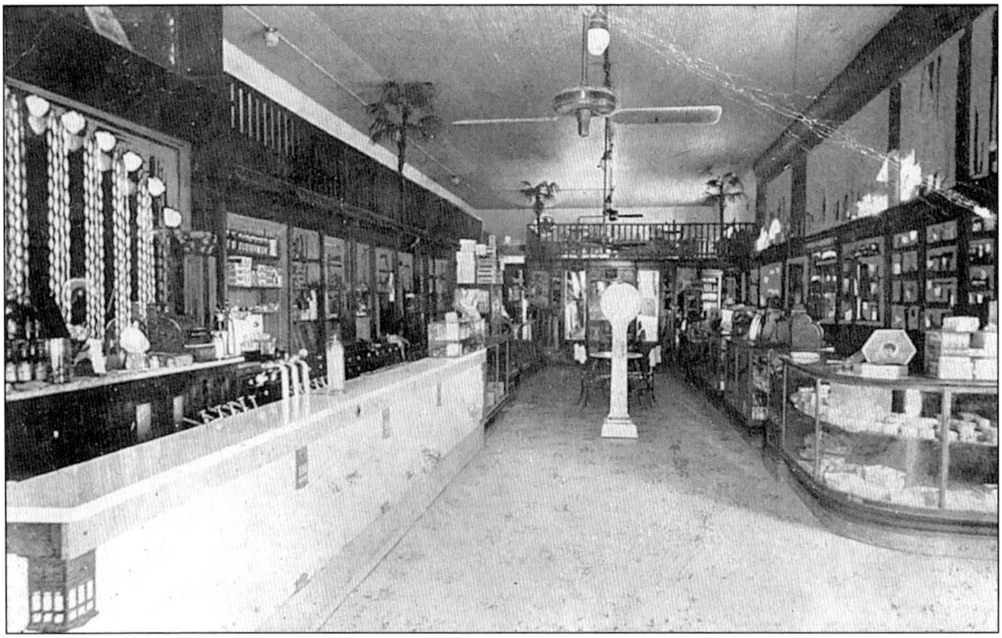

For over 100 years, travelers to Malvern, whether they came by wagon, train, or automobiles traveling Highway 67, have found one constant presence on Main Street, a block down from the 67 junction–Miller's Drug Store. Founded in 1890, the store has continued to operate on the same corner for over a century, always with a member of the Miller family behind the pharmacy counter. For much of that century, travelers found a treat at the drug store's soda fountain, seen to the left in this 1923 view, though today the counter is walled off and no longer in use. A selection of cigars can be seen in the case to the right, while a "your weight and fortune–1 cent" scale and several potted palms are also visible. Almost all the retailers that once lined Main Street have left, some to close and others to relocate to shopping centers, but Miller's has stayed and continues to prosper, as evidenced by the photo below. (1999 photo by Ray Hanley.)

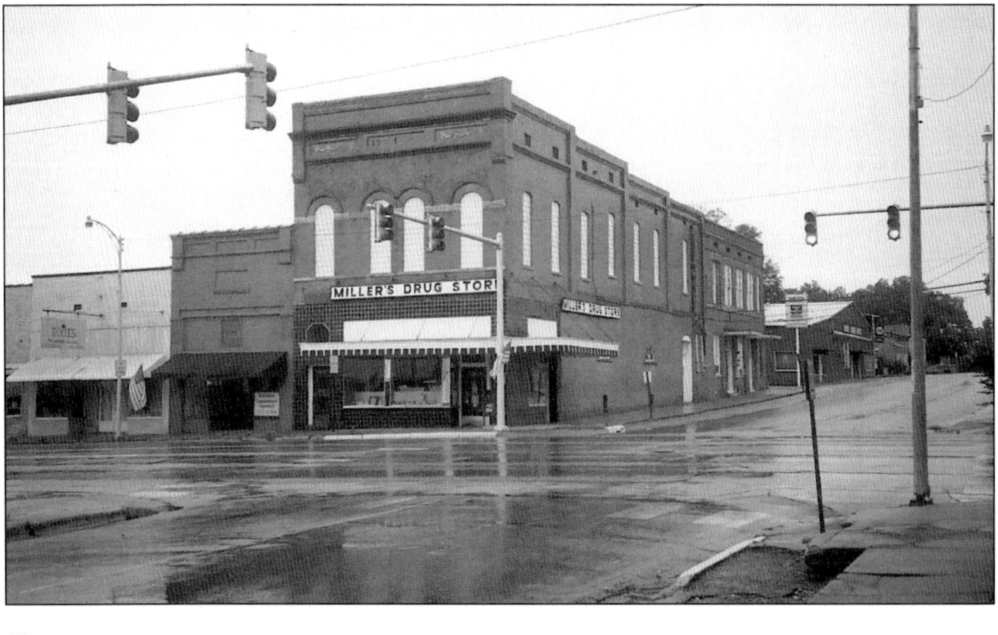

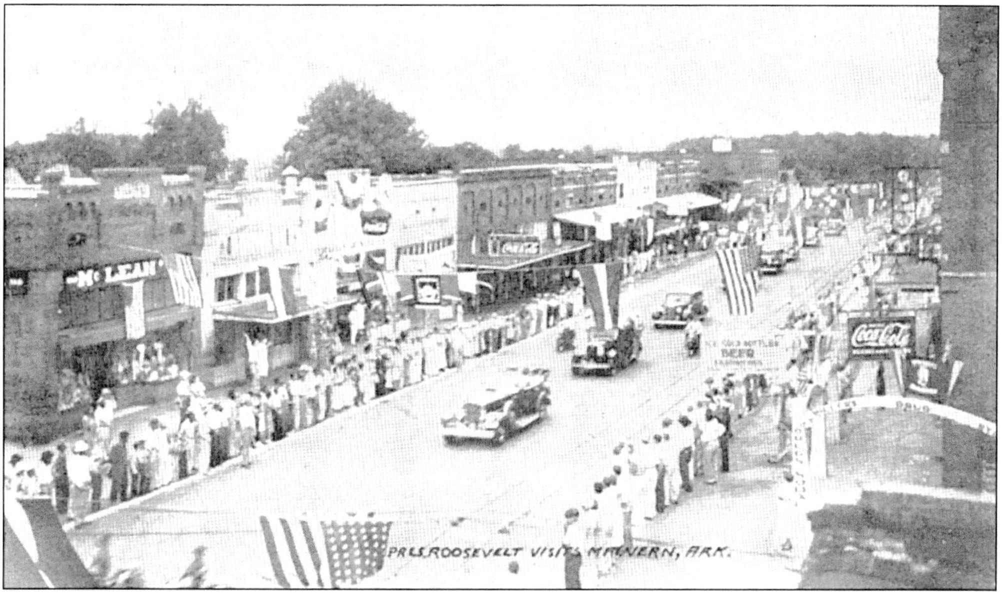

The intersection of Highway 67 and Malvern's Main Street has seen much history during the 20th century, but no occasion tops that of 1936 when Pres. Franklin Roosevelt passed down Main Street, here headed for the highway crossing a block up the street. FDR had come to Arkansas for the state's 100th birthday; he had come from Little Rock to Hot Springs by train and then to Malvern in an open-topped automobile. Miller's Drug store is in the lower right corner of the postcard, where a sign hangs over the street advertising ice-cold beer and sandwiches.

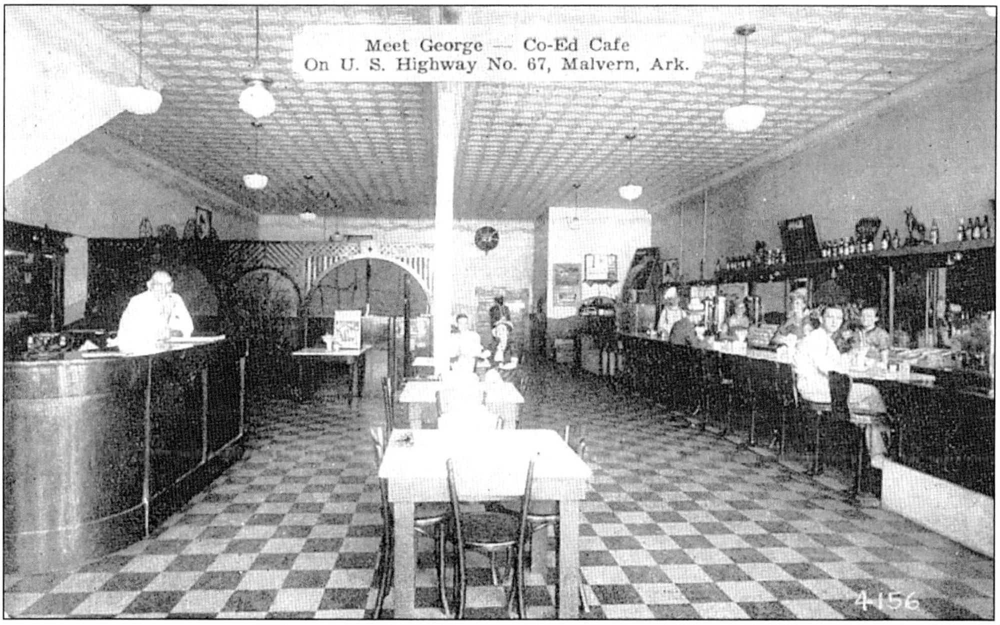

Travelers passing through Malvern on Highway 67 didn't have to look far for a place to eat. The Co-Ed Cafe, begun in the 1920s as the Elite Cafe, was located at the corner of Main and Highway 67. Diners could sit at a table in the middle of the restaurant or at the counter to the right. Across the shelf above the counter is a selection of bottled beers, something not displayed in Malvern today—the county voted dry around 1942. This card is from c. 1938.

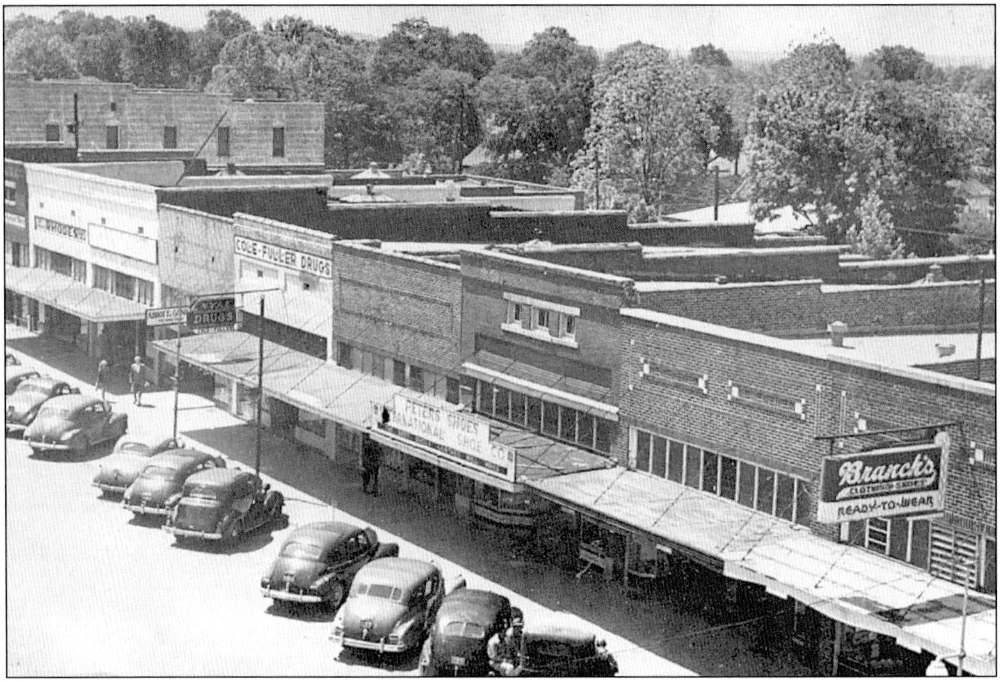

Competing with the tourist courts on the edge of town for Highway 67 travelers in search of a bed was the Keith Hotel, the three-story building located on the southwestern corner of Main and 67 and visible in the far left corner of the *c.* 1938 postcard above. A stroll out of the lobby could have brought a guest to Cole-Fuller Drug Store or Branch's Ready to Wear clothing store at the far right. In the center of the block is Peter's Shoes. This store advertised the products of the International Shoe Company, which, at the time, had a large factory on the north side of Malvern. The card below captured the Keith Hotel's desk clerk and a guest, who just looked up from his newspaper. The hotel, built early in the century, was especially popular with traveling salesmen whose business took them constantly up and down Highway 67.

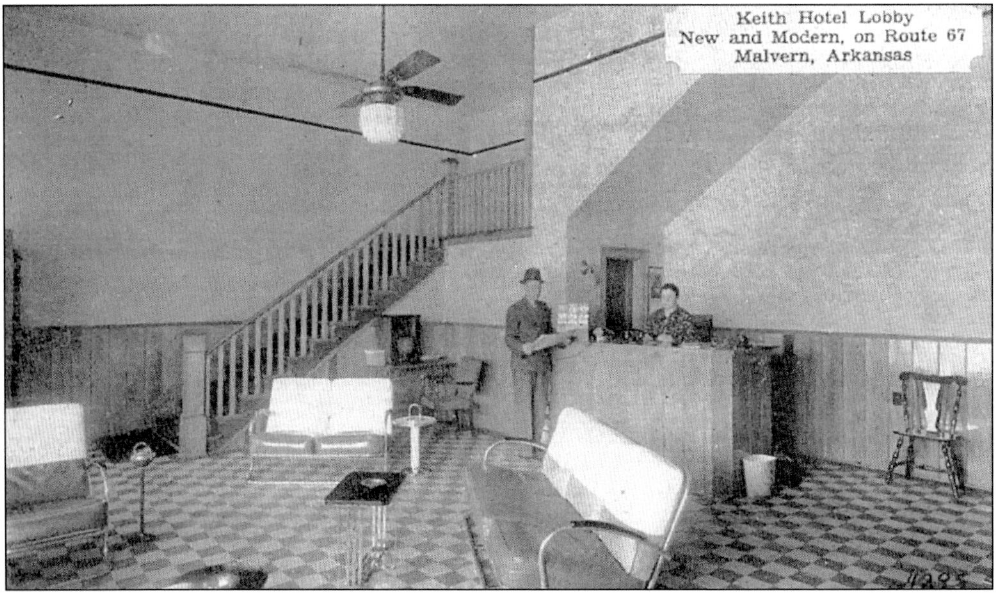

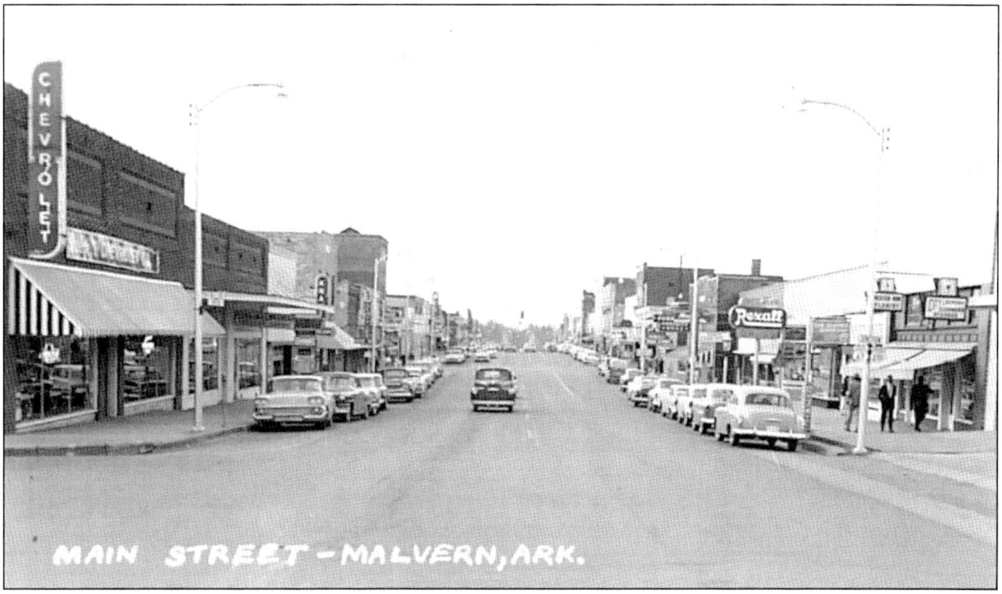

Time passes and things change, and such has been the case with the crossroads of Malvern. The photo above looks north on Main Street in the mid-1950s; the Keith Hotel is the tallest building on the left side of the street. For decades the intersection of Main Street and Highway 67, where the Keith Hotel stood for more than 50 years, was the center of town through which passed countless travelers from across the nation. Today, the traffic is gone, and most of the retailers, including the Chevrolet dealer to the left, have relocated to the north side of town, where a Wal-Mart anchors a typical shopping center of the 1990s. In the photo at right, the author returned to his hometown of Malvern with his young son and stood at the same intersection in 1999, the spot that would have once been the front of the lobby of the Keith Hotel. The hotel, a victim of age, changing tastes, and an interstate highway that took away the traffic, was torn down in the 1960s. (Photo by Diane Hanley.)

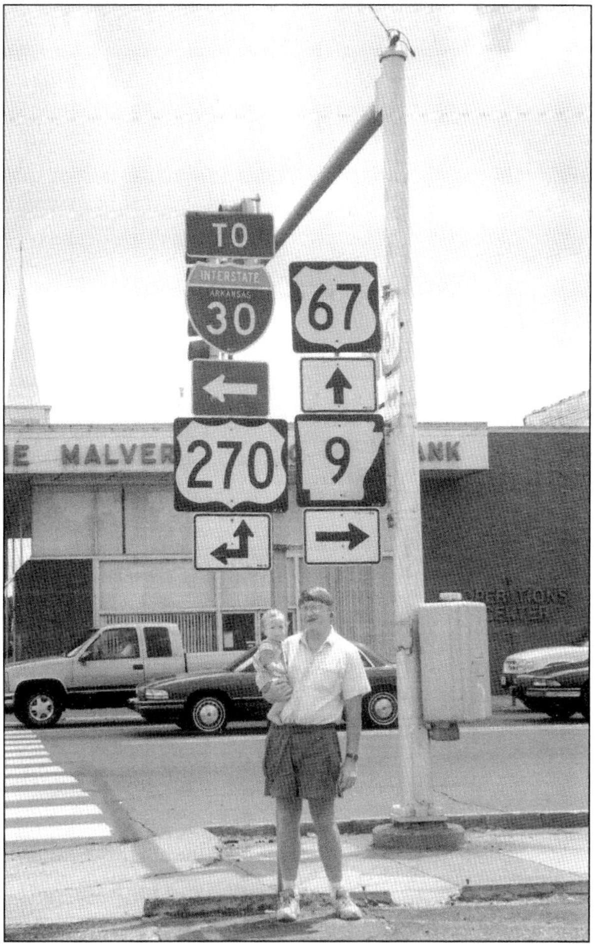

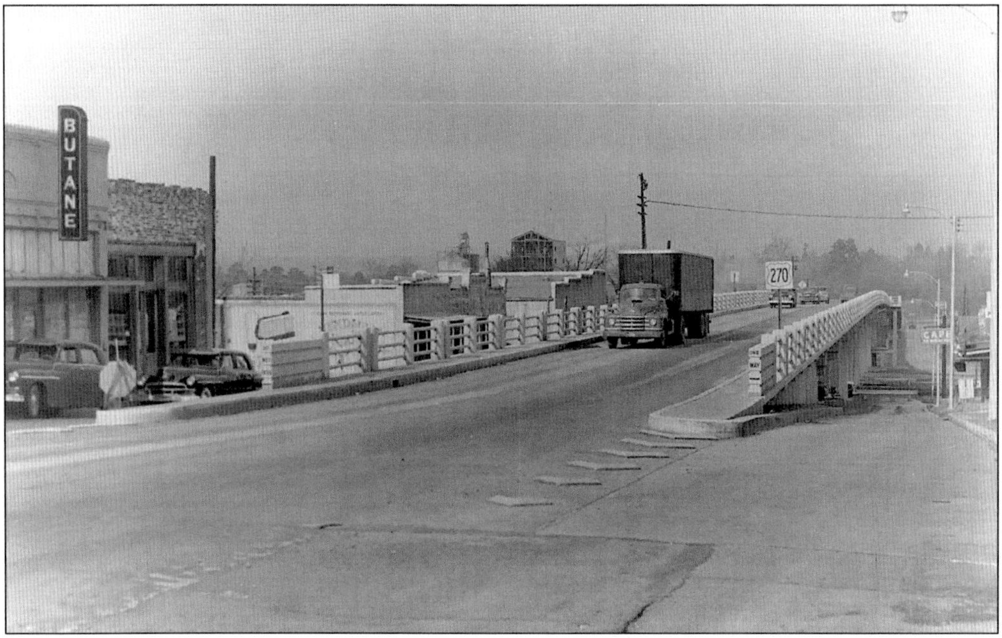

Traffic coming from Hot Springs and the north side of Malvern found it easier to reach Highway 67 in the mid-1950s because of a new viaduct. For decades, the highway from Hot Springs, first known as State Road 6 and then Highway 270, had to cross the dangerous railroad tracks at the bottom of the hill. The viaduct mitigated the dangerous crossing but cut off some visibility to the shops that run down the hill toward the train station, lying out of sight to the right and including places such as Pete's Pool Hall and the Depot Cafe.

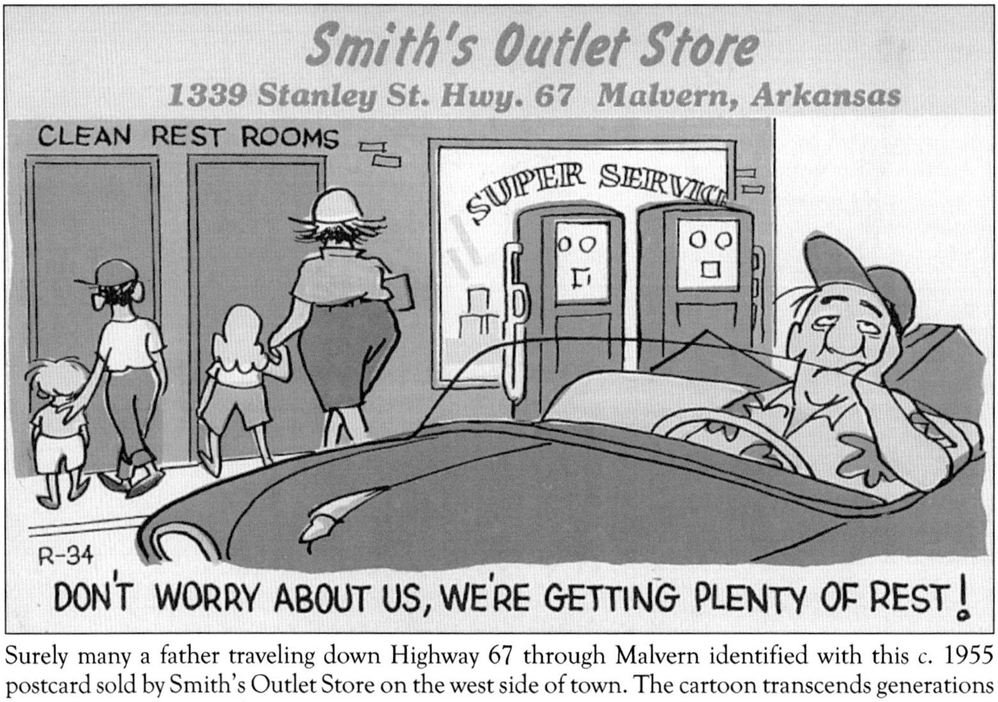

Surely many a father traveling down Highway 67 through Malvern identified with this *c.* 1955 postcard sold by Smith's Outlet Store on the west side of town. The cartoon transcends generations of family vacation travel.

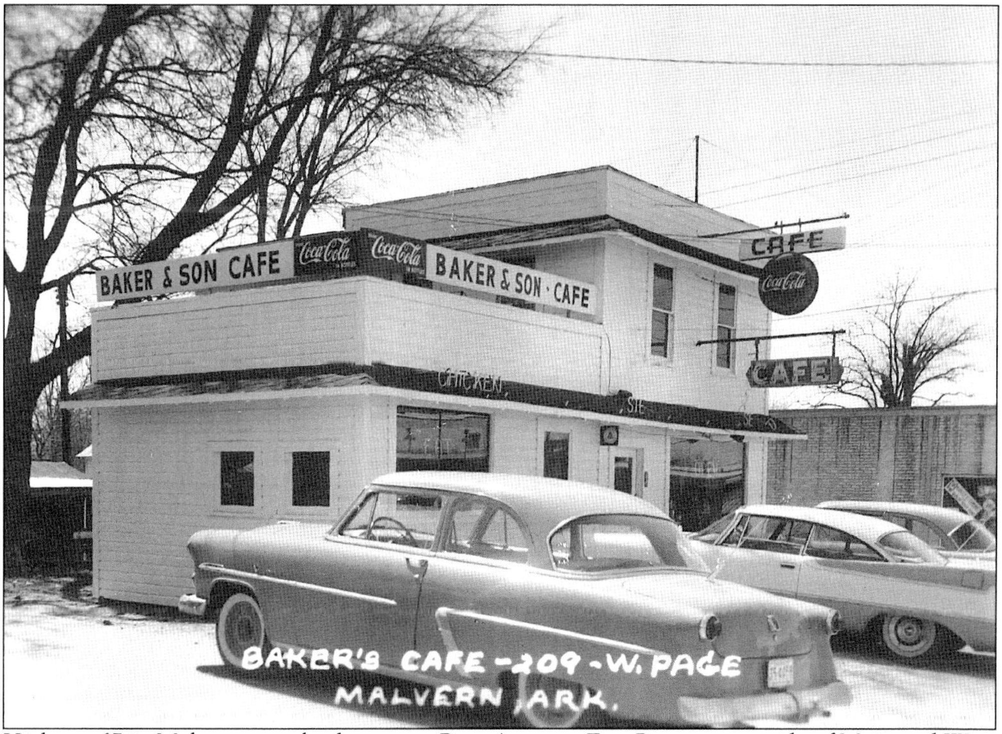

Highway 67 in Malvern was also known as Page Avenue—East Page on one side of Main and West Page after it crossed Main, passing the Keith Hotel before heading west. In the 1950s, a popular eatery on West Page was Baker & Son's Cafe, typical of the family-owned roadside diners of that era before the homogenized uniformity of the fast food chains began to emerge in the 1960s. The above image is dated c. 1957. The photo below finds Mr. Baker and his son long gone, along with the once bustling Highway 67 traffic. In a pattern repeated across the nation, a once-vibrant business serving the motoring public had gone under. The author sought out Baker's in 1999 and found instead the Malvern Pawn Shop occupying the building. (1999 photo by Ray Hanley.)

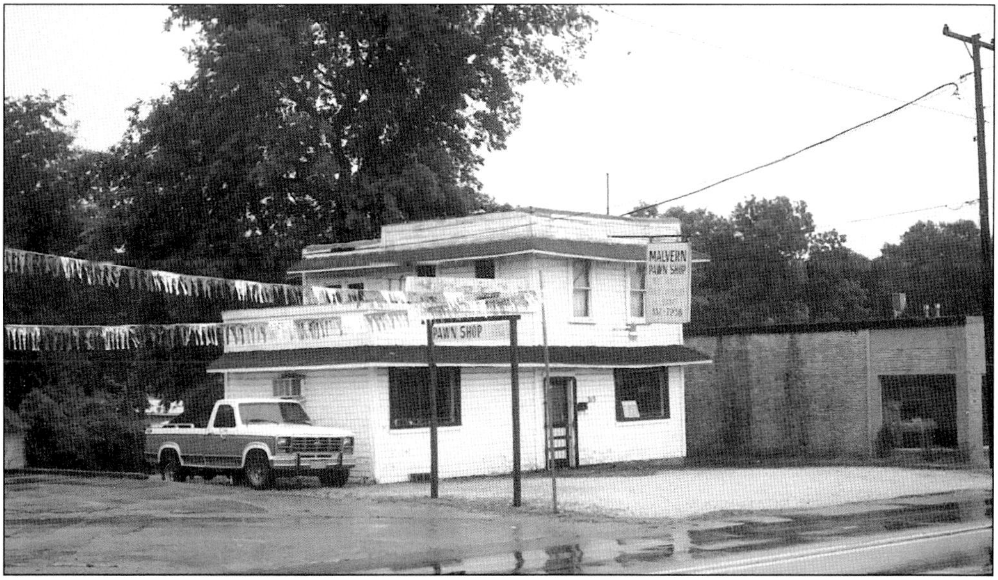

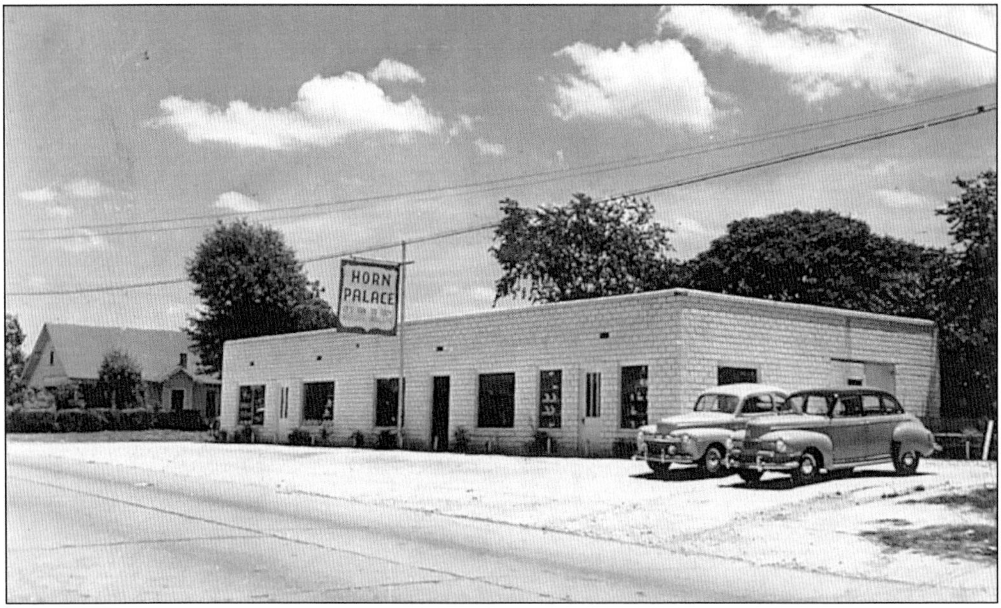

The term "tourist trap" was coined early in the age of the American automobile, and Highway 67 had its share of such attractions. One of these on the highway passing through Malvern was The Horn Palace, seen here around 1950 on West Page Avenue. Calling the long brick building owned by Clifford "Fats" Stovall a "palace" seems, 50 years later, a bit of a stretch, but it certainly had the horns. Among the souvenirs Dad could have loaded into the trunk while on vacation was furniture made of cow horns. If space was a problem, a raccoon skin or a pottery vase displayed in the store's window might have fit the bill. The business operated a cafe in one end and a gift shop in the other side. The Horn Palace closed in the 1950s, and the building was apparently razed.

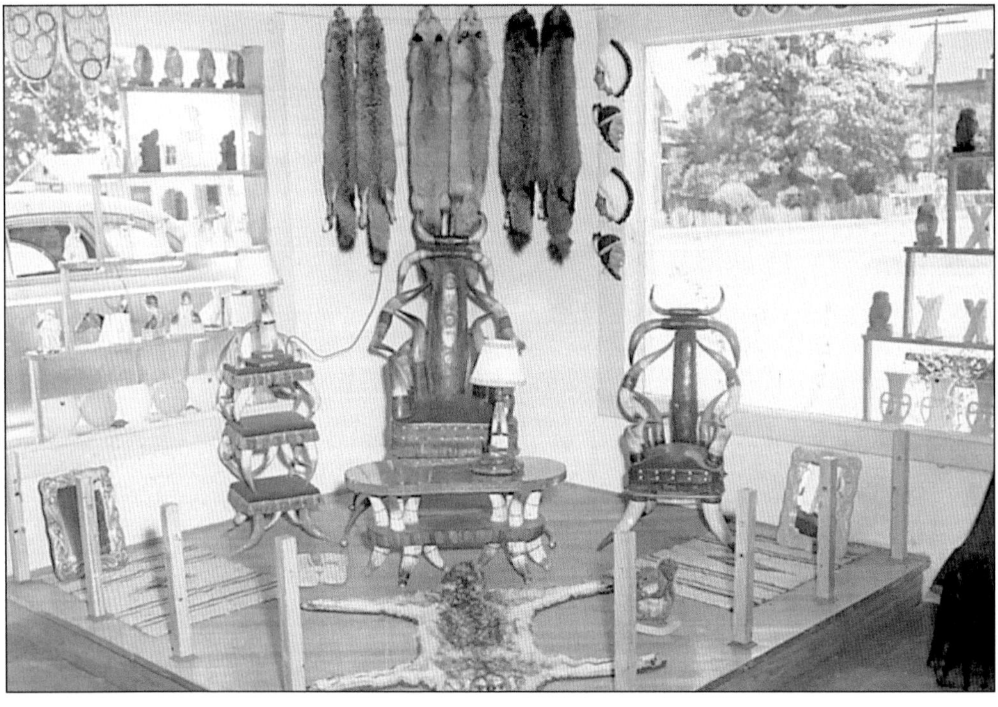

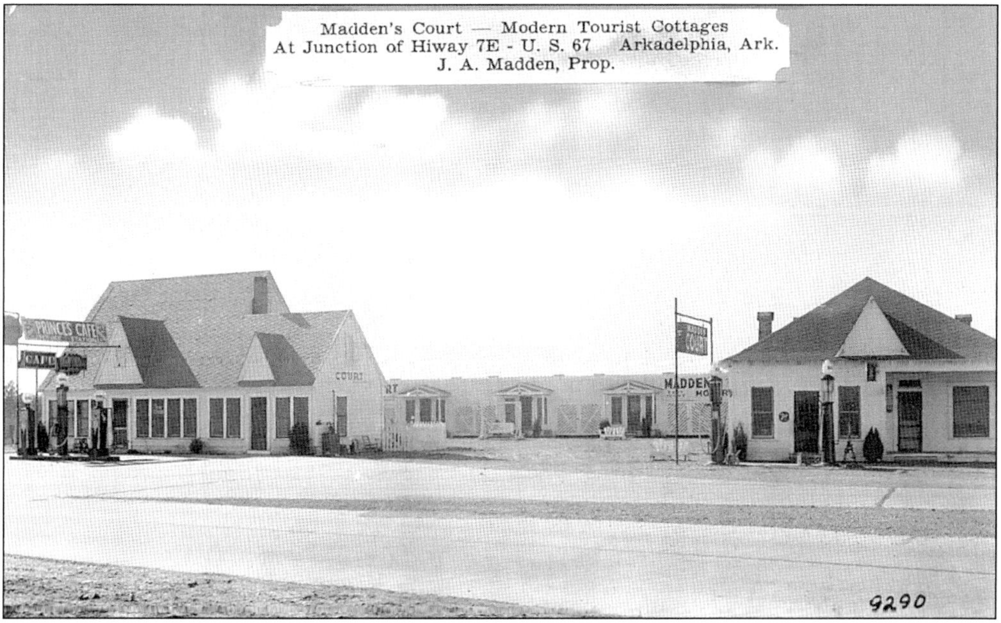

Heading west along the route of Highway 67, where the Malvern road met the route of the national Bankhead Highway coming from Hot Springs, the next bit of commercial activity to be found was at Caddo Valley, some 5 miles outside of Arkadelphia in Clark County. The juncture of two major highways gave rise to a host of businesses to serve the motoring public. One of these businesses was Madden's Court, which stood on the west side of Highway 67 for many years. In the above c. 1940 card, gravity-fed Shell gas pumps are in front of the Princess Cafe to the left, while the tourist court's office is in the building to the right. The court's cabins in the rear are joined by individual garages, each with doors that closed and locked. In the card below, made a few years later, the business was photographed from the air. The guest who sent this card stayed at the court twice, while traveling to and from San Antonio, Texas, in 1954. In the 1940s, near the Madden, there was a dance hall called the Bloody Bucket, recalled by old-timers as a wild place on a Saturday night. The Madden is gone today, and the area where it once thrived is now a sea of gas stations, franchised motels, and fast food outlets at the convergence of Highways 67 and 7 and Interstate 30.

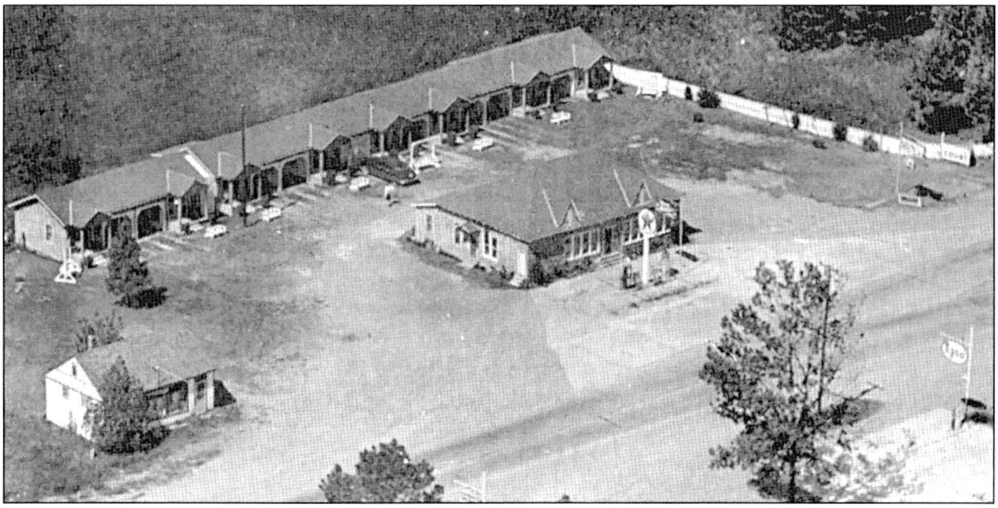

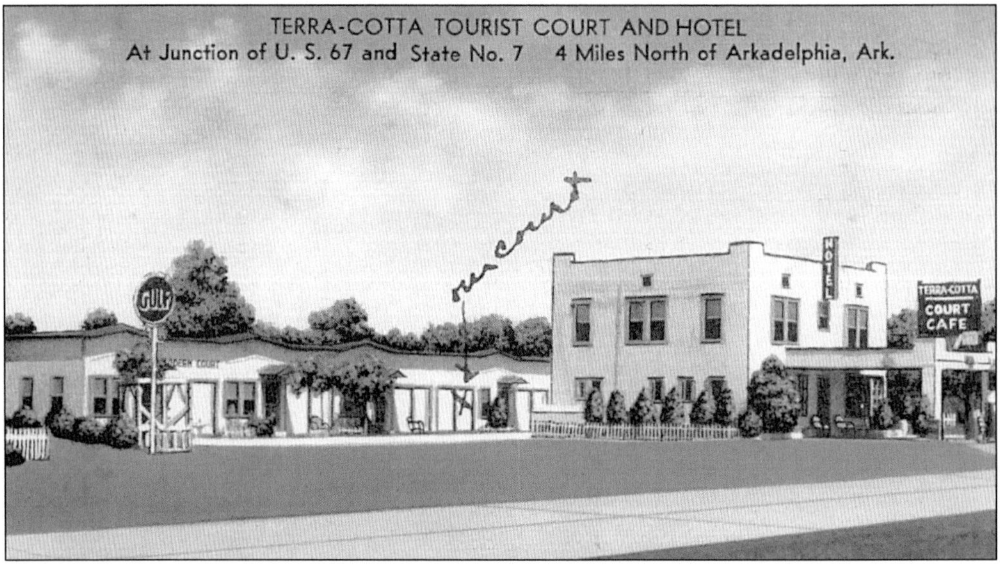

Another Caddo Valley lodging choice was the Terra-Cotta Tourist Court and Hotel, 4 miles north of Arkadelphia on 67 and almost across the road from the Madden Court. Reportedly, the Terra-Cotta was built by a man of Greek heritage, Vichy Malleus, who painted the buildings a terra-cotta color. The card was mailed by a guest of the court who marked her room with an "x" in 1945. "Staying right here for a good rest." The buildings are gone today, swallowed up in a franchised Interstate 30 exit area.

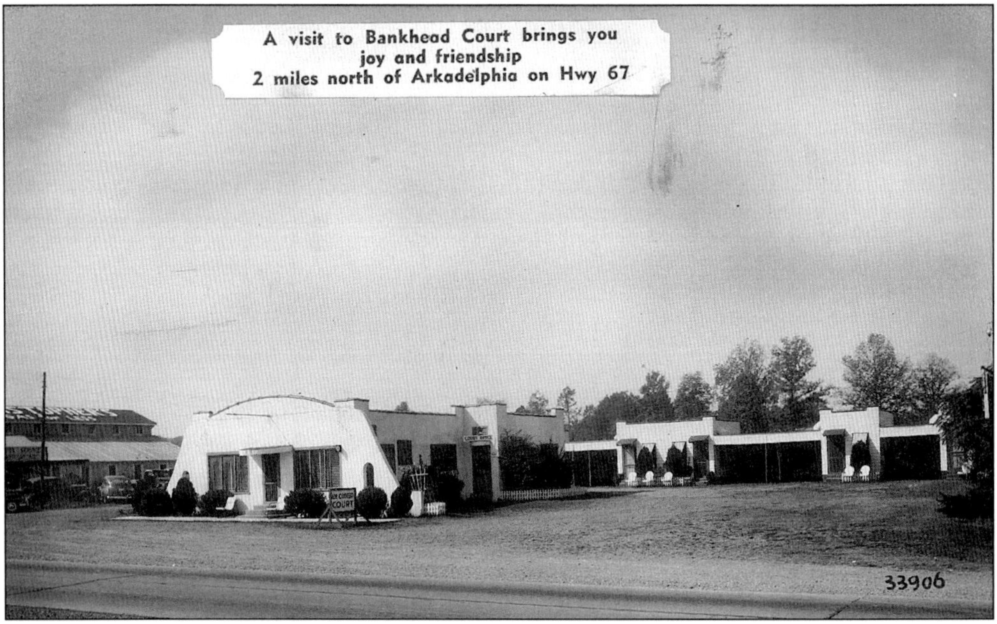

Moving down Highway 67 toward downtown Arkadelphia, travelers in need of a night's rest continued to have choices for a bed and a meal. The Bankhead Court promised "Joy and Friendship" and was apparently named for the Bankhead Highway that came through around 1920 and preceded the federal Highway 67 designation. The whitewashed court had a garage for each guest, a common feature in the 1930s and 1940s. The building to the left has a sign painted on the roof that reads, "STOP HERE, GAS FOR LESS."

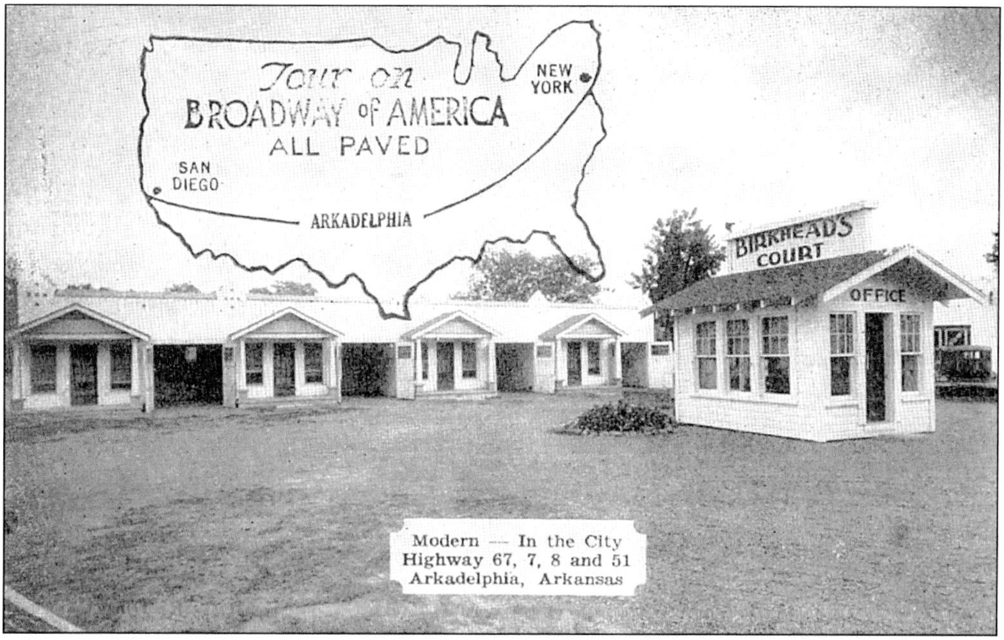

Highway 67 was completed through Arkadelphia in 1931, and when the paving was done, it was labeled the "Broadway of America" because it was a road that linked both sides of the continent. Arkadelphia civic leaders sought to capitalize on the town's location by advertising the city across the nation as an "overnight stop for tourists." In the 1930s, *Ripley's Believe it or Not* claimed that the small town had more service stations than churches. One business that prospered from the ever-increasing traffic volume was Birkhead's Court. Seen above around 1930, Birkhead's had a small group of cottages with the essential garages behind a small office. As seen in the *c.* 1940 card below, Birkhead's had added an Esso service station and a welding shop and featured "warm rooms" and locked garages. Today, all traces of these buildings are gone.

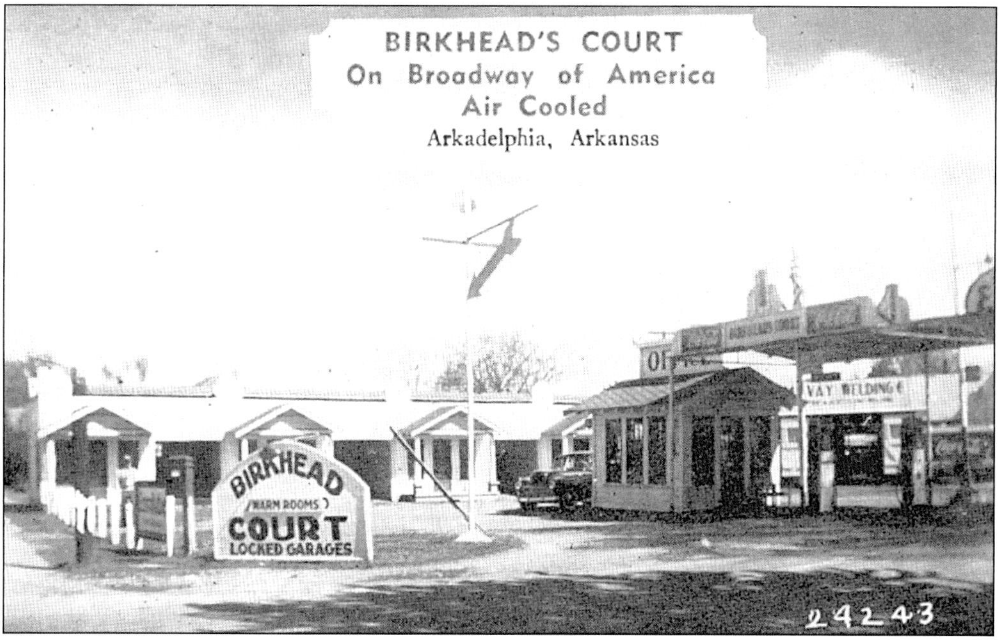

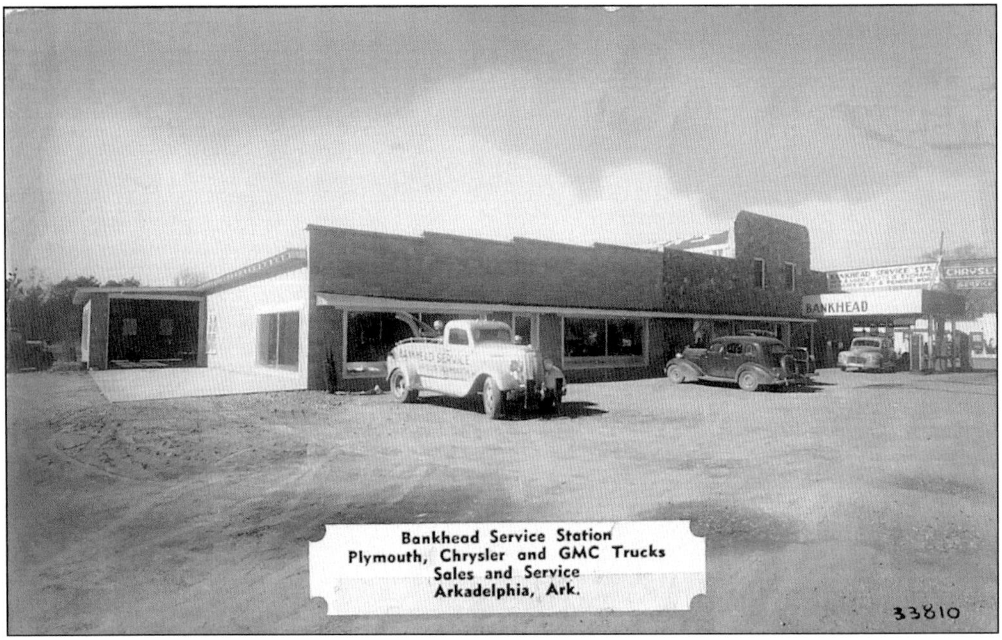

Two miles north of Arkadelphia on Highway 67 travelers passed Bankhead Service Station, a business that was also the Chrysler and GMC Truck dealership. The sign over the gas pumps reads, "New & Used parts, body & fender work." The business was operated by Roland Pennington, and upon his death in 1953, it ceased operation.

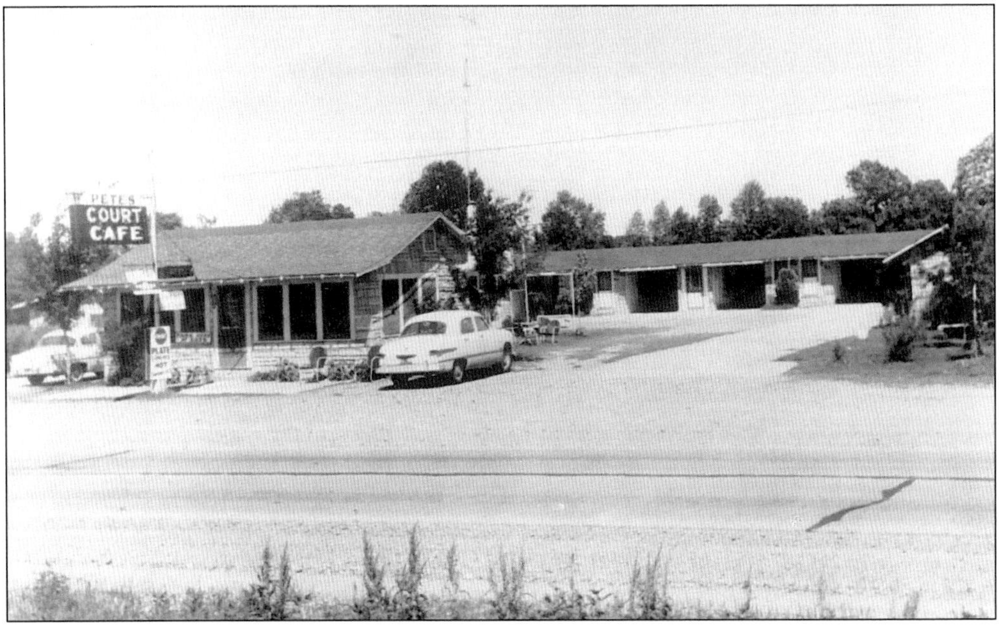

A stranded motorist whose car was in Bankhead's garage could have walked across the highway for a bed and meal at Pete's Court and Cafe. Pete Lecouris opened his court opposite the busy Bankhead's station around 1940 with a cafe and 12 cabins. The enterprising businessman also had a restaurant in downtown Arkadelphia. Pete's no longer operates today, but a portion of his court on the south side of the property still stands. (Courtesy of Clark County Historical Association.)

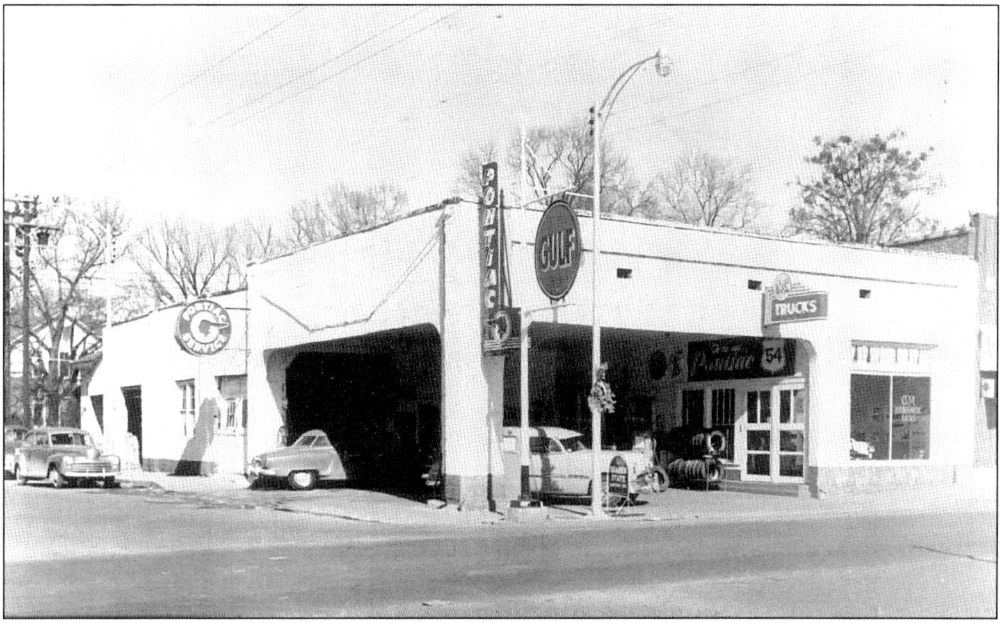

In stark comparison with the sprawling automobile dealerships of the modern era is Johnson's Gulf Station and Pontiac dealership, located on Highway 67 in Arkadelphia. The selection would have been limited to only a few cars in the dealer's small showroom; customers would almost always have ordered their car for delivery within a matter of weeks. Pictured here *c.* 1950, Johnson's was reportedly one of the first true full-service stations in the South. (Courtesy of Clark County Historical Association.)

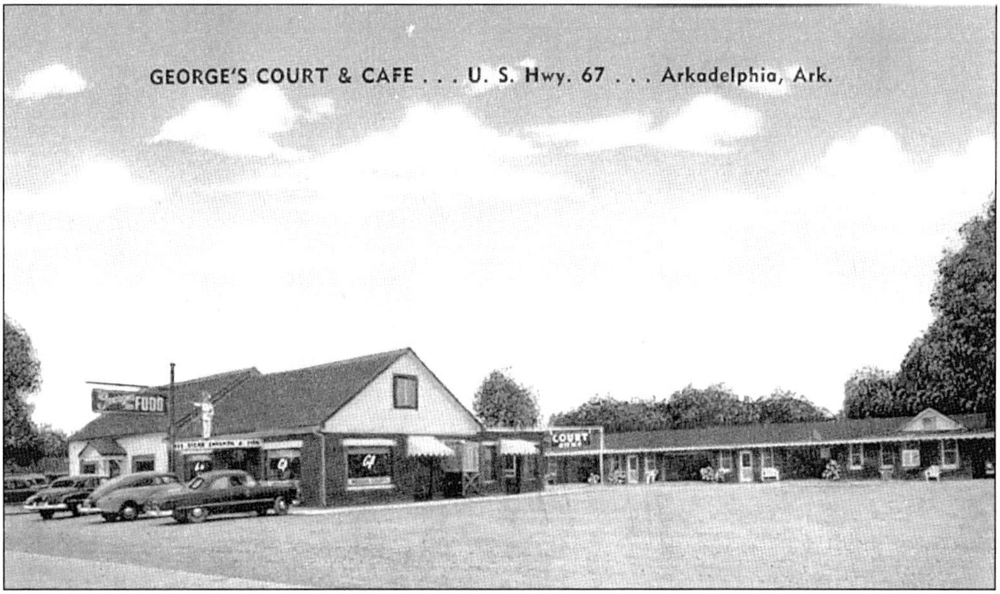

George W. Moore located his tourist court and cafe 1/2 mile north of Arkadelphia on Highway 67 in the 1940s. On the back of the postcard, Moore advertised "very modern brick units-Panel Ray Heat. We specialize in K.C. Steaks and Chicken Dinners." An indication of Mr. Moore's optimism about business volume is stamped by the printer on the back of the card–he ordered 12,500 of these cards in January of 1950. The business is gone today.

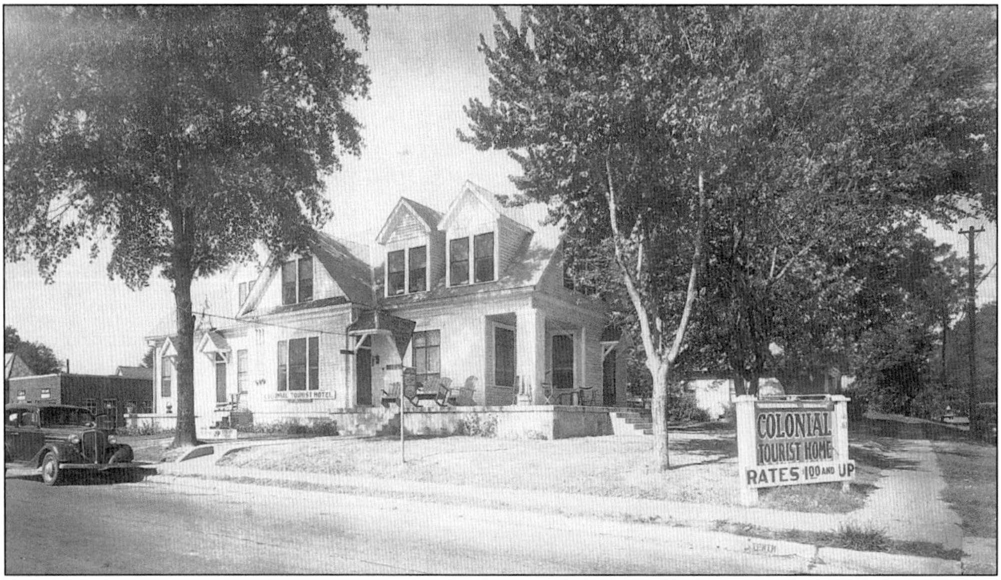

Travelers on a budget might have driven by the tourist courts on the Highway 67 approach into Arkadelphia and checked into the Colonial Tourist Home located on the corner of Tenth and Caddo, near downtown. The sign on the lawn advertised rooms at "$1 and UP," around 1945. A 1937 advertisement listed Mrs. Ida Ashford as the manager and promoted the lodging's fried chicken dinners for 35¢. The business, which began as Ward's Tourist Home in the 1920s, no longer stands.

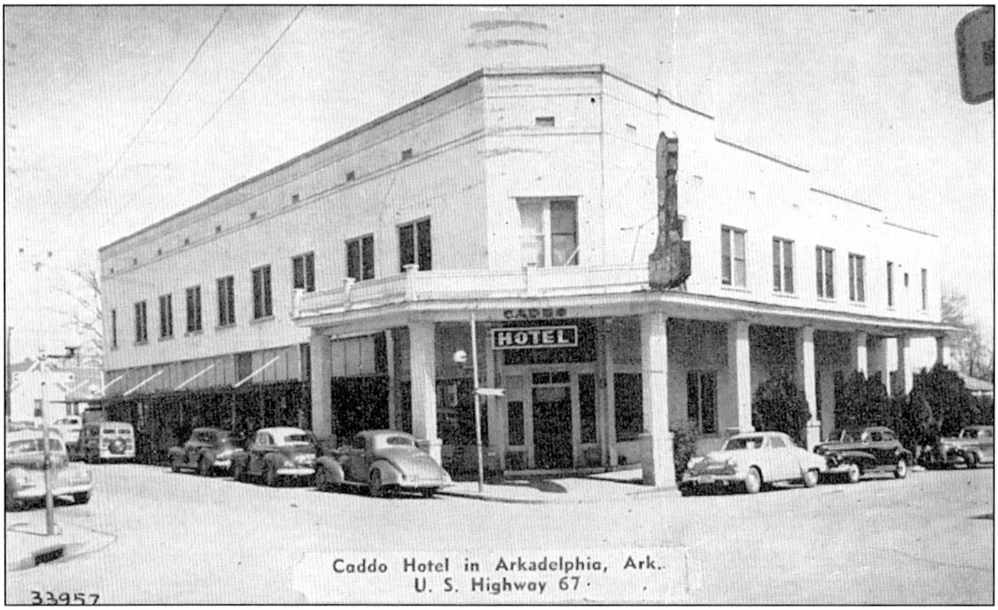

"Slept eight miles out, had breakfast here" were the 1947 words of a Massachusetts man who stayed at one of the Highway 67 courts and then ate breakfast downtown at the landmark Caddo Hotel. The building was erected in 1912 and originally housed a bank, but it was converted to a hotel around 1920. Eventually, the changing tastes of travelers, advancing age, and the coming of Interstate 30 a few miles out of town all resulted in the hotel's closure in the 1960s; it burned down in 1989.

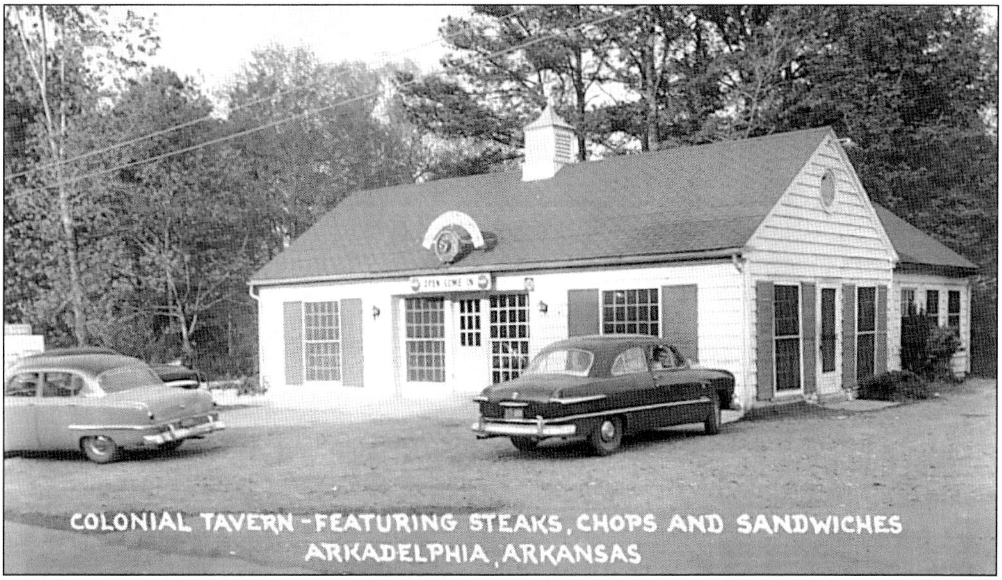

During the 1940s and 1950s, one of the more interesting Highway 67 dining choices was found across the road from Henderson College. The Colonial Tavern featured hearty meals of chops, steaks, and sandwiches in an effort to capture both travelers off the road and students and faculty of the two nearby colleges, Henderson and Ouachita Baptist College. The building was torn down some years ago, and the lot is vacant today.

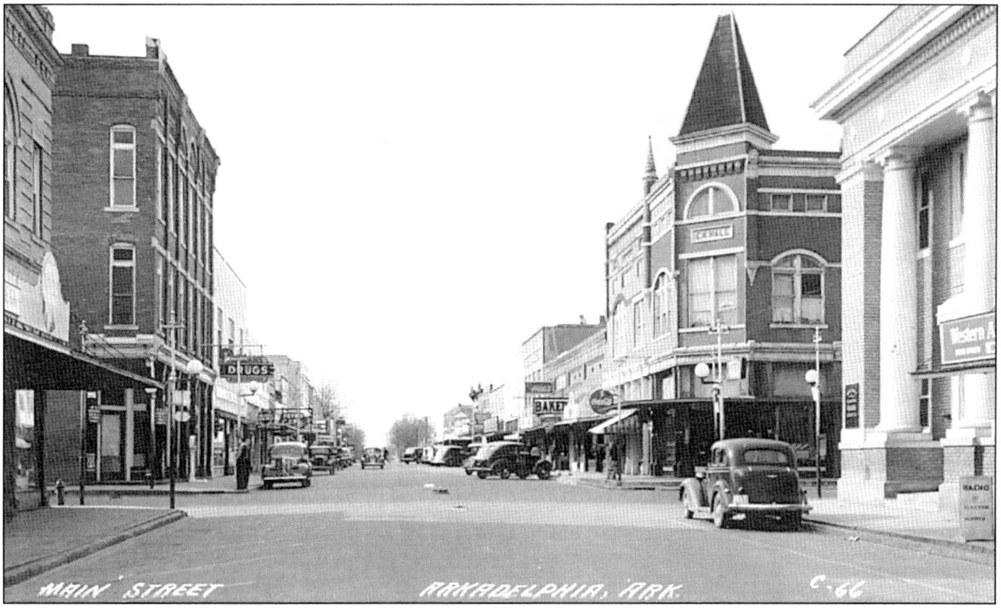

Motorists passing through downtown Arkadelphia on Highway 67 could have turned off a block or two for a drive around a business district of handsome, turn-of-the-century buildings in the era before the first outlying shopping centers. Today, most of the buildings in this c. 1945 photo are gone. The tall building with the steeple, the E.M. Hall building, housed a pharmacy among other businesses. A fire destroyed the building some years ago and the site is today a park. The Merchants & Planters Bank to the right was demolished years ago, and the buildings on the immediate left were destroyed in a tornado on March 1, 1997.

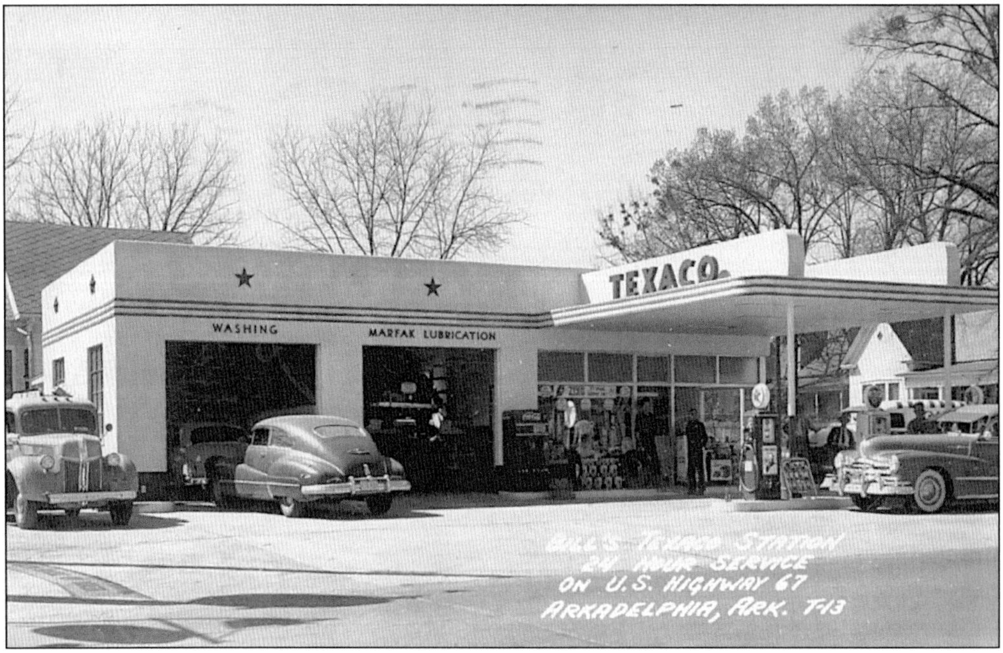

Bill's Texaco Station, seen here around 1950, was built in the style replicated by the major oil companies across the nation in that era. Bill's was an example of the last generation of full-service gas stations that preceded the rise of convenience stores with self-service gas pumps that are so familiar today. The station, located at the corner of Tenth and Caddo, is long out of business, but the building has been remodeled and today houses the Alliance Insurance Agency.

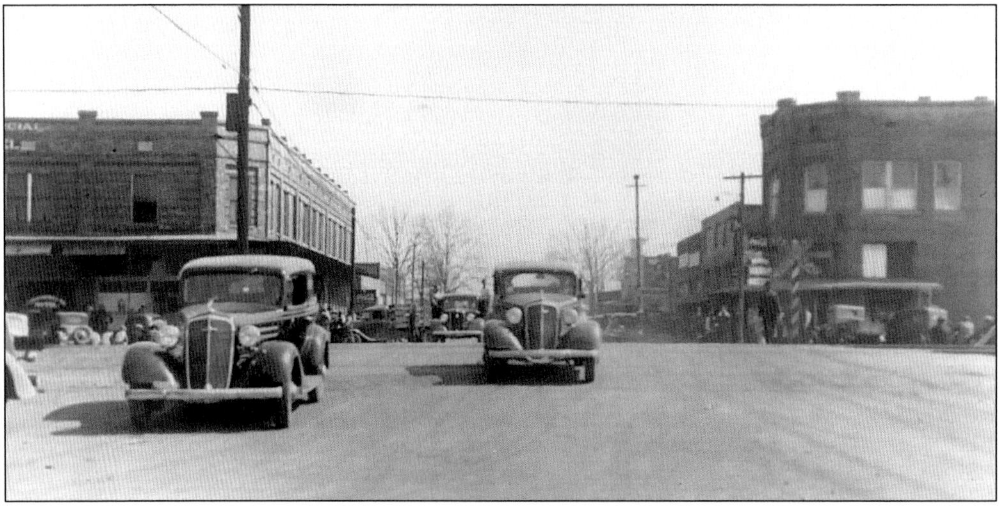

By the 1930s, the Bankhead Highway, which had come through Gurdon in the early 1920s, had been replaced by Highway 67. The photographer taking this photo was very likely standing on the edge of Highway 67, in the path of automobiles coming from the Gurdon business district that stretched along the train tracks for four blocks. The Commercial Hotel seen to the left dated from the turn of the century. It began by hosting people arriving in wagons and trains, then supplied bed and board for tourists driving automobiles like these down Highway 67. The hotel is gone today, and the traffic passes a couple of miles away on Interstate 30. (Courtesy of UCA Archives.)

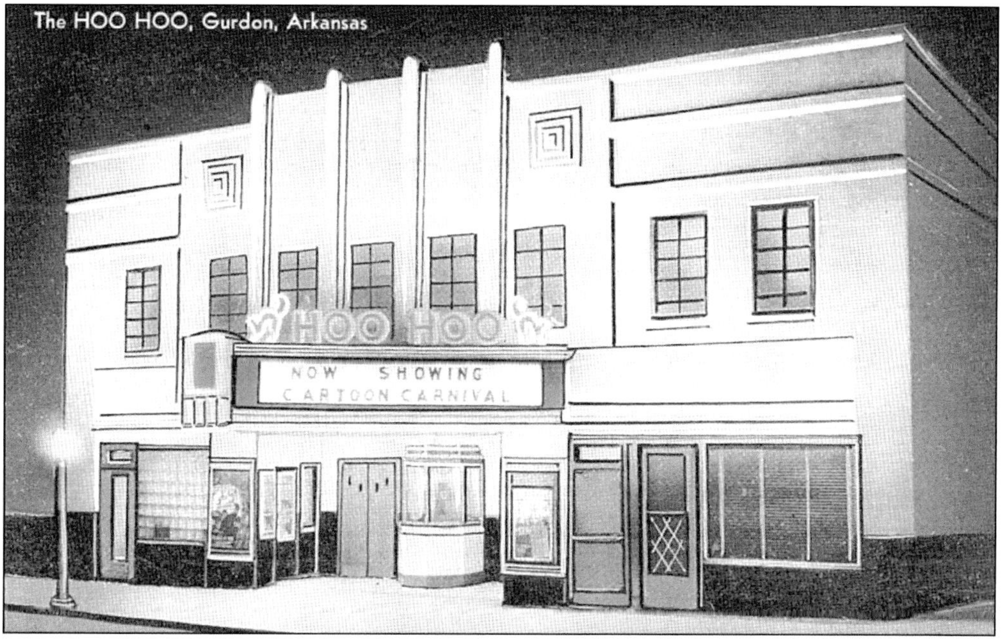

Motorists passing through Gurdon on Highway 67 at night could not have failed to notice the Hoo Hoo movie theater. The name was taken from the International Order of Hoo-Hoo, said to be the oldest industrial fraternal organization in the world. The worldwide forest products association was founded in Gurdon in 1892 by six conventioneers stranded by a delayed train. One of the men, a lumber trade journalist, added touches of humor, defining a "Hoo-Hoo" as "the alarming tuft of hair that grew on the top of the otherwise bald head of the soon to be first Snark of the Universe." The theater closed years ago and is only a shell today, though restoration is a future possibility.

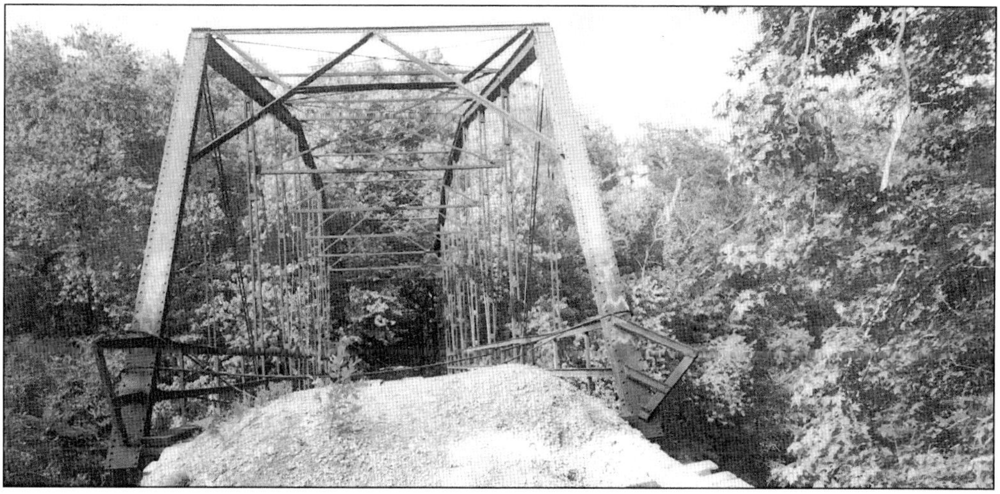

At the point where Highway 67 crossed from Clark County into Nevada County, engineers in the 1920s erected this iron bridge over the Little Missouri River. The narrow iron bridge served for several years before a concrete one re-routed the traffic. The bridge became a tourist attraction—it was one of the last surviving iron bridges still in use for local traffic, as late as 1990. Today it is closed, damaged by overloaded gravel trucks, but local citizens are trying to restore it, at least for pedestrian traffic. (Courtesy of Depot Museum at Prescott.)

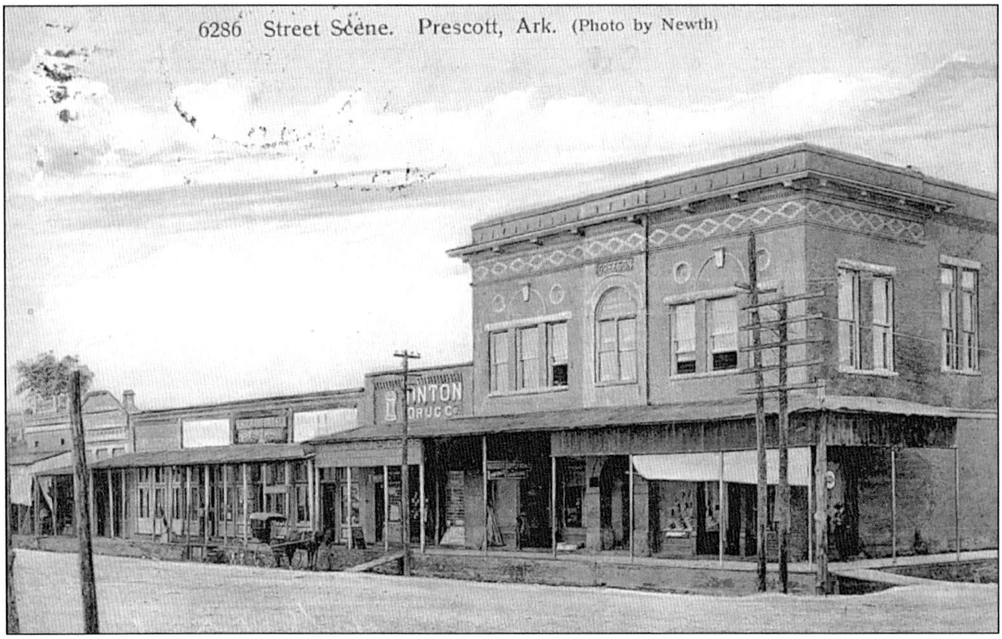

Proceeding down Highway 67 after leaving Gurdon, travelers came next to Prescott, the seat of Nevada County. It is said the town site, located on a Native American trail, was first settled and named Moscow in the 18th century. Prescott came into being in the 1870s, like Gurdon up the tracks, as a stop on the Cairo & Fulton Railroad. As shown in this postcard from 1908, the West First Street business block saw only wagons on a street that, within a few short years, would carry the traffic of busy Highway 67. The Prescott Opera House, which burned in 1908, is on the corner.

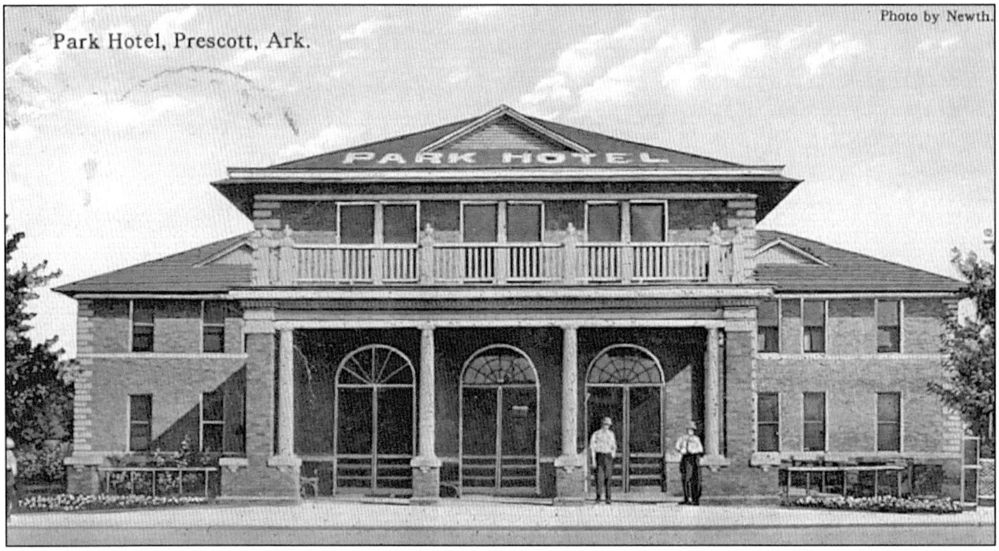

One of the first places for highway travelers to lodge in Prescott was the Park Hotel, which was originally erected as a hospital in 1915. The coming of the Bankhead Highway in 1922 resulted in the building's conversion to a hotel in 1921. In later incarnations, the same business was renamed the Hotel Allen, the Lawson Hotel, and the Loda Hotel. With its building torn down in the 1960s, the site is now occupied by a Pizza Hut.

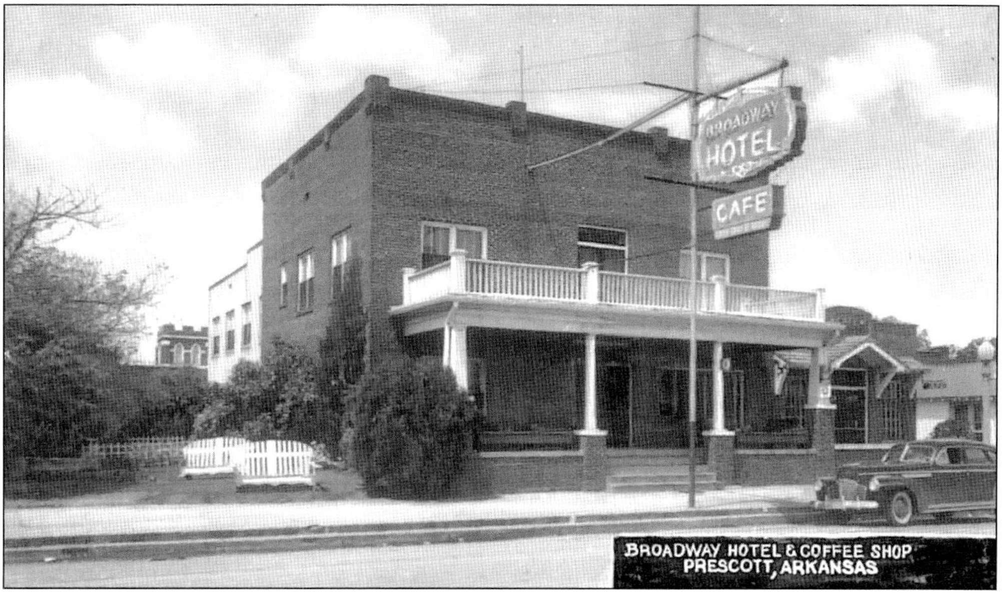

Highway 67 has thousands of human-interest dramas woven through its history, few of which will ever be recorded or remembered. A small hotel in Prescott might be the only exception. A young local man, Chester Hooker, went off to fight the Germans in World War II and earned a Bronze Star fighting in the Battle of the Bulge. Hooker returned home to Prescott and late in life purchased the Broadway Hotel, which had been built in 1919. The hotel took its name from the nickname that had been given to Highway 67, the newly improved road through town, also known as "The Broadway of America." The compact little hotel operated for almost 80 years and, in later years, served as long-term residential housing. In 1998, Hooker, in his late 70s and still running his small, well-maintained hotel a few steps from Highway 67, was killed in the hotel in a savage murder. To date, the crime remains unsolved. As seen in the 1999 photo below, the hotel building stands in good shape, awaiting a new owner. The sign that still hangs above the front of the hotel, extending over the street, carries the following quote from Hooker: "It's the heritage of everyone—we are only caretakers for a short time." The postcard above is from c. 1945. (1999 photo by Ray Hanley.)

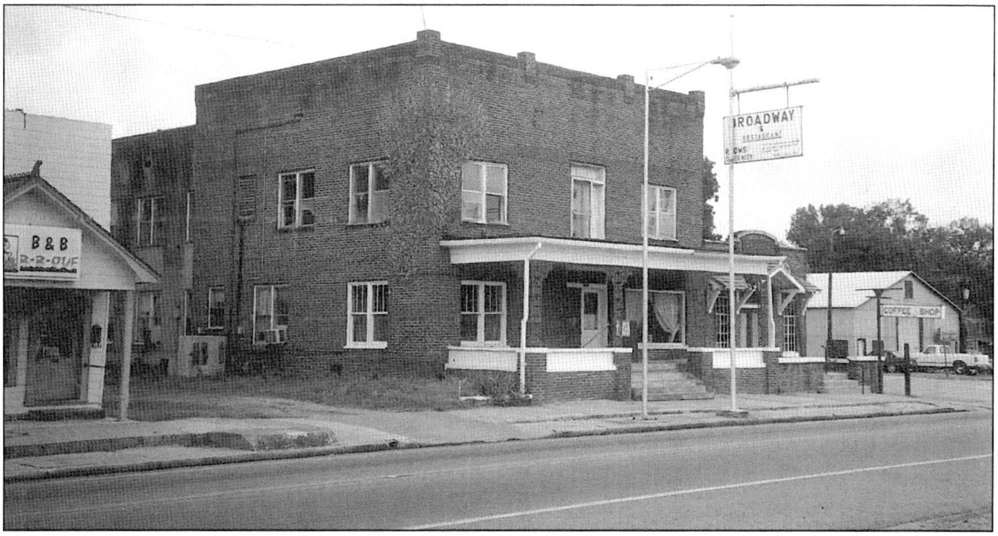

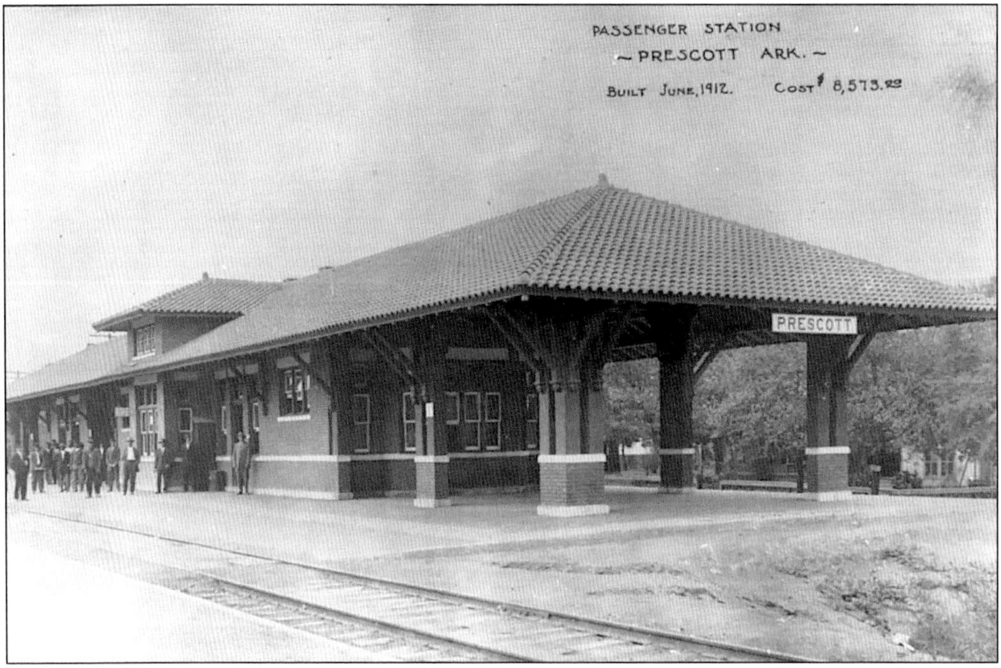

Across First Street, and today adjacent to Highway 67, is the Missouri Pacific depot built at a cost of $8,575 in 1912, when several passenger trains a day passed through Prescott. Today, the restored depot is home to the local historical museum, where visitors taking a break from the interstate 2 miles away can learn about the very interesting past of Nevada County.

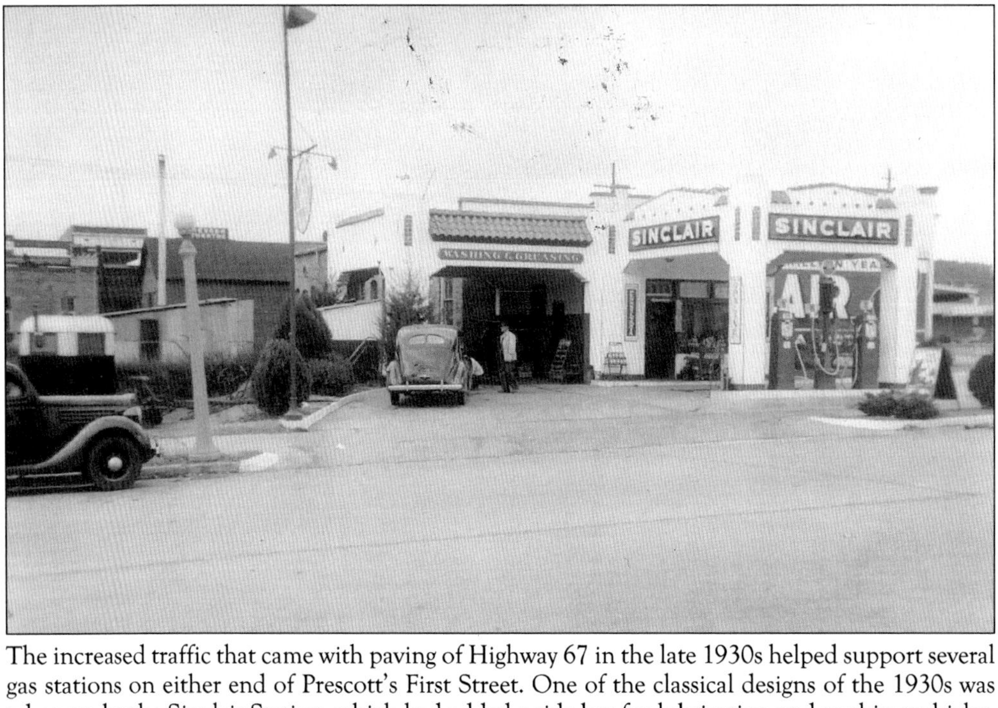

The increased traffic that came with paving of Highway 67 in the late 1930s helped support several gas stations on either end of Prescott's First Street. One of the classical designs of the 1930s was taken up by the Sinclair Station, which had added a side bay for lubrication and washing vehicles. (Photo courtesy of Depot Museum, Prescott.)

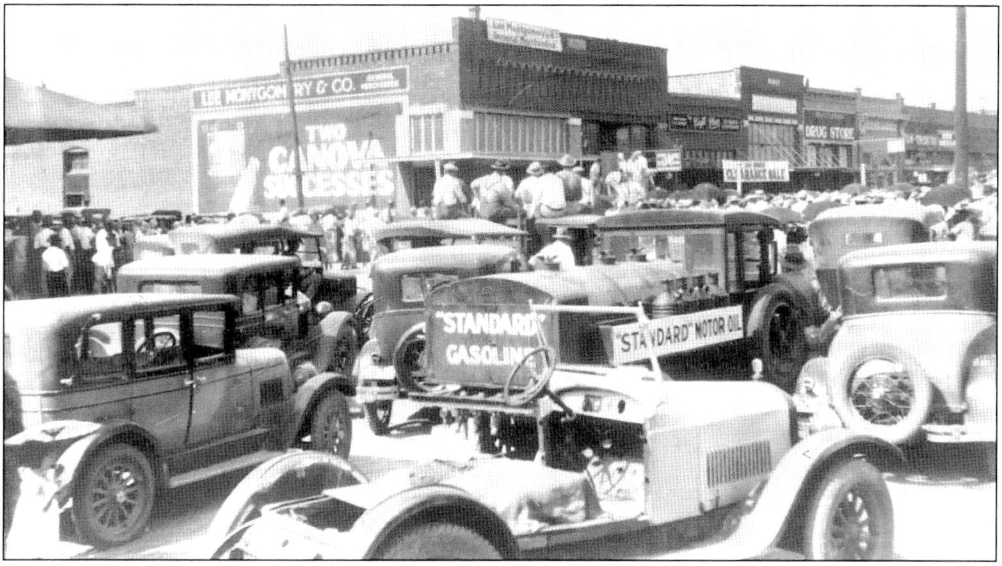

Though a small town, Prescott's First Street sometimes drew large crowds. In this case, the street was choked with parked cars and townspeople, apparently drawn by the chance to win a large cash prize announced at the Lee Montgomery & Co. store. For many years, Prescott merchants would hand out a ticket with every purchase, and on the last Wednesday in October, a drawing was held to find the lucky winner of $500 cash. In the photo above, a Standard Oil truck for transporting gasoline can be seen near a car with no doors or top. The 77 Service Station in the lower photo was the Texaco dealer; the two-story building beyond it, with a balcony packed with spectators, is the Saxon Hotel. These photos are from c. 1930. (Photos courtesy of Depot Museum in Prescott.)

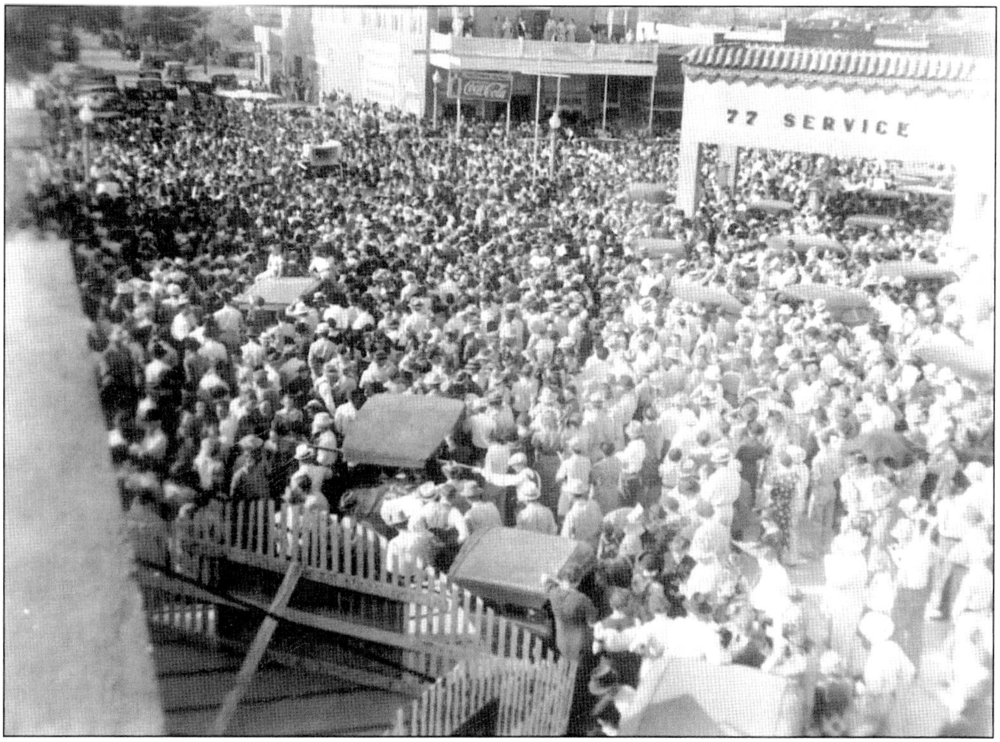

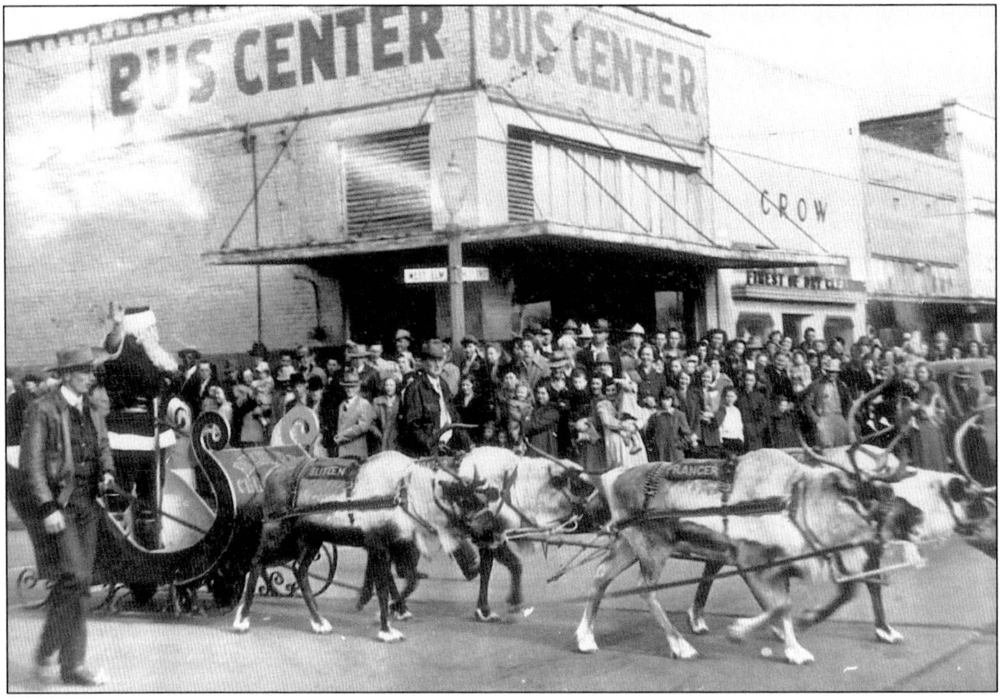

Passengers waiting for the next bus to pull in from Highway 67 in December 1940 would have been drawn out of the station at the corner of Elm and First Streets to watch Santa's sleigh pulled by live reindeer in the town's annual Christmas parade. (Photo courtesy of Depot Museum, Prescott.)

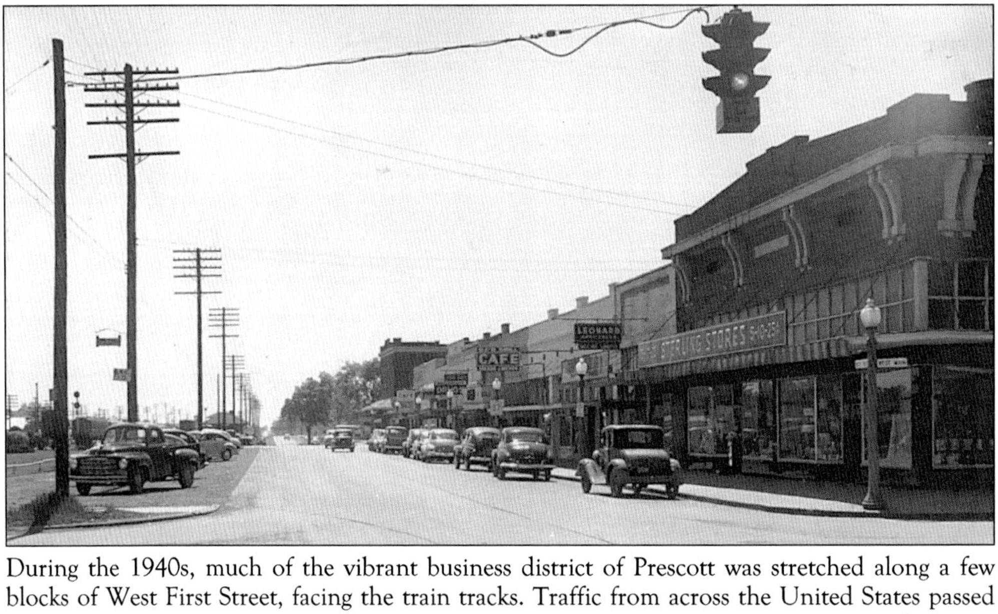

During the 1940s, much of the vibrant business district of Prescott was stretched along a few blocks of West First Street, facing the train tracks. Traffic from across the United States passed down Highway 67, a sign for which is in the center of the card on a lamppost in front of the D&D Grill. The large building on the corner of First and Main was the Sterling Store, once among the most common businesses on the main streets of small-town America. In the distance is Buchanan's Drug Store, a longtime presence on the street. The railroad tracks are just out of sight to the left.

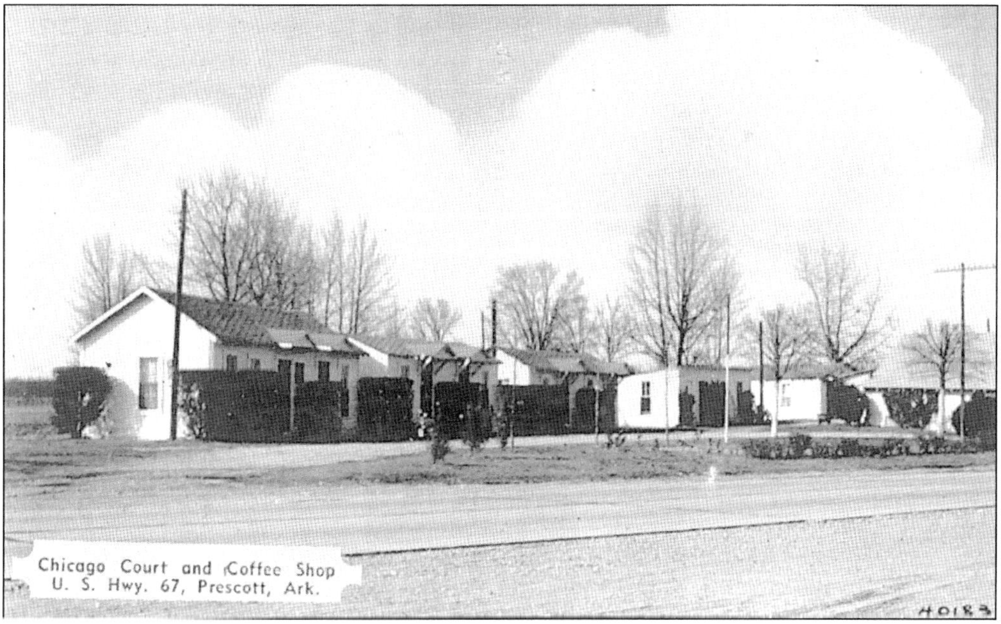

The Chicago Court and Coffee Shop was built on the north side of Prescott on Highway 67 and is seen here around 1940. The business was owned and operated by Mr. and Mrs. C.A. Malefyt, perhaps originally from Chicago and hence the big city name for the tourist court in small-town Arkansas. Today, the site is occupied by a private residence and a cattle pasture. If the Chicago Court on the north side of town had no vacancy, a short drive through town brought a motorist to Cummings' Court and Esso station. "Clean, comfortable, modern cabins, located 1/2 mile south of Prescott, Ark on U.S. Hwy 67, owned and operated by Alfred Cummings," read the printed caption on the back of the cards that would have been found in each of the cabins. Today, the court is gone, and a garment plant occupies the site.

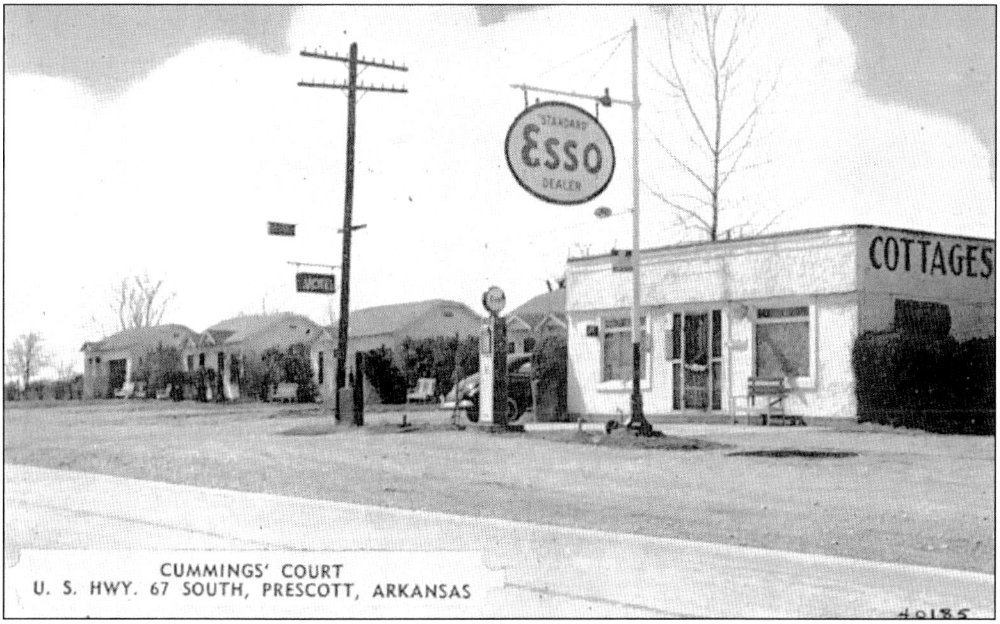

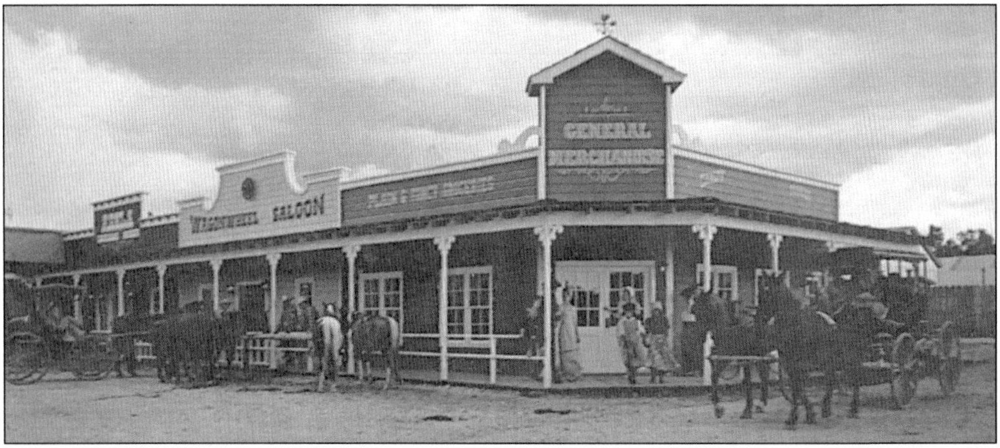

Emmet, Arkansas, located on Highway 67 at the Nevada/Hempstead County line, was home to one of the most novel tourist attractions between St. Louis and Dallas. In the 1950s, Arkla Gas Company (today Reliance Energy) erected a "re-creation of a typical thriving frontier town of the mid-1800's . . . authentic down to the last hand-split shingle. Manufacturing makes Arkla Village more than a monument—it is the home of Arkla Village Rocker, Carriages by Arkla, and Jim Key Harness." A part of the town is shown above, including the general store where souvenirs were sold and the Wagon Wheel Saloon where nothing stronger than root beer was served. The working village made carriages for sale to businesses for promotions and special events. The attraction also employed a variety of skilled craftsmen who demonstrated the art of 18th-century occupations. Visiting Cub Scouts in the photo below were learning about how cheese was once made and sold in the general store. When Interstate 30 took the traffic off Highway 67 in the 1960s, Arkla Village faded away, and today not a trace remains of the once-thriving attraction. (Courtesy of Arkansas History Commission.)

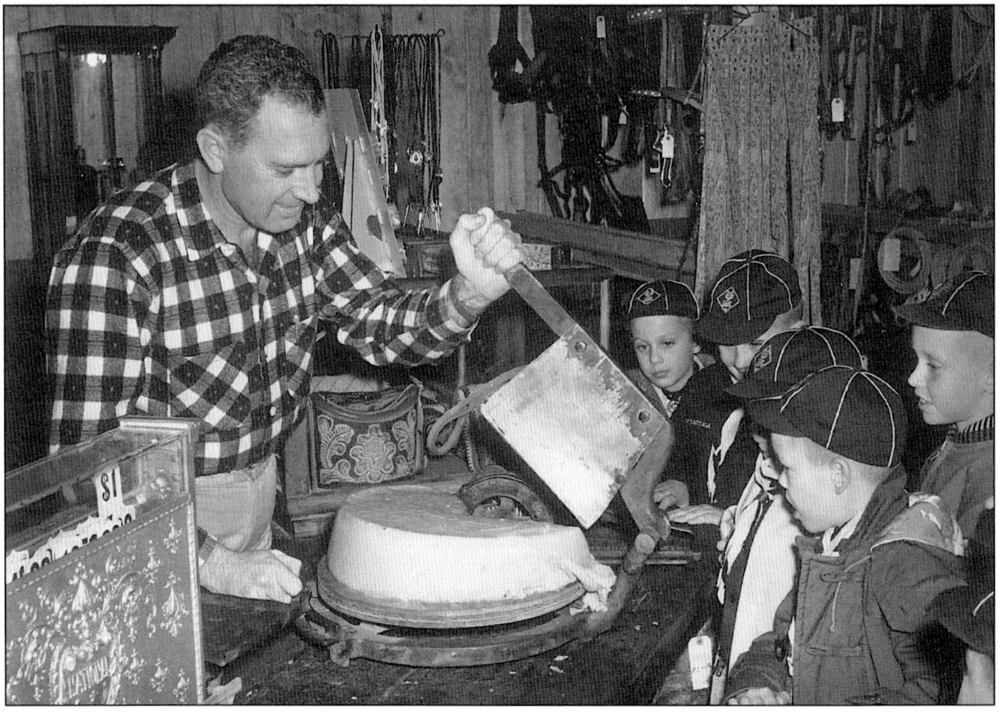

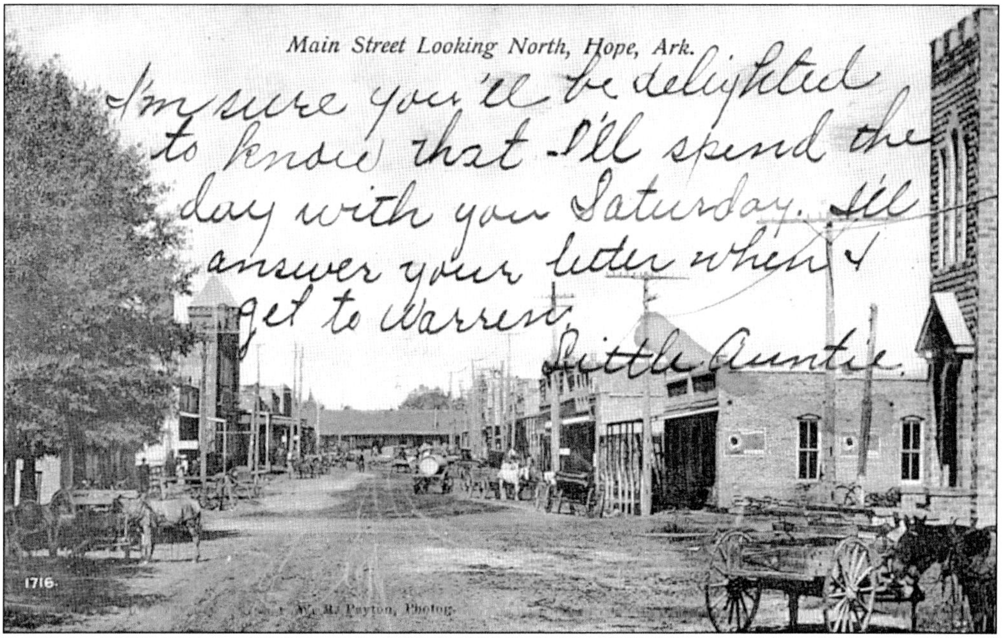

The route of Highway 67, and the nearby Bankhead Highway, in the early 1920s proceeded past Emmet into the Hempstead County seat of Hope, seen above around 1905. Like the towns of Prescott, Gurdon, and Arkadelphia north of it on Highway 67, the town of Hope was surveyed by the Cairo & Fulton Railroad, which followed the same general path as the military road of 1803. The town was named for Hope Loughborough, the daughter of a railroad director. The town grew outward from the rail station seen down Main Street in the distance. The photographer set up his camera in the dirt street at about the point Highway 67 would pass across Main Street in the next 25 years.

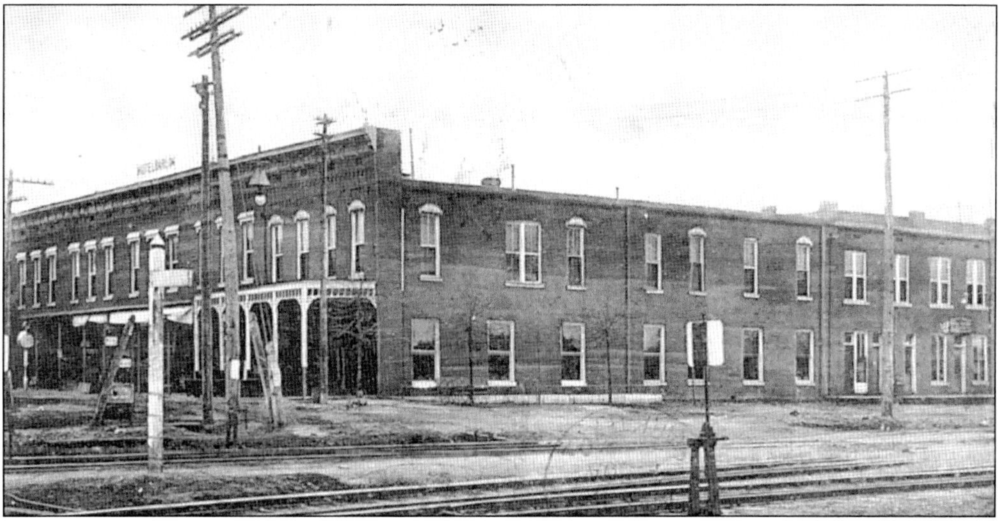

Hope's first large hotel, the Barlow, is seen above in 1908; it was built across from the rail station with the intent of lodging train passengers. The Barlow, first operating out of a large frame house, drew its name from owner John Barlow, who successfully marketed it for many years. Signs along the highway read, "Barlow Hotel—No Regrets," and the hotel indeed delivered, providing bowls of cut flowers on the tables and a bowl of whipped cream with each meal.

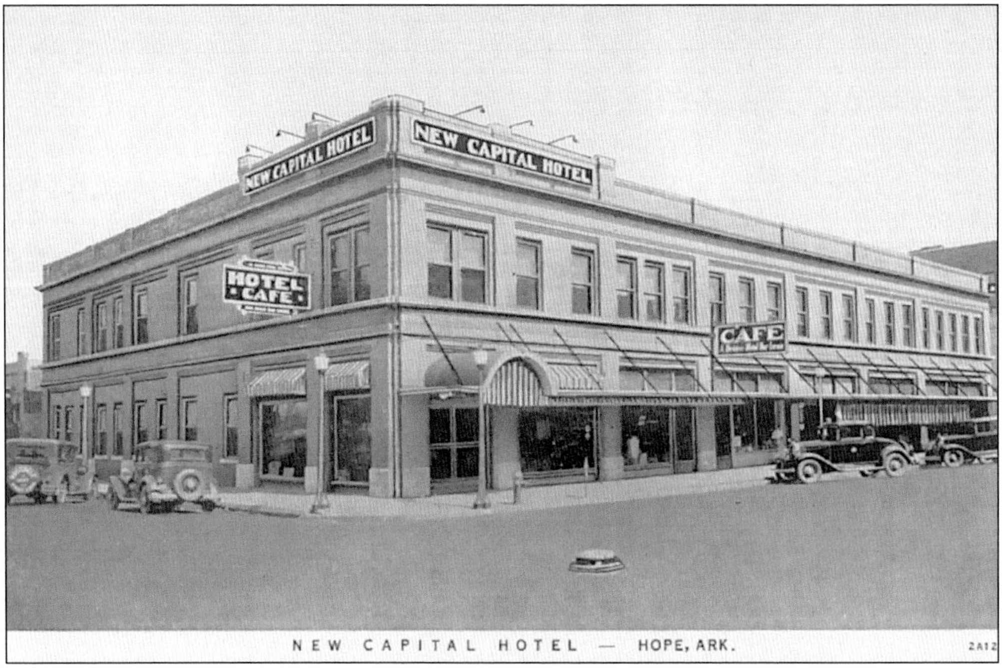

A later competitor of the Barlow, the Capital Hotel, was built by James Pilkington, the president of Hope National Bank. The Capital Hotel housed several other businesses, including a four-chair barbershop, a men's clothing shop, and a cafe. The Barlow burned some 30 years ago, and the Capital is also long gone.

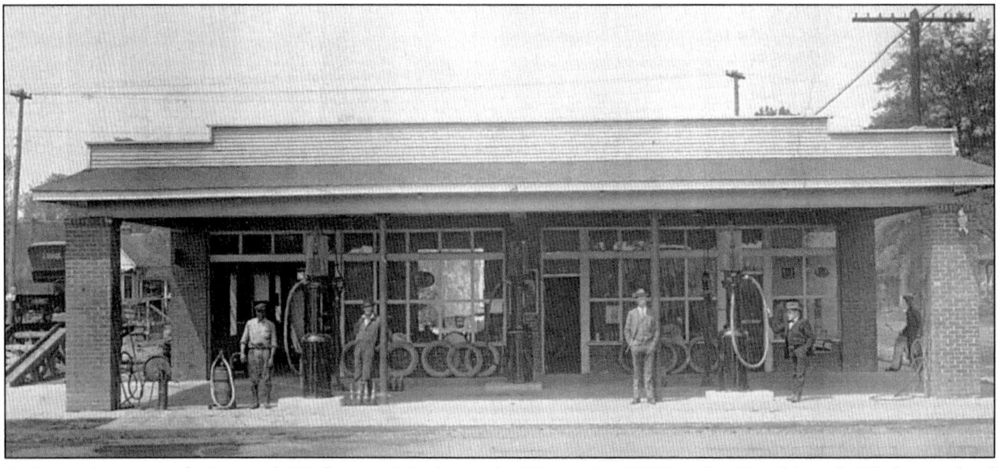

Before the completion of Highway 67 through Hope in 1930, the Bankhead Highway had preceded it around 1920. One pair of enterprising business partners who foresaw the profits to be made from the growing number of automobiles were two brothers, Thurman and Lester Rhodes, who opened Rhodes Brothers Service Station in 1924. Their location at Walnut and Division Streets prospered throughout the 1920s, only to decline when the new Highway 67 deviated away from the Bankhead route by a few blocks. Years later, an employee of the Rhodes brothers, Earley McIver, told stories about working there. He said the station had the first hydraulic lift for working on cars in Hope; it is visible at work on the far left in the above photo. McIver also remembered taking motorists over to the Barlow Hotel while their cars were being worked on. This photo shows the station in its first year, 1924.

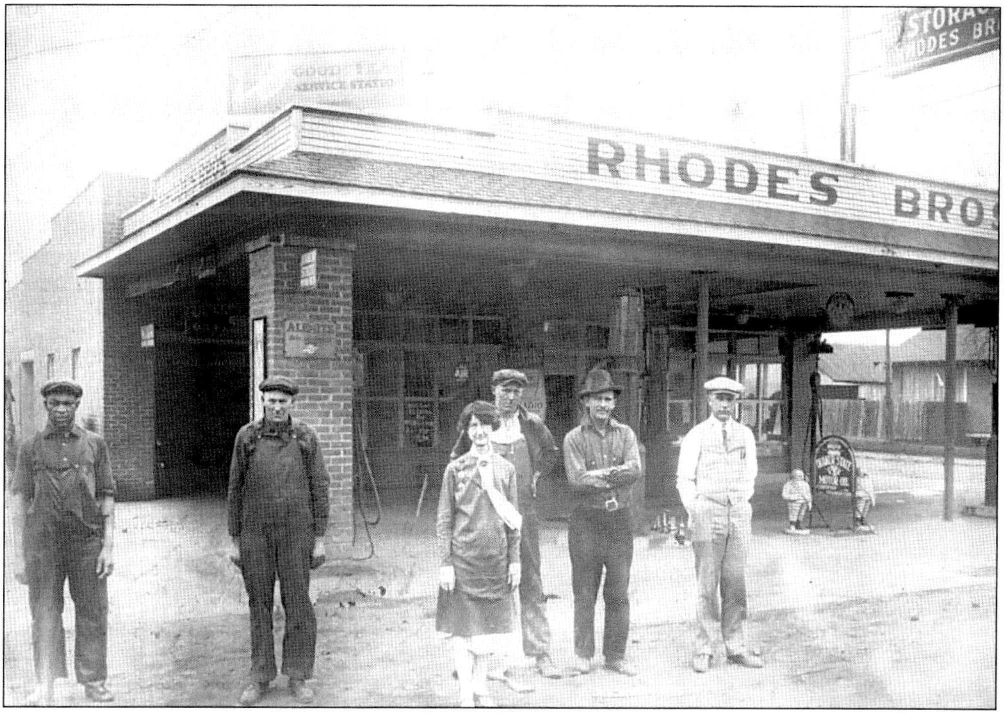

The Rhodes Brothers Service Station is pictured here a few years after its opening in 1924. From left to right are Batch, Earley McIver, Ethel Rose, Herbert Lewellan, John C. Turner, and Thurman Rhodes. (Courtesy of Mrs. Mary Nell Turner of Hope.)

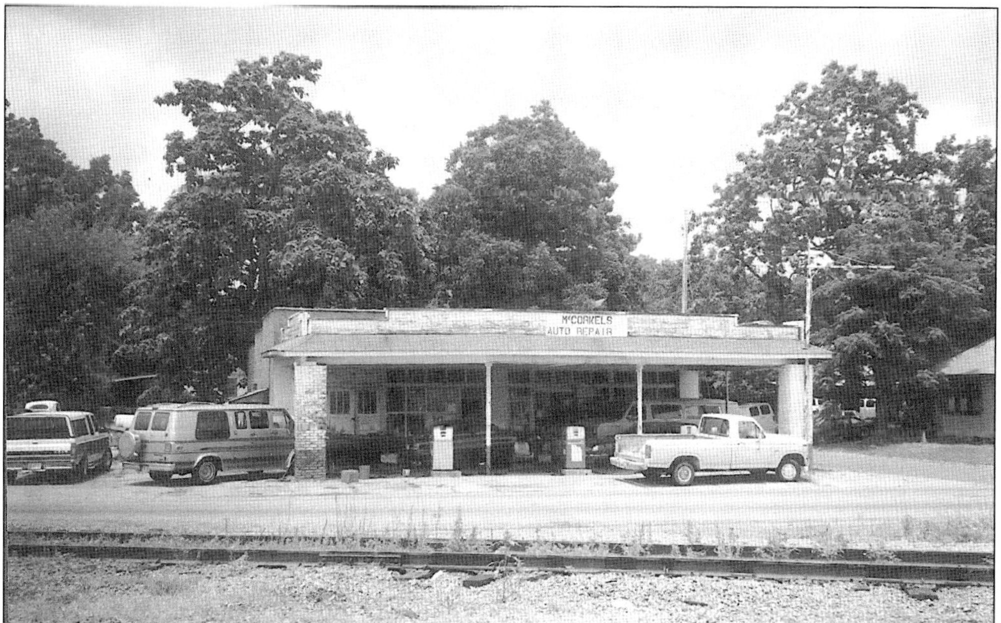

On a research trip to Hope in 1999, the author was amazed to discover that, after 75 years, the building the Rhodes Brothers erected in 1924 was not only still standing and remarkably unchanged in appearance, but still housed an automotive business—McCorkle's Auto Repair.

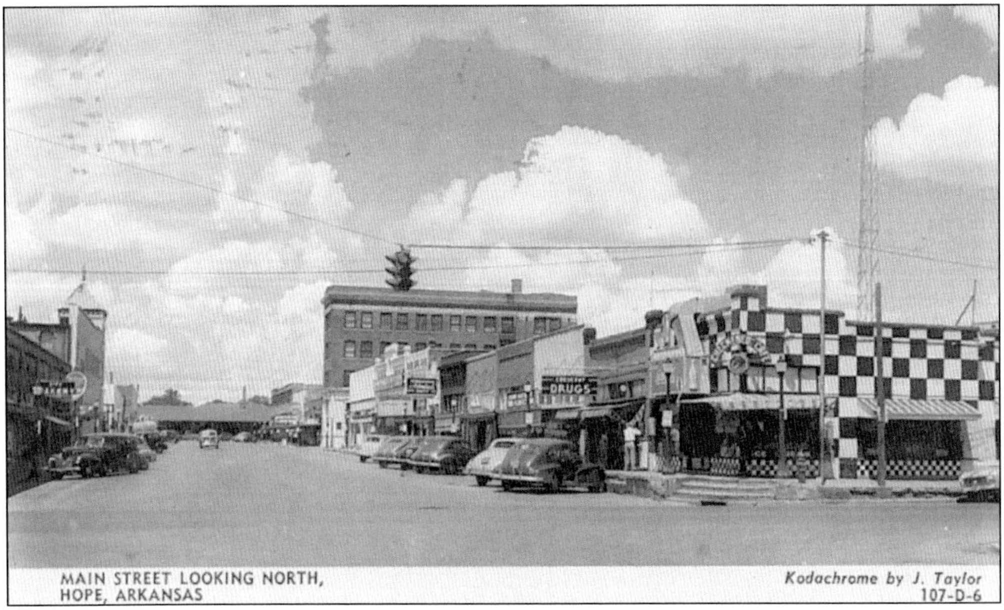

W.A. "Bill" Ramsey opened the Checkered Cafe in 1933 on Front Street and the Bankhead Highway, across from the depot, in Hope. The restaurant was open all night, and much of its clientele came off the frequent passenger trains. Among the most remembered diners was said to have been the gangster "Pretty Boy" Floyd. When the new Highway 67 came in a few blocks south, Ramsey relocated his café, seen above in the later 1940s, to Main and Third. In the *c.* 1940 interior view below, diners can be seen eating at checkered tables in a dining room with checkered floors. A daughter of Ramsey's said years later that her father hired a young boy to stand on the corner and wave travelers into the cafe, with the checkered exterior and interior making good on its name. Ramsey operated the cafe for more than 20 years before selling it; today it houses an office supply store.

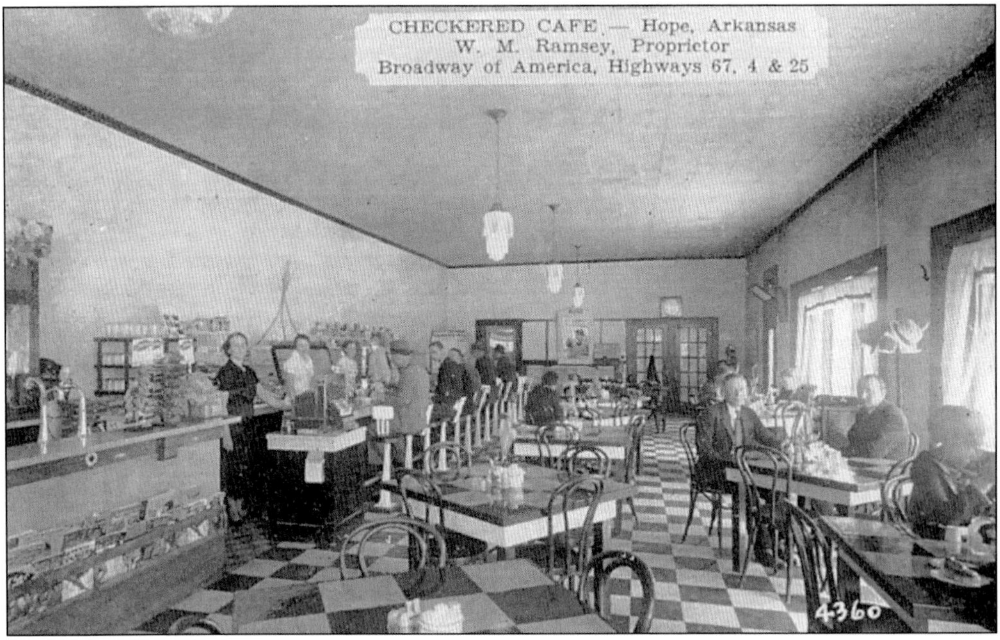

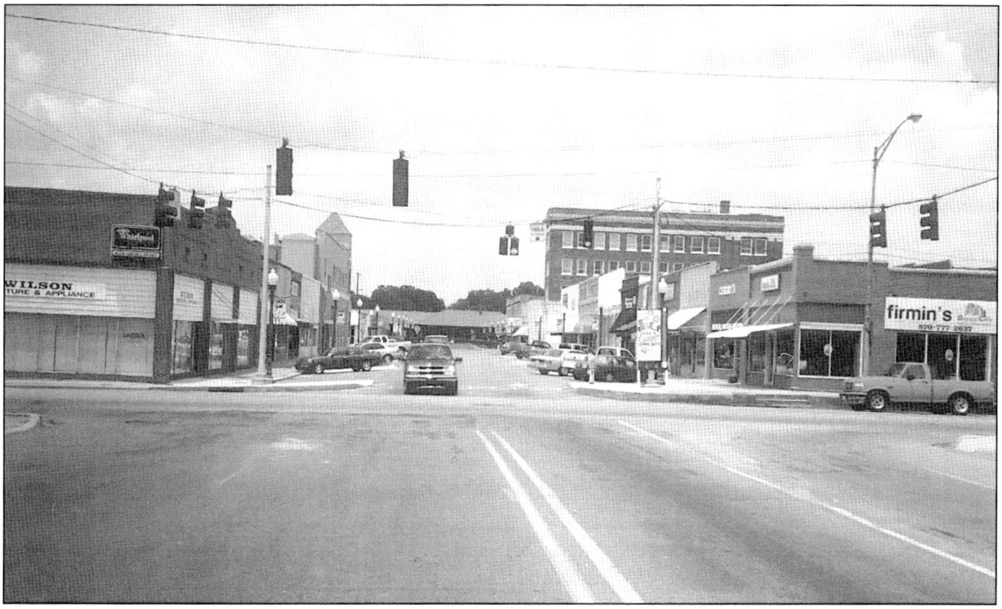

The opening of Interstate 30 in the 1960s took most of the traffic away, but Highway 67 still passes by the former Checkered Cafe, seen to the right as an office supply store. A look down Main Street today from the intersection with Highway 67 seems, at a glance, remarkably similar to the view on page 116 more than half a century earlier. Most of the stores have changed names, but in the distance, the Missouri Pacific depot is still seen. It hosts no passenger trains today, but instead houses the town's visitor's center, which details much of the life of President Bill Clinton, who was born in Hope in 1946, as well as native son Governor Mike Huckabee.

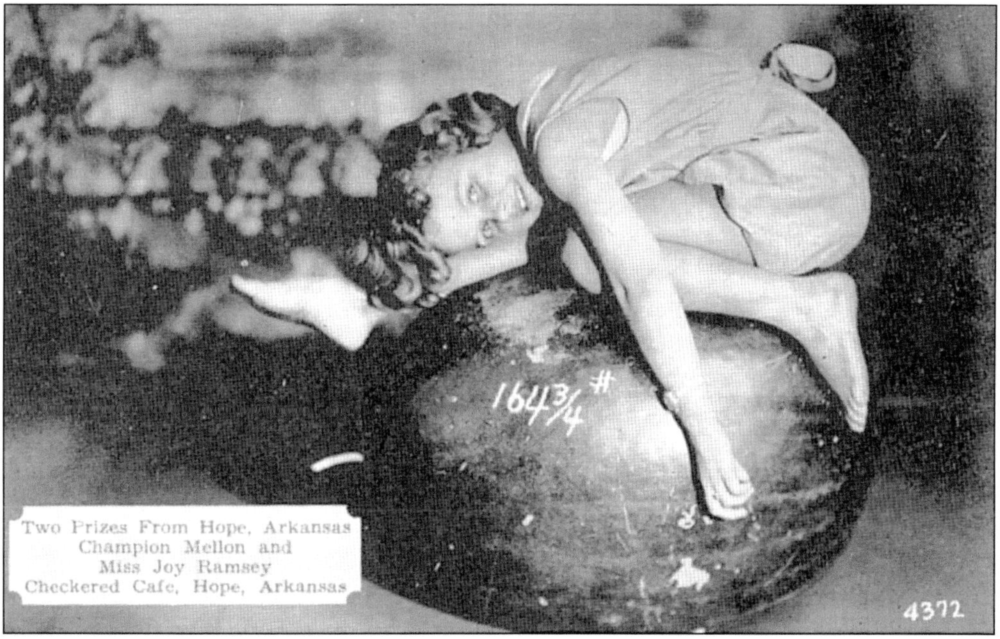

Hope has been famous for champion watermelons for many years, and the Checkered Cafe was the setting for this photograph of one of them around 1940. The girl posed on the 164-pound melon is Joy Ramsey, the daughter of the cafe's owner. Ramsey grew up, married, and still lives in Hope.

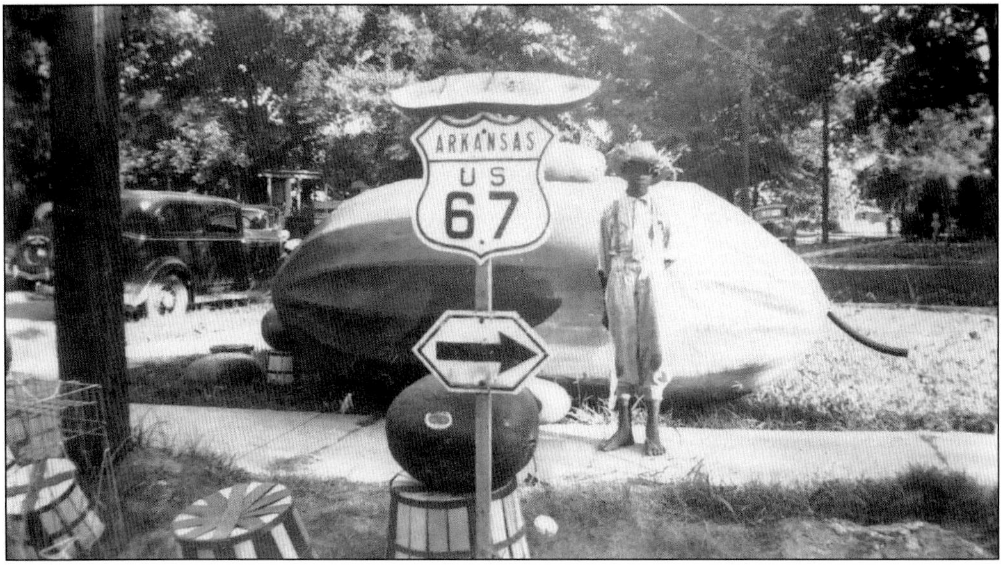

Before the election of native son Bill Clinton to the presidency in 1992, Hope's most identified symbol was the watermelon. For some 70 years, with few exceptions, one of the farms around Hope has produced the largest watermelon in the world. The above photo from the late 1930s captured a common sight seen by Highway 67 motorists during the season—a roadside watermelon stand. The large watermelon prop behind the child would have been a traffic stopper intended to boost sales. The town's first prize melon in 1925 weighed 136 pounds, and it was shipped to President Calvin Coolidge at the White House. In recent years, the new record was set by a 260-pound watermelon, insuring that Hope retains the honor of being "Watermelon Capital of the World."

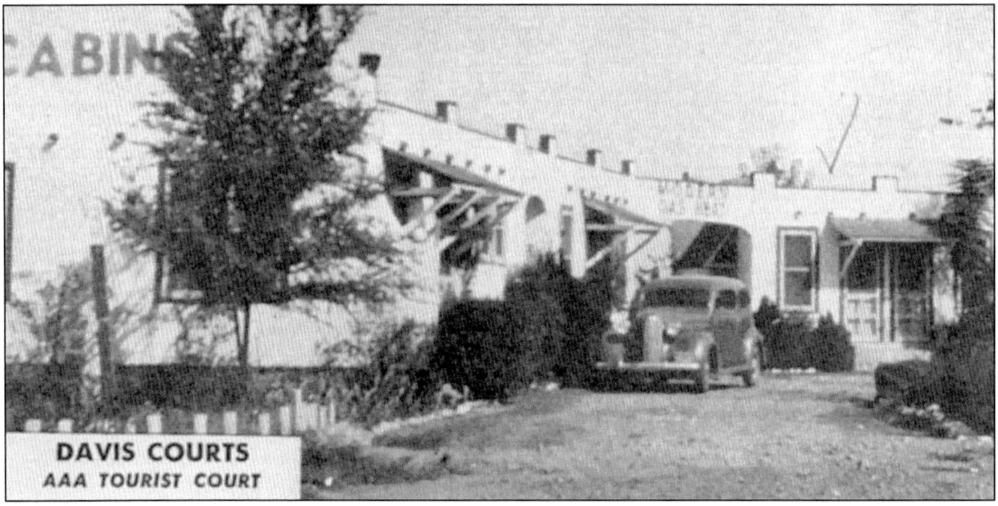

Like the other towns on Highway 67, Hope had tourist courts spring up with the coming of the automobile traffic on the "Broadway of America." One of these, the Davis Courts, was erected on the east side of town in the late 1930s. At the time of this c. 1940 card, the motel was operated by Mr. and Mrs. Linus Walker, who proclaimed on the card that their court had a prized rating by the American Automobile Association. Remarkably, the court still sits beside the highway, little changed on the outside. It is still in business, providing more long-term stays since being bypassed by the interstate.

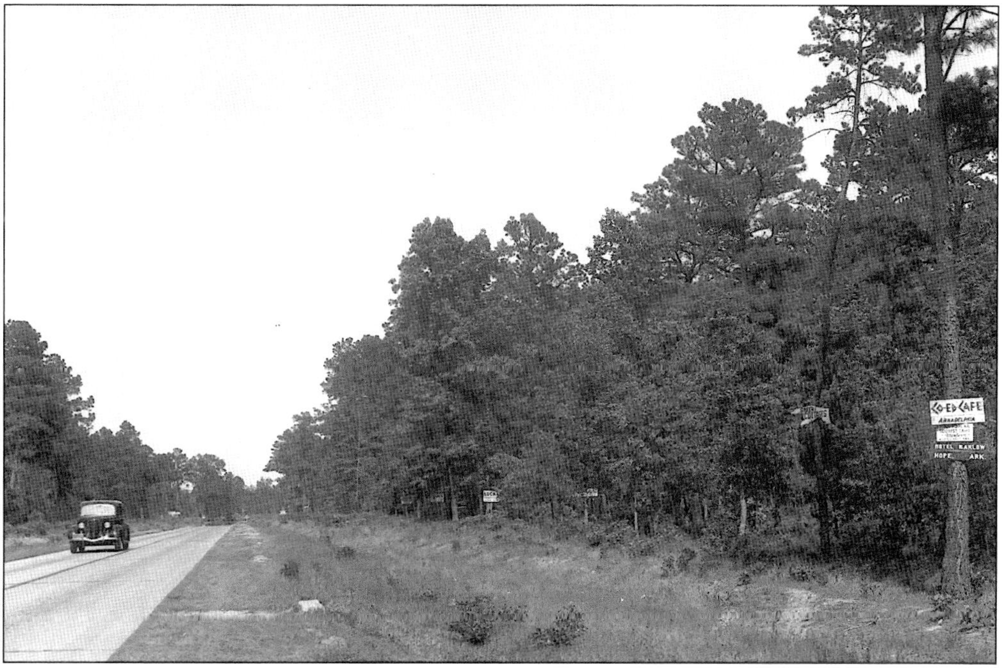

South of Hope, Highway 67's concrete slab passed through woods and pastures, but even between towns there were commercial messages, as seen here in 1940. In the photo above, looking north toward Hope, numerous signs nailed to the trees to promote businesses located up the road are visible. One sign is for the Barlow Hotel in Hope, another is for the Co-Cafe in Arkadelphia, and one is for the Poplar Tourist Camp in Little Rock, 100 miles up the road. The photo below, on the highway about a mile north of Fulton and the Red River, shows Cox's One Stop Service Station. W.E. Cox and his five sons opened the business when the Highway 67 came through the area in the early 1930s. Cox's offered cabins, Esso gas, Texaco and Quaker State motor oil, and, reportedly, some of the best dining on the road. It was said that people came from Texarkana and other towns, sometimes standing in line for half an hour to get a seat in the Cox's dining room. The business closed years ago, but some of the buildings still remain. (Courtesy of UCA Archives.)

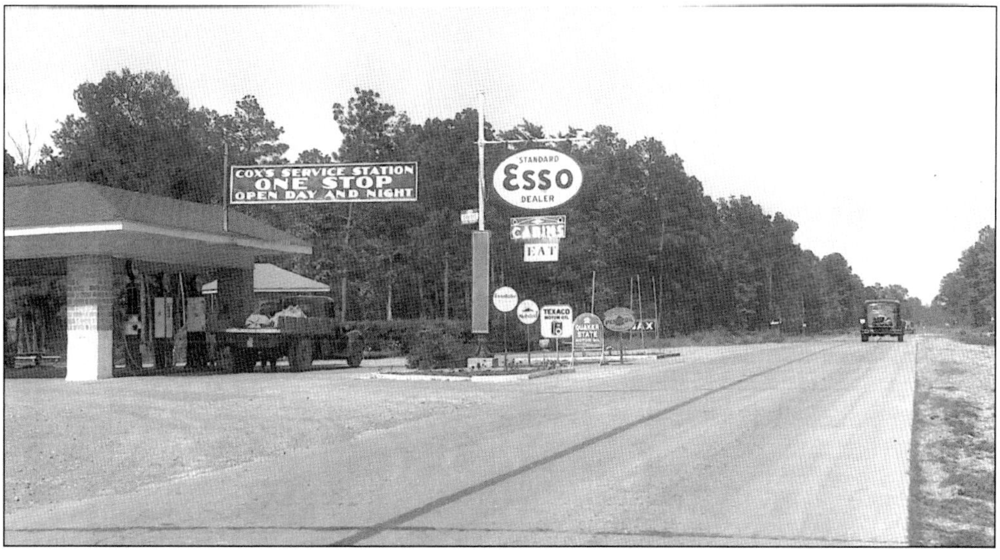

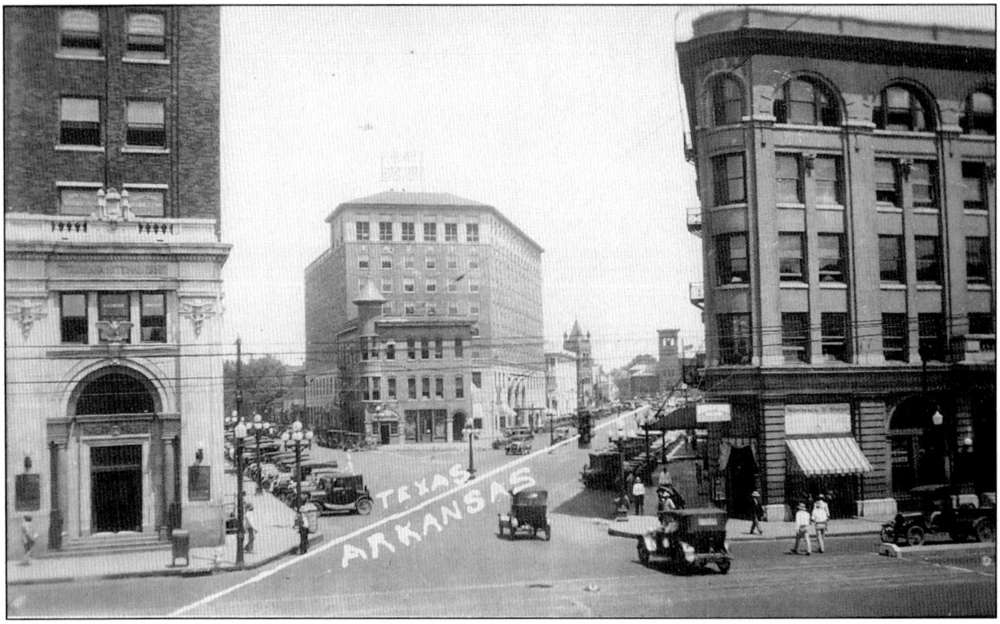

Until a highway bridge was built over the Red River around 1930, automobiles had to use a ferry at Fulton to cross from Hempstead County into Miller. Once across the river, few motorists wasted much time before heading for Texarkana. The town, taking its name from a combination of Texas, Arkansas, and Louisiana, grew up straddling the state line between Arkansas and Texas. Highway 67 traffic would have crossed Stateline Avenue; some visitors may have detoured a couple of blocks to spend a night at the towering Hotel Grim, seen in the center of this 1920s photo.

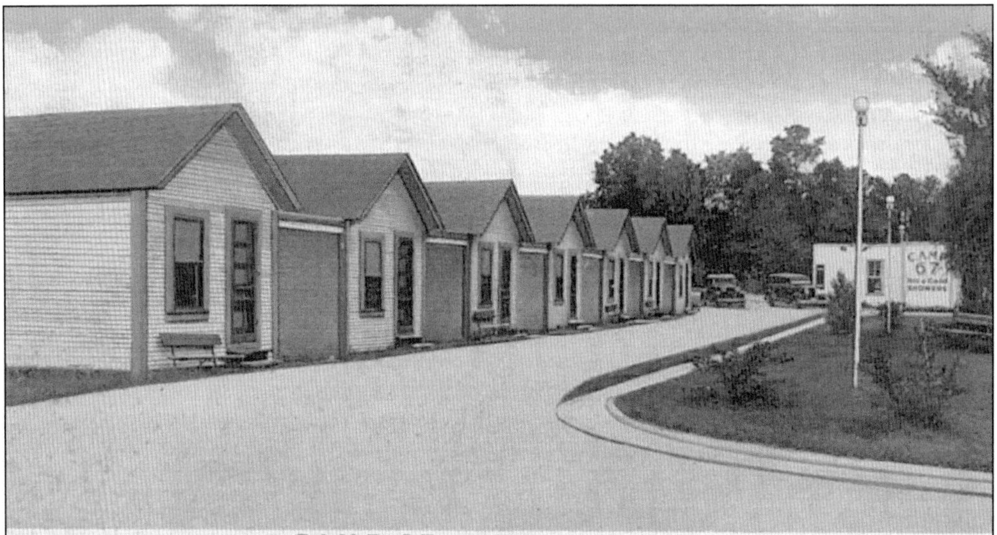

CAMP 67 — TEXARKANA, U. S. A.

Travelers not able or willing to pay for the Hotel Grim, might have chosen the more rustic Camp 67 located at East Broad and Ninth Streets. W.J. Nichols Jr. was listed as the proprietor on the card, which advertised the camp as "Clean, Comfortable, Courteous, with Hot and Cold Showers." The showers were in the common building next to the office in the distance. A tourist court, gas station, and restaurant of one sort or another operated on this site from 1929 to 1960; today only a gas station remains there.

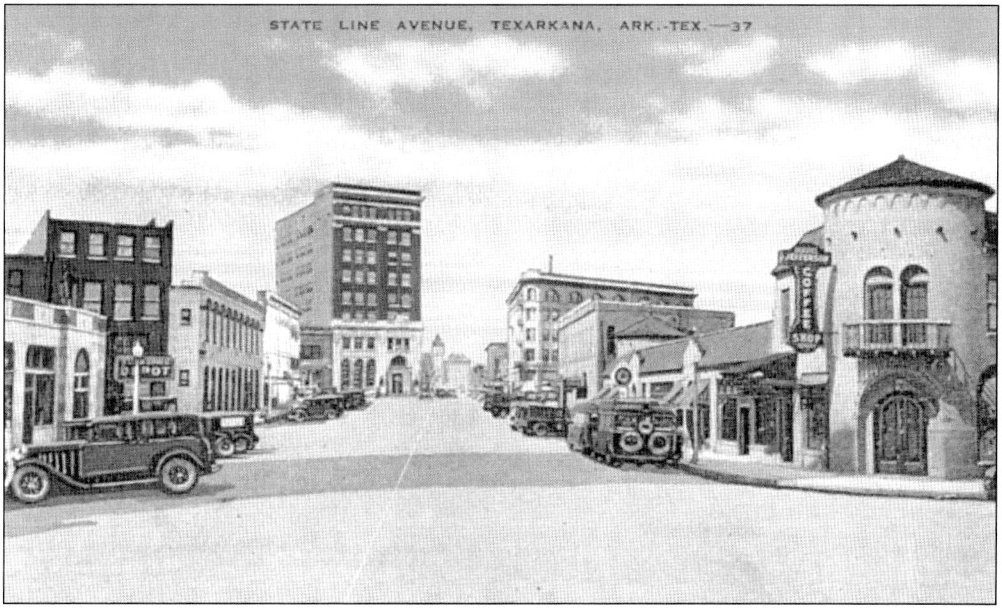

Highway 67 travelers wanting a quick meal before heading on down the road to Texas could have stopped at the Jefferson Coffee Shop, pictured here c. 1945, on the Arkansas side of Stateline Avenue. The round, Spanish-styled building, seen to the right at 100 Stateline, operated from 1931 through the 1960s, but faded away with the coming of Interstate 30 some 30 blocks to the north. The card below showing an interior view of the Jefferson was mailed in 1947. The ad on the back of the card read, "Modern in Every Way. Serving Better Foods at Popular Prices, Completely remodeled in 1946." The shop was managed by Thomas Asimos and Victor Scott.

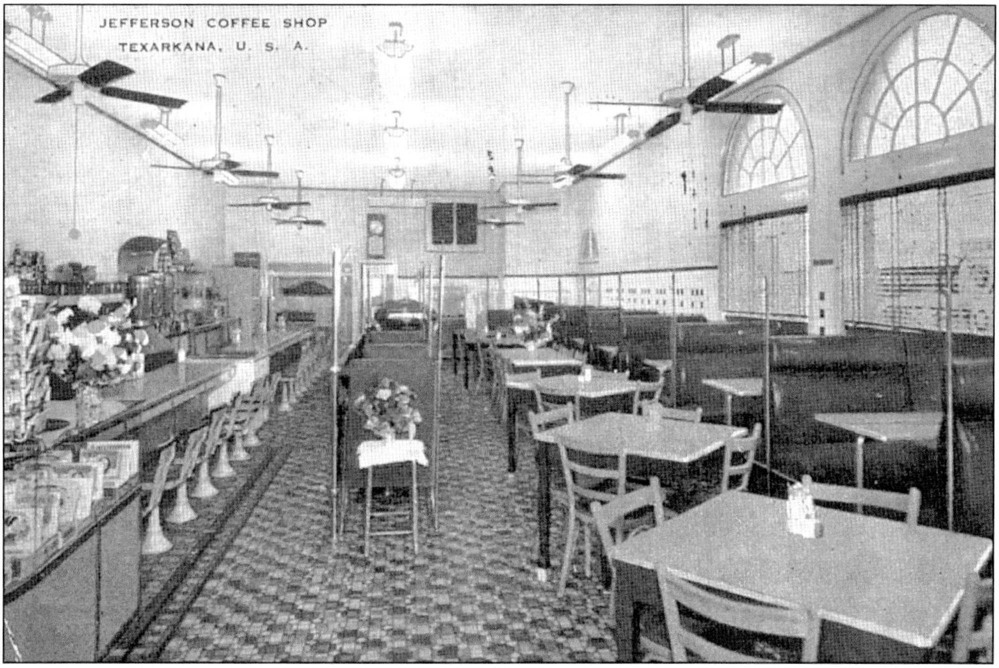

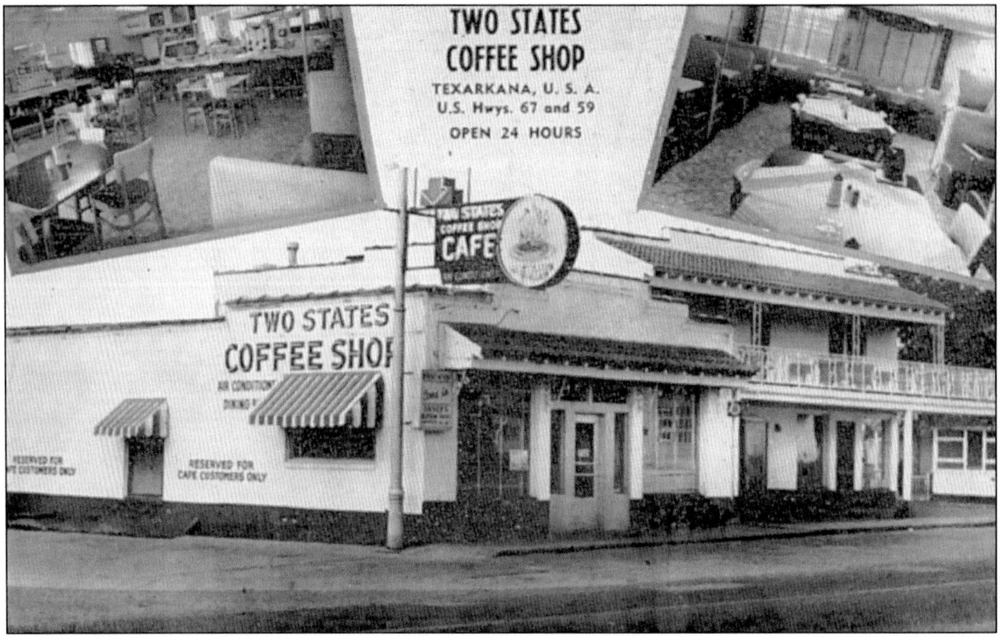

The Two States Coffee Shop was opened around 1940 at 824 West Seventh, an area that, historically, had been home to Texarkana's African-American community. The coffee shop was open 24 hours a day, was air conditioned, and made much out of its border state location. On the card below the calendar on the wall behind the cashier within the Texas shape was furnished by East Funeral Home, and it indicates that the photo was taken the weekend of January 4–5, 1947. The Two States prospered until the new interstate came in the 1960s, when, like so much of Highway 67's commerce, the restaurant faded and closed.

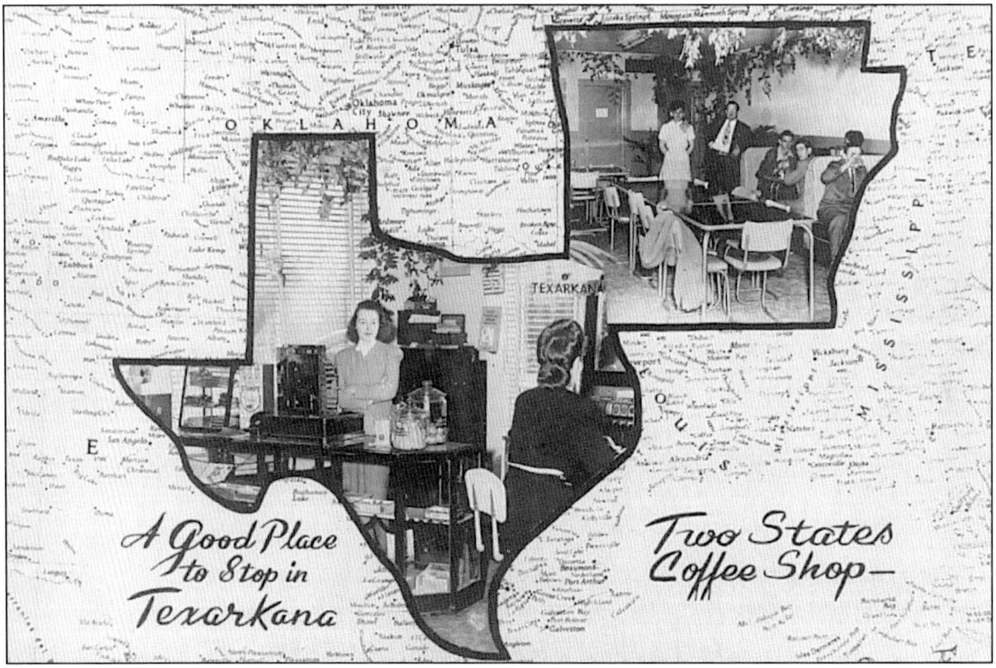

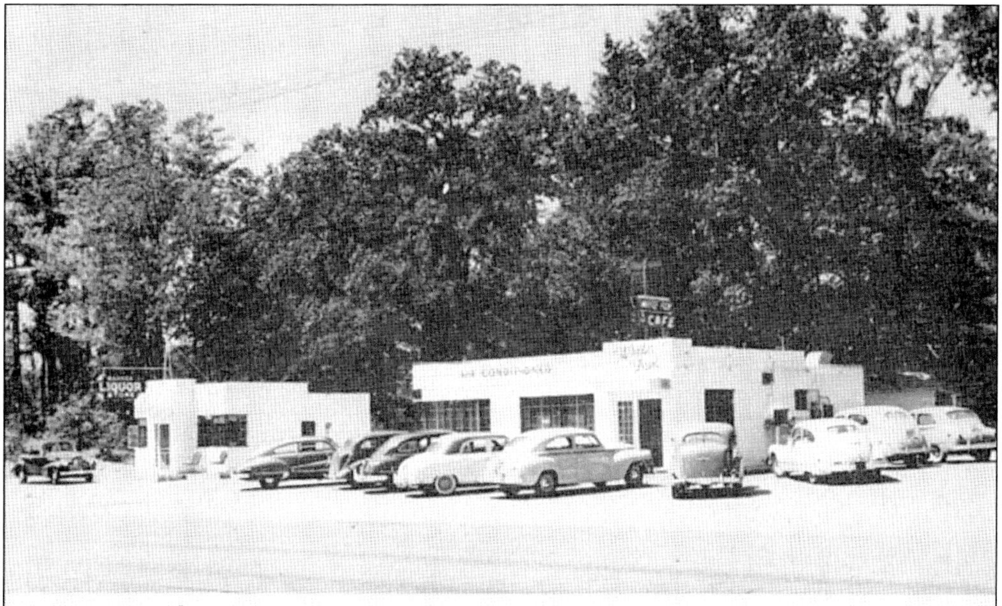

WHITE FOX CAFE - Little Rock Highway - Texarkana, Ark.

The White Fox Cafe on the Mandeville Road section of Highway 67 opened around 1950 and is seen here around that same time. As the name suggests, the building was white, as was the adjacent liquor store to the left. The White Fox closed in the 1960s, another victim of the coming of the interstate. Below is The Coffee Cup, which operated from 1940 to 1959 at 217 East Seventh. Mailed in 1949, this postcard carried the following message: "We have stopped to eat (as usual)." The advertisement on the card offered this about the diner, "Opens 5:45 Mornings, closes 12:30 Nights, Is modernistic and has plenty of parking space." The front of the card carried the added draw, "Recommended by Duncan Hines and Approved by A.A.A."

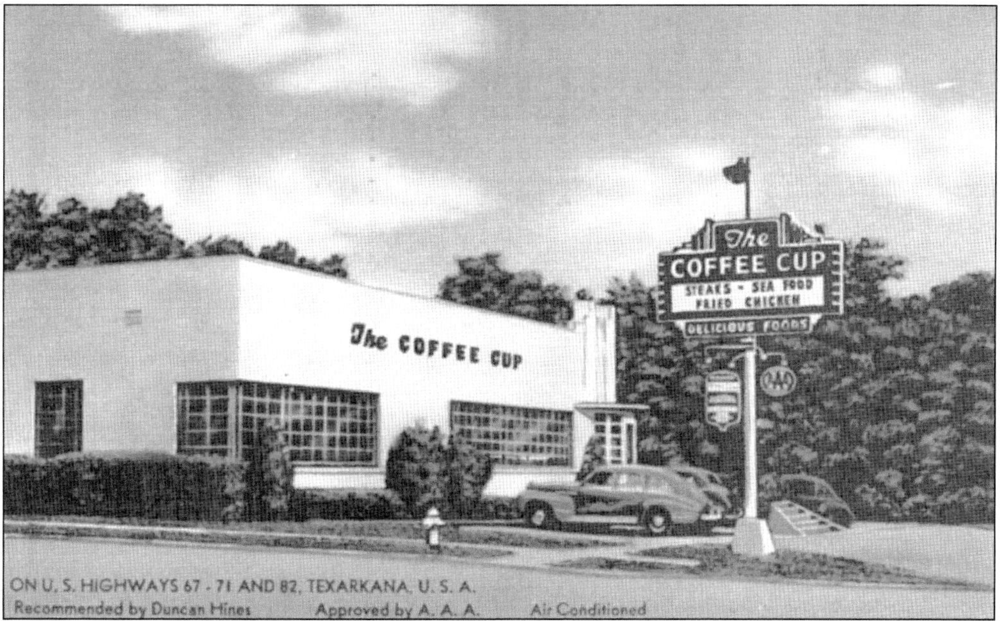

ON U. S. HIGHWAYS 67 - 71 AND 82, TEXARKANA, U. S. A.
Recommended by Duncan Hines Approved by A. A. A. Air Conditioned

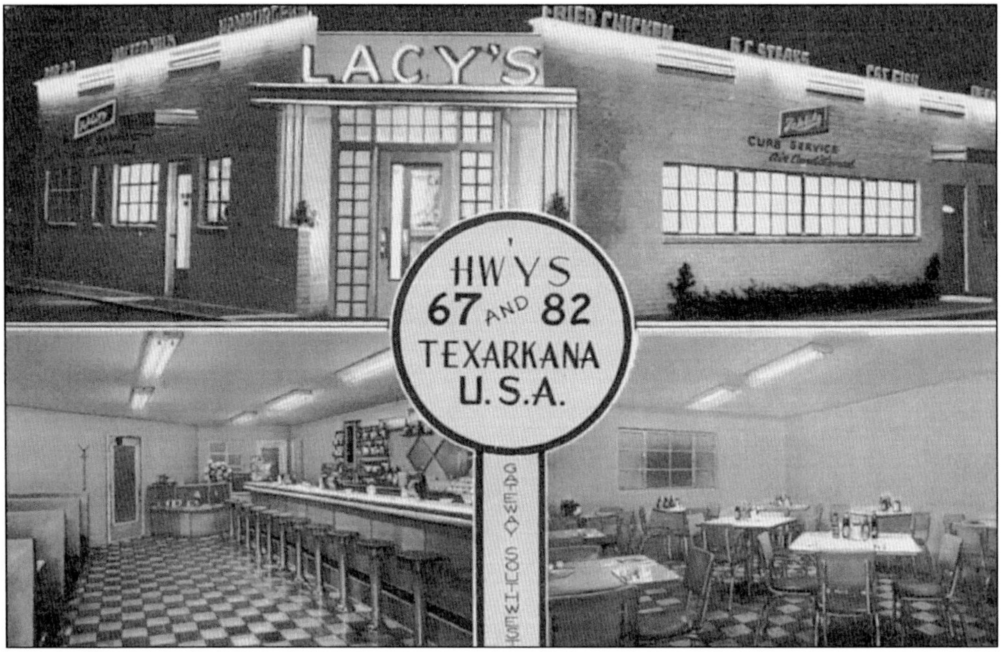

The junction where Highway 67 coming from the east intersected Highway 82 on the east side of Texarkana was home to Lacy's, one of the larger diners on the road. The advertisement on the back of the card offered a suggestion on how to describe the dining experience at Lacy's—"Gosh we had a wonderful meal! Such delicious milk-fed fried chicken, wonderful, tender Blue Ribbon Steaks and Aunt Minnie even ate a full course dinner. P.S. The beer was really cold!" Once the "Home of Home Cooked Food," Lacy's is no more, for it closed years ago.

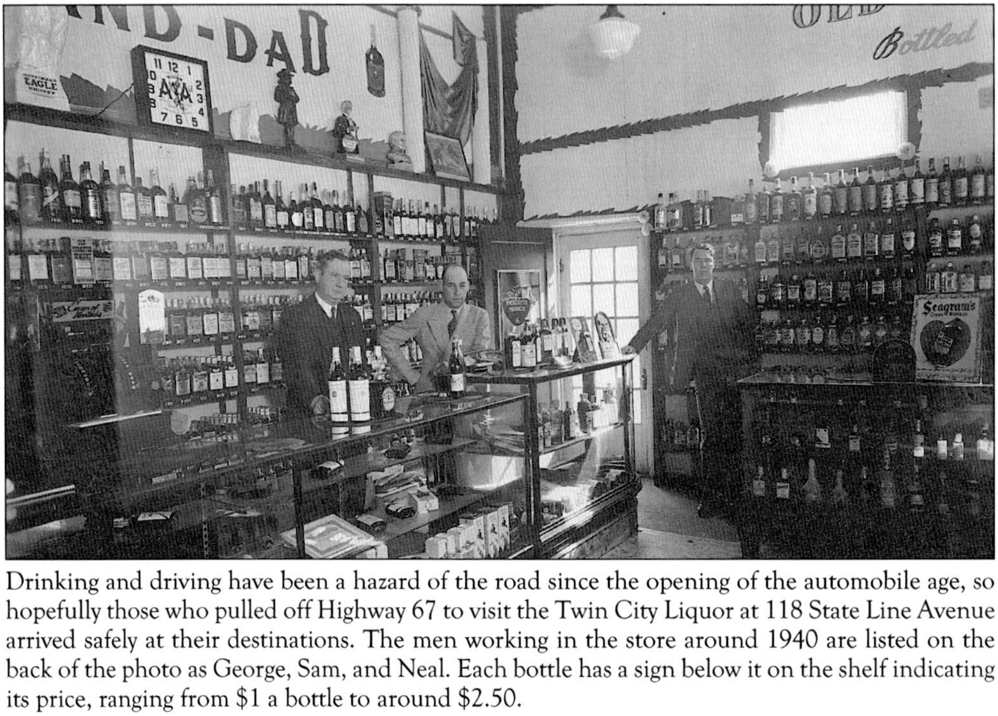

Drinking and driving have been a hazard of the road since the opening of the automobile age, so hopefully those who pulled off Highway 67 to visit the Twin City Liquor at 118 State Line Avenue arrived safely at their destinations. The men working in the store around 1940 are listed on the back of the photo as George, Sam, and Neal. Each bottle has a sign below it on the shelf indicating its price, ranging from $1 a bottle to around $2.50.

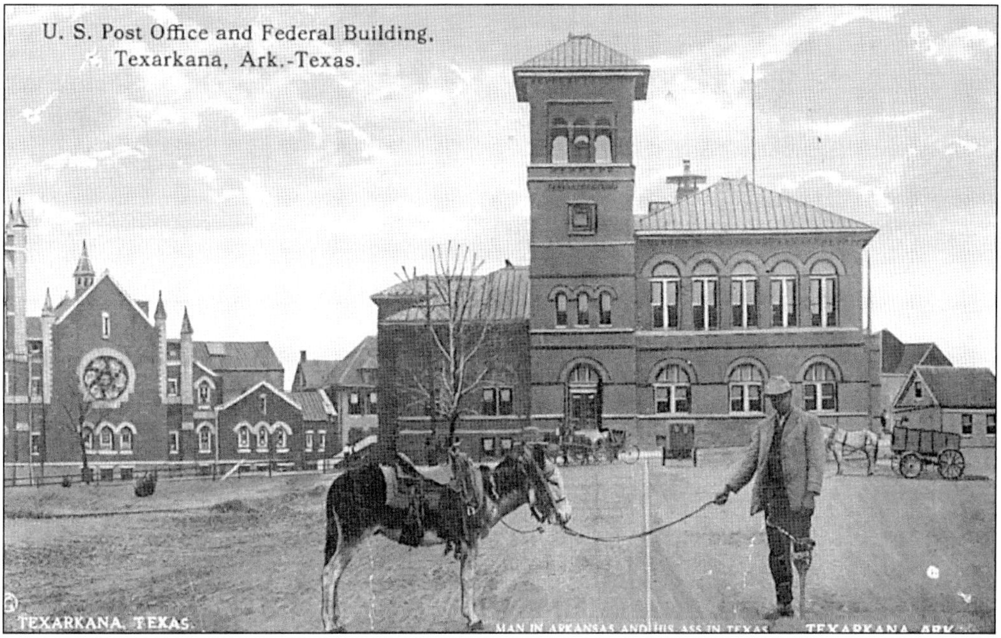

The journey down Highway 67 from Corning to Texarkana on Highway 67 would have covered more than 300 miles and passed through some of the state's most diverse and historic areas. At Texarkana, the motorist who stayed on the road would enter the state of Texas, eventually passing through Dallas and finally reaching the Mexican border at Presidio in far west Texas. A common Texarkana souvenir available in various forms for many decades was a postcard captioned, "Man in Arkansas, and his ass in Texas." The top card, in which the man has a wooden leg, was made against the backdrop of the federal courthouse around 1910. Forty years later, the town had a new federal courthouse on the same site, and yet another "man and his ass" came out to pose for a postcard, straddling the state line around 1950.

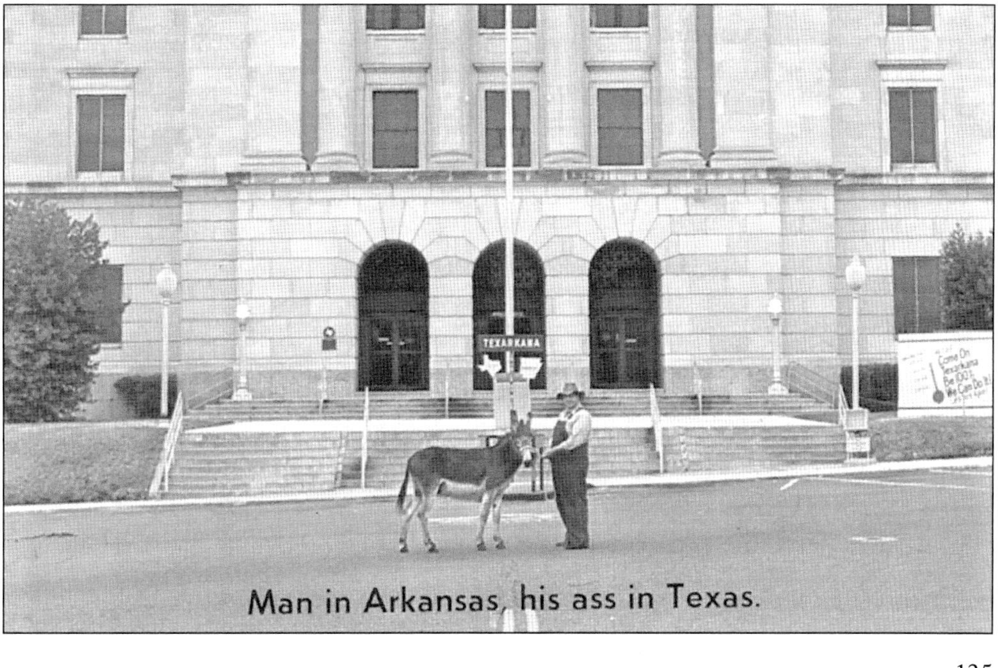

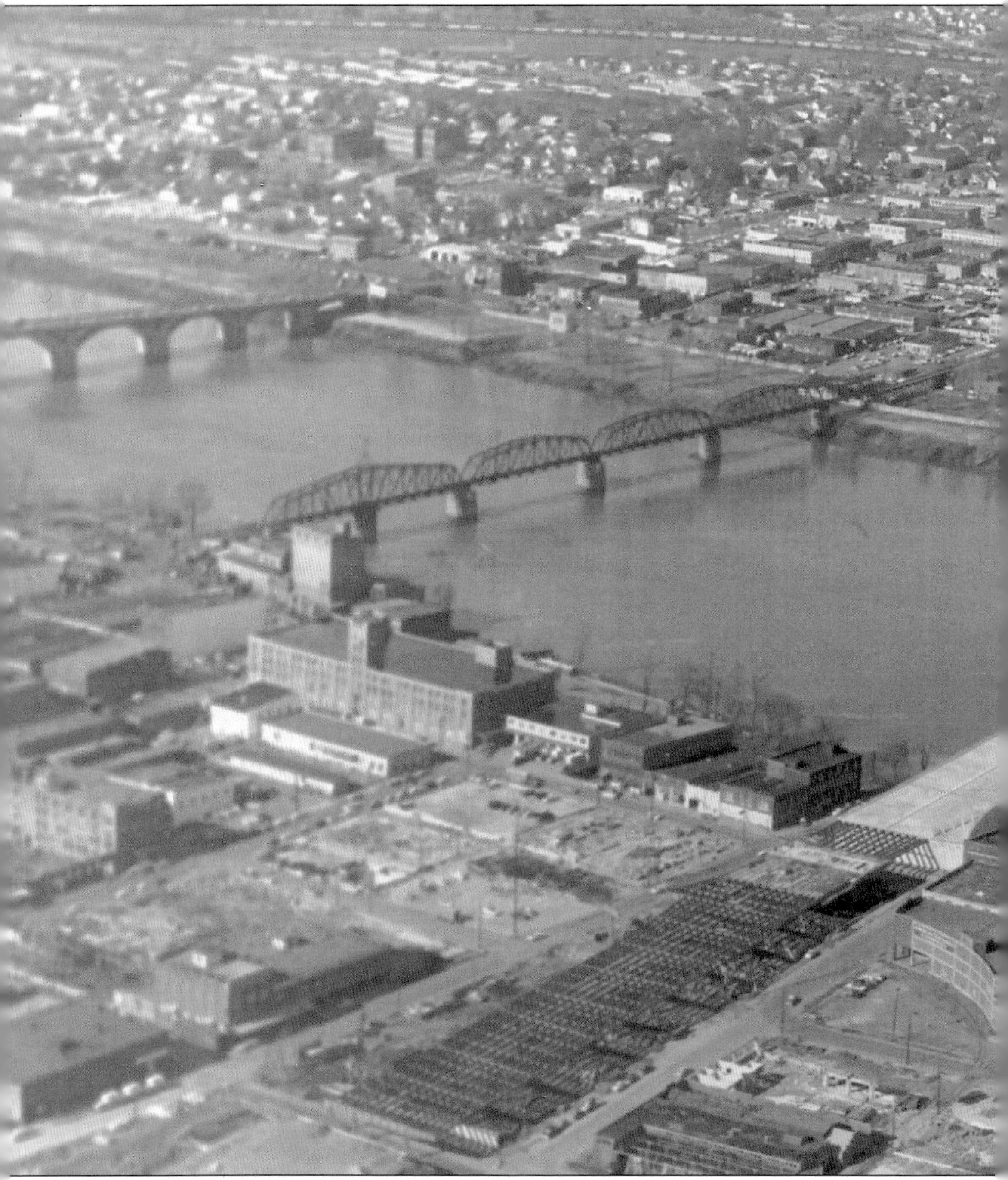

The process of replacing Highway 67 with a four-lane freeway, by covering it over or routing the traffic away, would take some four decades to complete. Still, the beginning of the end for the historic road and the pace of life it represented was symbolized in the bridging of the Arkansas River at Little Rock by Interstate 30 in 1959–1960. This aerial photo was taken from the Little Rock side of the river, looking across to North Little Rock. The approaches to the finished bridge were still under construction, but the future of the Arkansas driving experience was soon to

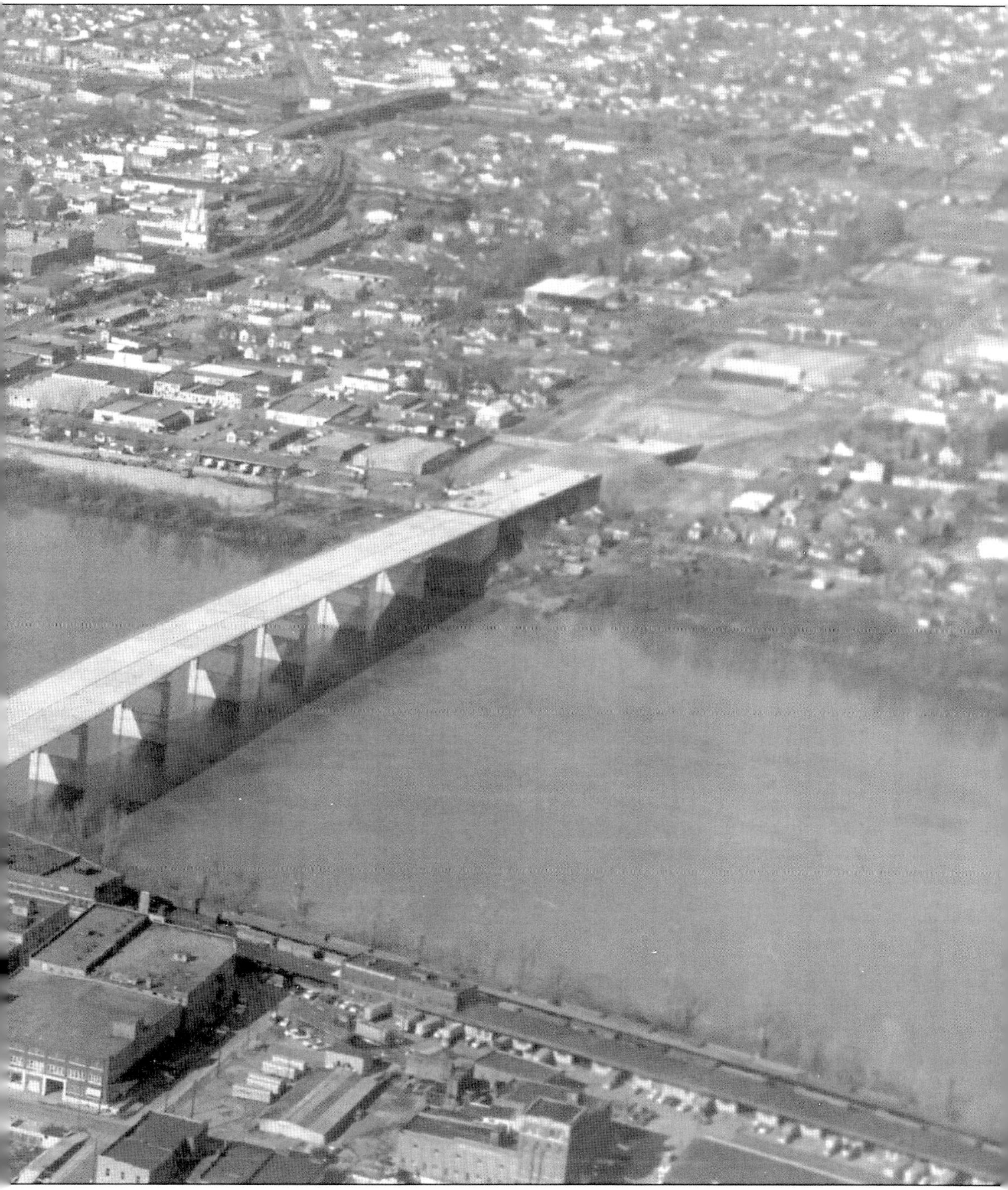

change drastically. It was a necessity, for the old Highway 67 could never have handled the huge volume of traffic and the thousands of large trucks that today move at all hours on Interstate 30. In addition, the new interstates are much safer, and the trip is much quicker. However, as this book hopefully shows, a part of the heritage of Arkansas was left behind as the hundreds of family-owned tourist courts, cafes, and "tourist traps" closed and the "Mother Road of Arkansas" faded into memory.

INDEX